Critical Theory and Contemporary Europe

Critical Theory and Contemporary Society

Series Editor

Darrow Schecter

ABOUT THE SERIES

Critical Theory and Contemporary Society explores the relation between contemporary society as a complex and highly differentiated phenomenon, on the one hand, and critical theory as a correspondingly sophisticated methodology for studying and understanding social and political relations today, on the other.

Each volume highlights in distinctive ways why (1) critical theory offers the most appropriate concepts for understanding political movements, socio-economic conflicts and state institutions in an increasingly global world, and (2) why critical theory nonetheless needs updating in order to keep pace with the realities of the twenty-first century.

The books in the series look at global warming, financial crisis, post-nation state legitimacy, international relations, terrorism and other issues, applying an interdisciplinary approach, in order to help students and citizens understand the specificity and uniqueness of the current situation.

Darrow Schecter,
Series Editor,
Reader in the School of History, Art History
and Humanities, University of Sussex, UK

BOOKS IN THE SERIES

- *Critical Theory and Film* Fabio Vighi, Senior Lecturer and co-director of the Žižek Centre for Ideology Critique at Cardiff University, UK

- *Critical Theory and Contemporary Europe* William Outhwaite, Professor of Sociology at Newcastle University, UK

- *Critical Theory, Legal Theory, and the Evolution of Contemporary Society* Hauke Brunkhorst, Professor of Sociology and Head of the Institute of Sociology at the University of Flensburg, Germany

- *Critical Theory in the Twenty-First Century* Darrow Schecter, Reader in the School of History, Art History and Humanities, University of Sussex, UK

- *Critical Theory and the Digital* David Berry, Department of Political and Cultural Studies at Swansea University, UK

- *Critical Theory and the Contemporary Crisis of Capital* Heiko Feldner, co-director of the Centre for Ideology Critique and Žižek Studies at Cardiff University, UK

Critical Theory and Contemporary Europe

WILLIAM OUTHWAITE

continuum

Continuum International Publishing Group

The Tower Building
11 York Road
London SE1 7NX

80 Maiden Lane
Suite 704
New York NY 10038

www.continuumbooks.com

ISBN: HB: 978-1-4411-1626-0

Library of Congress Cataloging-in-Publication Data
Critical theory and contemporary Europe / William R. Outhwaite. – 1st ed.
p. cm. – (Critical theory and contemporary society)
Includes bibliographical references and index.
ISBN-13: 978-1-4411-1626-0 (hardcover : alk. paper)
ISBN-10: 1-4411-1626-5 (hardcover : alk. paper)   1. Critical theory–Europe.
2. Europe–Economic conditions–20th century.   3. Business cycles–Europe–
History–20th century.   4. Communism–Europe–History–20th century.
5. Europe–Politics and government–20th century.   6. European Union.   I. Title.

HM480.O98 2012
330.94–dc23
2011038965

Typeset by Newgen Imaging Systems Pvt Ltd, Chennai, India
Printed and bound in the United States of America

Contents

Preface

In this book, I am taking both critical theory and contemporary Europe in a broad and flexible sense. My main focus is on Europe since 1945, but the earlier history of Europe and critical theory's response to it continues to influence the current state of critical theory, which was shaped by the inter-war conjunction of fascism (and Nazism), Stalinism and liberal capitalism. I include under the rubric of critical theory any writer linked to the Institute for Social Research before and/or after the Second World War and some pursuing work recognizably in this tradition, whether or not they had or have close institutional or personal connections with leading representatives of critical theory.[1] Although Norbert Elias, for example, had no substantial contact with the Institute, his 'Studies on the Germans' (Elias, 1989) can usefully be read alongside Klaus Eder's much later book on political modernization in Germany. And although Slavoj Žižek is hostile to Frankfurt critical theory, notably to what he sees as its failure to address Stalinism (Žižek, 2001), his own work is closely related to critical theory in a broader sense. A narrower definition of critical theory would tie it more tightly to the work of Max Horkheimer, Theodor Adorno and Herbert Marcuse in the earlier period and that of Jürgen Habermas, Albrecht Wellmer and Axel Honneth in the later twentieth and twenty-first centuries, but in relation to Europe such a restriction would make little sense. Habermas provided in 1984 a valuable overview of the principal protagonists (including himself), while including a warning:

> The suggestive fiction of a unitary school should not divert too much energy to self-thematisation in the history of ideas. We would do better to turn to the problems themselves, to see how far one can get with the ruthlessly revisionist exploitation of the stimulative potential of such a diverse tradition of research.[2]

Critical theory began with an orientation to what has been called the 'diagnosis of the time(s)' (Zeitdiagnose), meaning in this case the political crisis in Europe and the coming World War. The term was brought to the English-speaking world by Karl Mannheim, in an essay of 1941, followed by a book with the same title.[3] The idea however has a much longer history. Hegel wrote famously that philosophy is 'its time captured in thought',[4] and his own philosophy aimed to do this. Tocqueville's *Democracy in America*, written in the 1830s, suggested that the current state of (North) America showed the future for France and the rest of Europe. Max Horkheimer in 1932 launched the Institute's journal, the *Zeitschrift für Sozialforschung*, with the remark that it was 'principally oriented to a theory of the historical course of the present epoch'.[5] The first issue opened with a short essay by Horkheimer, 'Remarks on Science and Crisis', and one by Friedrich Pollock, the Institute's financial director and Horkheimer's closest associate, on 'The Current Situation of Capitalism and the Prospects of a Planned Economy'. As Furio Cerutti noted in 1984, the original plan to integrate philosophy and social science 'was embedded from the beginning in an open-dialectical understanding of the present as history'; this soon became problematic with the rise of Nazism and the War.[6] When, a year later, the journal had to be published in France, he added that the associates of the Institute saw in theory 'a factor for the improvement of reality'.[7] As he wrote in a later essay, what distinguished critical theory from 'traditional' theory was the theorist's reflective attitude to his or her historical location as a background to their more specialized work.[8] Habermas's theorizing has been fundamentally shaped by his response to the historical context of Germany in and immediately after the Second World War, and some of his earliest work directly addressed that context. More recently, Axel Honneth has put the concept of diagnosis of the times at the centre of his own work.

Critical theory made a distinctive contribution to theorizing post-war Europe and the European crisis out of which it had emerged. The first generation theorists (notably Adorno), who had been prominent in theorizing Nazism and other crisis phenomena in the inter-war period, insisted after the War on addressing the horror of Nazism and the Holocaust, in a generally unsympathetic context. Habermas's work, too, is crucially shaped by the memory of Nazi irrationality and the regime's misuse of science and technology.[9] Unimpressed by post-war affluence in capitalist Europe and North America, where Marcuse's *One Dimensional Man* (1964) was highly influential, the critical theorists were also without illusions about Soviet socialism, about which Marcuse and others also wrote. They welcomed but also criticized the student and youth movements of 1968, having provided much of the analysis which motivated these and subsequent alternative social movements. Their neo-Marxist analysis of capitalist crisis tendencies and of advanced capitalist culture shaped the thinking of the Left worldwide.

In the 1980s, Andrew Arato and others developed a critical theory of state socialism in association with local critics; much of the most valuable analysis of post-Stalinism, for example that of the 'Budapest School' of the circle around Georg Lukács until his death in 1971, was shaped by critical theory.

This was continued in the analysis of post-communist transition after 1989, notably by Claus Offe and Ulrich Preuss in Germany and Arato in the United States. Meanwhile a third wave of critical theory was being developed by Axel Honneth, Seyla Benhabib and others, also addressing contemporary social issues such as European xenophobia. Habermas has been increasingly concerned with the future of the European Union (EU) and other issues of contemporary relevance in his work from the mid-1990s to the present, and critical theory has inspired much contemporary work on deliberative democracy and the question of a European public sphere.[10]

Notes

1 For a similarly broad approach, see, for example, Stephen Eric Bronner, *Of Critical Theory and its Theorists*, Oxford: Blackwell, 1994. As in a fast food stall, there are Hamburgers as well as Frankfurters: Jan Phillip Reemtsma's Hamburger Institut für Sozialforschung has done important work on controversial historical and contemporary issues and publishes a journal, *Mittelweg 38*, and a book series. There is also an Institut für kritische Theorie (InkriT) in Berlin, linked to the Marxist journal *Das Argument*.

2 Jürgen Habermas, 'Drei Thesen zur Wirkungsgeschichte der Frankfurter Schule', in Axel Honneth and Albrecht Wellmer (eds), *Die Frankfurter Schule und die Folgen*, Alexander von Humboldt-Stiftung: Symposium 1984, Berlin, De Gruyter, 1986, p. 11. See also Albrecht Wellmer's contribution in the same volume, pp. 25–34.

3 Karl Mannheim, *Diagnosis of Our Times: Wartime Essays of a Sociologist*. London: Kegan Paul, Trench, Trubner & Co, 1943.

4 G. W. F. Hegel, *Philosophy of Right*, Preface, various editions.

5 Max Horkheimer, 'Vorwort', *Zeitschrift für Sozialforschung*, 1(1), 1932, p. III.

6 Furio Cerrutti, 'Philosophie und Sozialforschung. Zum ursprünglichen Programm der kritischen Theorie', in Axel Honneth and Albrecht Wellmer (eds), *Die Frankfurter Schule und die Folgen*, Alexander von Humboldt-Stiftung: Symposium 1984, Berlin: De Gruyter, 1986, p. 257.

7 Max Horkheimer, 'Vorwort', *Zeitschrift für Sozialforschung*, II(2), 1933, p. 161.

8 Max Horkheimer, 1937, 'Traditionelle und kritische Theorie', *Zeitschrift für Sozialforschung*, VI(2), pp. 245–94. Various translations.

9 See Matthew Specter, *Habermas: An Intellectual Biography*, New York: Cambridge University Press, 2010, for a comprehensive discussion of Habermas's work in the context of contemporary issues.

10 I am grateful to a number of friends who read earlier versions of this text. Any errors are of course mine. I was unfortunately too late to take account of the excellent book by Christian Fleck, *A Transatlantic History of the Social Sciences* (London: Bloomsbury, 2011).

1

Theorizing the European crisis of 1914–45

Although the Institute for Social Research had been founded in 1923 and officially inaugurated as an independent research institute attached to the University of Frankfurt in 1924, it was only in 1930, when Max Horkheimer became Director, that what we now know as critical theory became its dominant approach. The early orientation of the Institute had been solidly Marxist (there was initial discussion of calling it an 'Institute for Marxism') and its founding members were all close to the German Communist Party. The Institute's first director, Carl Grünberg, identified himself and the Institute at the opening ceremony with 'the view . . . that we are in the midst of the transition from capitalism to socialism' (Dubiel, 1994: 5; see also Jay, 1973; Bottomore, 1984). While the economists and economic historians Henryk Grossmann, Karl-August Wittfogel and Friedrich Pollock remained from the earlier period, under Horkheimer's directorship the Institute's centre of gravity shifted from economics to a broader interdisciplinary approach, inspired by a similarly broad conception of philosophy focussed on the understanding of the contemporary world.

By now, as well as the unexpected and ambiguous success of the Bolsheviks in Russia and the failure of revolutionary Marxism to take root elsewhere in Europe, the contemporary scene was marked by two other phenomena: the economic crisis of 1929, and the strength of the German form of fascism (national socialism). The Institute members began an empirical investigation of workers' consciousness in 1929 directed by Erich Fromm. Its initial results contributed to their awareness of the gravity of the situation, which in turn saved them and the Institute itself when the Nazis came to power.[1] Fromm's study may have been inspired in part by a contemporaneous ethnographic inquiry into white collar workers in Berlin by Adorno's close friend Siegfried Kracauer, later famous for his book on German cinema 'From Caligari to Hitler'. Although Fromm's material was not published as a book until 1980, it fed into the Institute's *Studien über Autorität und Familie* of 1936.[2] The focus on authoritarianism was continued in the US study of *The Authoritarian Personality* by Adorno and others,[3] unpublished studies of anti-Semitism towards the end of the War[4] and the post-war German *Gruppenexperiment* (1955).[5] These related projects, briefly discussed below, pick up from earlier work on the German working class[6] and combine a neo-Marxist approach with an attention to psychological dynamics.

In Kracauer's brilliant study he repeatedly distances himself from 'vulgar-Marxist' categories of class and ideology, a 'roof nowadays riddled with holes'.[7] Anti-capitalist intellectuals, he complains, concentrate only on manifest outrages and neglect the misery of everyday life. 'How is everyday life to change, if even those whose vocation is to stir it up pay it no attention?'[8] Walter Benjamin, in an enthusiastic response, described Kracauer as a 'rag-picker at daybreak'.[9] 'And it is not as an orthodox Marxist, still less as a practical agitator, that he dialectically penetrates the existence of employees, but because to penetrate dialectically means: to expose.'[10]

Kracauer wrote in April 1930 to Adorno:

> The situation in Germany is more than serious . . . We are going to have three or four million unemployed and I can see no way out. A disaster is hanging over this country and I am convinced that it is not just capitalism. That capitalism may become bestial is not due to the economy alone.[11]

Although Fromm, in his retrospective introduction to his own study, is rather dismissive of Kracauer's,[12] the two can be seen as complementary. Fromm and his associates used a (rather over-long) questionnaire, submitting the responses however to a qualitative and, to use a later term, 'symptomatic' reading.

> . . . we relied on the basic rule in psychological work that the individual's statements about their thoughts and feelings, however subjectively honest, can not be taken literally but need to be interpreted. Or to put it more exactly: it is not *what* someone says which is important but *why* he says it.[13]

It is worth noting here that this interpretative approach to empirical research is continued in all the Institute's subsequent work.

Of the nearly 600 respondents, roughly two-thirds were manual workers and the rest mostly white-collar employees, drawn from urban centres in and south of Frankfurt and northwards to Berlin and the Rhineland. They were mostly communist, left socialist Unabhangige Sozialdemokratische Partei Deutschlands (USPD) or social democrat supporters, with 7 per cent supporting the bourgeois centre and right parties and only 3 per cent the Nazis, a third of them white-collar workers. Despite this strong support for the political left and centre-left, broadly representative of the country as a whole,[14] Fromm was concerned about the weakness of many respondents' political beliefs and the inconsistency between their formal political responses, reflecting the line of the respective parties, and other attitudes to authority in the family, gender issues etc. A simple contrast between conservative authoritarians and leftist 'liberals', as we would now say in America, was not sustained, nor was there much of a link between these two positions and a petty-bourgeois or proletarian class position respectively.

> Although the Left had the political loyalty and votes of the great majority of workers, it had largely not succeeded in changing the personality structure of its adherents in such a way that they could be relied upon in critical situations. (Fromm, 1984: 228)

Even more worryingly, a significant proportion of socialists, and a somewhat smaller (p. 230) proportion of communists, displayed authoritarian attitudes:

> These people were filled with hate and anger against everyone who had money and who appeared to enjoy life. That part of the socialist platform which aimed at the overthrow of the propertied classes appealed to them. On the other hand, items such as freedom and equality had not the slightest attraction for them, since they willingly obeyed every powerful authority they admired; they liked to control others in so far as they had the power to do so. Their unreliability finally came into the open at the point where a programme such as that of the National Socialists was offered to them. This programme not only corresponded with the feelings which had made the Socialist programme attractive but also appealed to that side of their nature which Socialism had not satisfied or had unconsciously opposed. In such cases they were transformed from unreliable leftists into convinced National Socialists. (Fromm, 1984: 43)

This is a retrospective judgement, probably made in 1937–38, but it is complemented by the analysis of the handful of Nazi respondents in the study. Their preferred reading matter was not, as one might have expected, nationalist or militarist literature but rather leftist social criticism, reflecting the populist emphasis of Nazism before it attained power (Fromm, 1984: 139).

The pessimistic nature of this analysis may explain the Institute's hesitancy to publish in the late 1930s what material had been successfully rescued from Germany. Some of it appears however in Fromm's contribution to *Studien über Autorität und Familie* (1936). Horkheimer, increasingly under Adorno's influence, fell out with Fromm, who was eased out of the Institute in 1939, taking the materials with him (Bonss, 1984: 2). Most of the Institute members' analyses of the crisis were in fact completed in exile or after the return of the Institute to Frankfurt in 1950; it remains of course a major topic of critical theory up to the present.

Herbert Marcuse, who had been part of the Institute since 1932 and worked in its Geneva office, relocating to New York in 1934, was not so much eased out as kept at arm's length for over two decades by Horkheimer, again under Adorno's influence.[15] Marcuse published in 1934 one of the Institute's earliest analyses of totalitarianism and other articles in the *Zeitschrift*, and contributed to *Studien über Autorität und Familie*. Horkheimer, having invited him to join him in California in 1941 to work on a project on dialectics later encouraged him to seek other work; he joined the Office of Strategic Services in Washington in 1942 and worked there for the rest of the War.

The dialectics project continued with Adorno

It was in fact people associated more with the Institute than with the critical theory project in a narrower sense who were most active in the analysis of fascism and Nazism in the early stages. The Sinologist Karl August Wittfogel, who had joined the Institute in 1925 and was its only active Communist, abandoned a planned trip to China in order to work instead on fascism and Nazism. From 1931 until his arrest in 1933 he published a massive flow of articles in the communist press and completed a lost book on Nazism.[16] Of the articles reprinted by the Kommunistischer Bund in 1973, one is a crude expression of the Kommunistische Partei Deutschlands' (KPD's) 'social-fascism' line,[17] but the next, under the pseudonym Hans Petersen, emphasizes the origin of Nazism in 'petty bourgeois political activists rather than capitalist interests.[18] Wittfogel also secured a scoop by getting hold of an early programme of the Italian fascists which had immediately been suppressed.[19]

Having rejoined his Institute colleagues in New York in 1934 and working at the Institute of Pacific Relations there, Wittfogel contributed to the *Studien über Autorität und Familie* and occasionally to the journal, but not to subsequent Institute projects. He became strongly anti-communist and his *Oriental Despotism* (1957) presented communist totalitarianism in the Soviet Union, and incipiently in China, as a natural successor to Asiatic despotism. Already in the winter of 1937–38, at an Institute seminar, he had claimed that the Soviet Union needed a second revolution to restore popular power over the bureaucracy (Ulmen, 1978: 209). According to Ulmen (1978: 211), Wittfogel only once used the term 'critical theory', which he defined as aiming at a holistic understanding of society. Although this is not very different from Horkheimer's original formulations, Wittfogel did not share the suspicion of systems and theoretical closure that came to define the work of Horkheimer and Adorno.

Another former active communist who had held a scholarship from the Institute and published an article on the history of science in the first issue of the *Zeitschrift* was Franz Borkenau, whose book, *The Totalitarian Enemy*, (London, Faber, 1940), was an early example of theories of totalitarianism. For Borkenau, 'The German–Russian pact . . . has brought out the essential similarity between the German and the Russian systems.'[20] The Institute had published his book in Paris in 1934 but, as Wiggershaus notes,[21] without endorsing it in Horkheimer's preface.

Franz Neumann, also a member of the Institute in New York, had better luck than Wittfogel: his book on Nazism, *Behemoth* (1942) was extremely influential in the United States. Neumann, like Wittfogel, had been politically active, in his case ending his Weimar career as principal lawyer to the SPD. Fleeing to London, where he took another undergraduate degree and a PhD with Harold Laski, he was invited to New York by the Institute. Here he was employed as a lawyer and lecturer and published two articles in the *Zeitschrift* but was denied the permanent attachment that he had been promised.[22] When *Behemoth* was almost complete, Horkheimer wrote encouragingly to Neumann that 'This publication will document the fact that our theory is still the best guide through the maze of present-day social conditions.'[23] He followed this up after publication with a mild reproach that Neumann had neglected 'some anthropological issues'.[24] As Keith Tribe has shown, *Behemoth* is in fact rather far from the dominant perspectives in the Institute.[25]

Another associate of the Institute kept very much at arm's length was the legal and political scholar Otto Kirchheimer. Kirchheimer had already published substantial works on the subversion of the Weimar constitution throughout the history of the republic; in exile in Paris he worked on criminal and constitutional law and published in Germany in 1935 a pseudonymous critique of the law and state of the Third Reich. Invited to New York as a research assistant, he edited a manuscript that became the Institute's first English-language publication[26] and published a number of articles in the *Zeitschrift* on the Nazi legal order and a still influential article on 'the structure of political compromise' (1941).[27] Like Neumann, he later had a successful academic career in New York.

Against all this output, that of the core members of the Institute, Horkheimer, Pollock and, from 1938, Adorno, seems for a long time rather thin.[28] Horkheimer's *Dämmerung* (1934), published in Switzerland under a pseudonym, contained some observations on the contemporary scene up until 1931 but no sustained analysis.[29] With the exception of his article on 'Science and Crisis' (1932), his work until *Dialectic of Enlightenment* and his contemporaneous studies of anti-Semitism are concerned almost entirely with purely philosophical topics. The same is true of Adorno's work on philosophy and on music, coinciding with his collaboration on the radio research project. Pollock, the business manager of the Institute, wrote little except two articles in the final volume (1941) of the *Zeitschrift* (by then appearing in English as *Studies in Philosophy and Social Science*). Leo Lowenthal worked exclusively on literature until the later stages of the war, when he collaborated on the work on anti-Semitism and authoritarianism. Finally, Felix Weil, whose money had founded and sustained the Institute, published review articles on the New Deal and on the German arms economy.

For the US public, it was *The Authoritarian Personality* (1950) that was the core of critical theory's contribution to the analysis of the European crisis. The Institute itself, while engaging actively in contract research on anti-Semitism and related issues, did little to address the aspects of the rise of Nazism and the outbreak of war which were of greatest concern. Horkheimer is renowned for the remark that 'he who does not wish to speak of capitalism should be silent about fascism'.[30] The Institute spoke of capitalism, while often in euphemistic language, without having much directly to say about fascism.

If, however, Adorno had been slow to address Nazism as a whole,[31] he made up for this in the post-war years. The Institute's first large research project, begun in 1950 with support from the US High Commission for Germany (HICOG), was a study of contemporary German attitudes to the Third Reich and the subsequent Occupation, involving what was called a *Gruppenexperiment* and would now be called a focus group methodology. The stimulus for the group discussions was a fictional letter to his home newspaper by an Allied soldier stationed in West Germany. Topics covered were attitudes to democracy, war guilt, Jews, the West, the East, rearmament and to Germany and Germans. As with Fromm's Weimar study, the results were somewhat alarming. To quote Wiggershaus:

> The attitudes of those taking part in the discussions . . . were largely negative, not only towards the Soviet Union but also towards the Western

powers. Approximately two thirds of the speakers expressed ambivalent attitudes to democracy . . . [and] . . . half of the speakers rejected any shared guilt for the atrocities of the Third Reich. Two statistical groups stood out in particular for their negative qualities: farmers and academics [i.e. participants with higher education; the translation is misleading here]. The farmers all without exception denied any share in national guilt; the academics denied it virtually without exception. Of the farmers who expressed views about the Jews, more than three-quarters proved to be radically or considerably anti-Semitic. The academics . . . were noticeably withdrawn on the subject of the Jews. Of those who did express an opinion, over 90 per cent were radically or considerably anti-Semitic.[32]

The leading sociologist René König, while strongly supporting publication of the book, thought that the implications of the results were too 'devastating' for it to be wise to print full summaries of the discussions.[33] It could be argued that the stimulus letter was likely by its nature to evoke defensive responses, but the authors reject this suggestion,[34] and the stimulus letter, presented in its definitive version (after various revisions in the early stages of the study) on pages 501–3, does seem extremely measured in its positive and negative judgements.

Chapter 5 of the study, by Adorno,[35] is a detailed qualitative discussion of 'Guilt and Defence' (Abwehr) and points in particular to 'the rigid rejection of any feeling of guilt' as 'the symptom of an extremely dangerous social psychological and political potential'.[36] The authors note however that attitudes to democracy had become more positive over the period between the research for the study and its publication.[37] Even in the case of 'our national socialist participants', it was generally not possible to determine whether what was at issue was 'the residue of fascist ideology or the expression of a persisting anthropological disposition'.[38]

The results may have further encouraged Adorno to emphasize the theme of 'working through the past' in his influential lectures and radio broadcasts. In 1950 he had already published an article in the *Frankfurter Hefte* on the 'resurrection' of German culture after the War.[39]

Before returning to settle in Frankfurt, Adorno and Horkheimer had already written a good deal in the 1940s on the European tragedy. This writing was partly shaped by the Institute's projects on anti-Semitism but was foreshadowed by Horkheimer's essay on 'The Jews and Europe', published just after the War began in 1939 but completed nearly a year earlier. As Wiggershaus notes, 'It was his first essay on the topic of fascism, and the first on fascism by anyone in the Horkheimer circle since the articles by Pollock and Marcuse in 1933 and 1934.'[40] Horkheimer had however written a short forward to an article on the planned economy, including the following claim:

> Humanity does not in any sense have a choice at present between the liberal economy and the totalitarian state order, since the one necessarily turns into the other, precisely because the latter today best serves the liberal demand for the continuation of the private ownership of the most important social resources.[41]

Wiggershaus goes on to conclude:

> Marcuse, the critic of ideology, Fromm, the social psychologist, Mandelbaum and Meyer, the economists, and Horkheimer, the social philosopher, were thus all united in their agreement with the dominant communist interpretation of the period, according to which fascism was both the logical consequence of liberalism and the form of political domination which monopoly capitalism adopted.

In 'The Jews and Europe', writing more boldly, Wiggershaus suggests, than he would have done in English for a US audience that Horkheimer had again immediately made a link with capitalism.

> Anyone who wants to explain anti-Semitism must intend national socialism . . . The new anti-Semitism is the emissary of the totalitarian order into which the liberal order has developed. One must go back to the tendencies of Capital . . . Anyone who does not want to talk about capitalism should also be silent about fascism.

This essay, published in German in the last issue printed in Paris, had been followed by a whole series of analyses in English of Nazism, making up, or failing to make up, for lost time.

Fascist rule in Europe, and specifically in Germany, evoked a triple response from the critical theory tradition. First, there was a need to explain it, if what Horkheimer had called in a preface 'conceptual thinking' (begreifendes Denken) was to mean anything. The Institute's official position, if it can be called that, was the fairly orthodox communist view, represented by Horkheimer's essay just cited, that monopoly capitalism, under certain circumstances, secured its continuation by authoritarian means. If explanations in this form were seen to be inadequate (and, as we have seen, others linked more loosely to the Institute had attempted to go further), Horkheimer and Adorno had provided, in *Dialectic of Enlightenment*, a kind of explanatory antithesis. Here, instrumental reason itself, in pursuing mastery of nature (including human nature) turned into its opposite. Neither form of explanation was satisfactory.

The second response was one of reflection on the past and stabilizing an inherently unstable set of memories. The punishment of perpetrators had been carried out briskly, if incompletely, by the allies, and was at a standstill by 1949, when the two German states were established. What was missing, as documented in the *Gruppenexperiment*, was an adequate reflection on issues of guilt or complicity.

Adorno in particular returned again and again to this issue, anticipating the much later global discussion of the Holocaust. For the most part, however, he and Horkheimer accepted the need to work with colleagues whose political pasts were questionable – an attitude that we can perhaps understand better after 1989. As Wiggershaus points out,

> When the rebuilt Institute of Social Research was reopened, there were eight chairs of sociology in West Germany . . . Only three of these were held by émigrés or anti-fascists. One of the two émigrés was Horkheimer. The other was René König. In Berlin, Otto Stammer . . . had been banned from teaching and publishing. His academic career only started at the end of the Third Reich . . . The other five sociology professors had all had a more or less normal academic career under Nazism . . .[42]

To take an extreme example, it is interesting to see the passion with which Horkheimer, in his private notes published posthumously, rejected the idea of trying and punishing Eichmann as 'simple-minded and shocking' 'The trial is a repetition: Eichmann will do harm a second time.' (p. 196)[43]

The third response is to attempt to strengthen political and intellectual defences against any repetition of fascist authoritarianism. Adorno and Horkheimer were not political practitioners,[44] though Horkheimer was Rektor of the University of Frankfurt and Adorno was also very influential in the media.[45] Their contribution was essentially their presence in Frankfurt, the re-establishment of the Institute and their defence of the values that had been suppressed under Nazi rule and were still weak.

My main concern here is to show how all three responses are continued in subsequent work in critical theory, broadly conceived. The first, explanatory response is perhaps best represented by Klaus Eder's book of 1985 *Geschichte als Lernprozess?* on political modernity in Germany. If it is appropriate to speak of generations of critical theorists, Eder belongs to the third. Born in 1946, he was one of the young sociologists working with Habermas at the Max Planck centre in Starnberg from 1971 to 1983.

The question of Germany's historical relation to democracy had cropped up as a topic in the *Gruppenexperiment*: participants 'often refer to history and deny, in contradiction to the facts, that there was ever a democratic tradition in Germany'.[46] As Eder shows in great detail, there *were* traditions of this 'Western' kind; the pathology of political modernity in imperial Germany is, rather, the result of their *relative* weakness. As a result, other traditions were consolidated which undermined the democratic 'normative premises' of modernity.[47] Just as an individual may fail to develop a reflexive and post-conventional moral awareness, so a society may abandon or weaken its capacity for moral reasoning. Eder suggests three ways in which this may happen. One is the displacement of moral coordination by non-moral forms of coordination based on self-interest. This can be seen in the development of liberalism in an economistic direction or towards social Darwinism. A second form is the sealing off of group morality, notably in nationalism ('my country, right or wrong'). Historical memory, too, becomes partial. A third form is the subordination of individual or collective interests to an authority figure within the group, with the result that learning is displaced by prescription.[48] Eder is concerned with the early stages of this process in Germany in the late eighteenth and nineteenth centuries and the name Hitler does not appear in the book, but it is clear that Nazi ideology is a particularly good example of these processes, combining a model of life as a 'Darwinian' combat between nations and 'races' with the subordination of moral and legal reasoning to the decision of the national leader. The individualization of politics in the cult of the 'great man' is a further element of this pathological development.[49] The irrationalist direction taken by German thought in the second half of the nineteenth century can be seen 'in the social Darwinist reformulation of radical democratic positions, the utilitarian reformulation of liberal positions and the state-metaphysical reformulation of conservative positions'.[50] Even in social democratic thought, 'politics is reduced to a midwife of social revolution'.[51] In Germany a particular association of legal theory with administration and the elevation of the state bureaucracy to the representative of the national interest amount to a survival of principles of absolutist rule against a background of democratization. Bismarck, in particular, managed at the end of the 1870s to steal the political clothes of the conservatives, the liberals and even the social democrats, in what Eder calls 'the creation of a civil religion, a modern collective consciousness, from above'.[52]

Eder's book can usefully be compared with that on *The Germans* by Norbert Elias, published in 1989, the year before his death, though mostly written a good deal earlier. Elias, born in 1897 in Breslau (now Wrocław), worked from 1930 to 1933 in the Frankfurt sociology department as Karl Mannheim's assistant. The department was housed on the ground floor of the Institute building; relations between Mannheim and Horkheimer were cool, but Elias had more contact with his assistant, Leo Lowenthal. Elias had just completed his habilitation thesis on court society, finally published in 1969, when he was forced to leave for exile (*not*, he used to insist, just emigration)[53] in France and then England, where he remained until 1962, teaching in schools and, from 1954, at Leicester University. He then taught in Ghana and West Germany, before finally settling in Amsterdam.

Elias' book is a good deal wider-ranging than Eder's, but they converge on the theme that, as Elias puts it,

> two streams of middle-class politics can be recognized in the nineteenth and early twentieth centuries, one idealistic-liberal and the other nationalistic-conservative. In the early nineteenth century, one of the main points of both was the unification of Germany . . . It was of great significance for the development of the German middle-class habitus that these plans failed. The shock caused by this was deepened when one prince, the King of Prussia with his adviser Bismarck, managed to satisfy the craving for a united Germany militarily, through a successful war, when the middle classes had failed to do so by peaceful means.[54]

In Elias' account, this aristocratic victory combined with longer-standing cultural traditions and territorial anxieties in Germany to make it vulnerable to authoritarian politics in the crisis of the late 1920s.[55]

The second response to Nazism, the critical attitude to historical memory or its repression, has been addressed most directly by Habermas in the second generation of critical theory and Helmut Dubiel in the third generation. The defensive responses documented in the *Gruppenexperiment* are paralleled by Habermas's memories as a teenager in the immediate post-war years.

> At the age of 15 or 16 I sat before the radio and experienced what was being discussed before the Nuremberg tribunal; when others, instead of being struck by the ghastliness, began to dispute the justice of the trial, procedural questions, and questions of jurisdiction, there was that first rupture, which still gapes. Certainly, it is only because of the fact that I was still sensitive and easily offended that I did not close myself to the fact of collectively realized inhumanity in the same measure as the majority of my elders.[56]

In 1953 Habermas was schocked again when his friend Karl-Otto Apel pointed out that Heidegger had just reprinted without comment a lecture from 1935 which referred to the 'inner truth and greatness' of the National

Socialist movement that had been in power since 1933. His response was a newspaper article in which he attacked the failure of Heidegger and the West German popularion as a whole to 'risk' a 'confrontation (*Auseinandersetzung*) with what happened, with what we were'.[57] As Wiggershaus notes in his short biography of Habermas, 'The article broke with the taboo on addressing or even critically mentioning earlier or retrospectively important connections with national socialism. . .'[58]

Habermas's developing work was fundamentally shaped by the memory of Nazism, from his early participation in a survey of the political consciousness of students, through his anxieties about the post-war public sphere and his critique of technocracy to his involvement with the student movement in 1967–68 and his developed theories of communicative action and discourse ethics and law to, finally, his 'postnational' vision for Europe.[59] The relation to the past returned more directly in his intervention in 1986–87 in what came to be known as the 'historians' dispute'. This concerned both the work of historians themselves – in particular the maverick right-winger Ernst Nolte, who had claimed that the Holocaust was a partly defensive imitation of terror in the Soviet Union – and also attempts by conservative politicians to draw a thick line under the past and present a positive image of West Germany. In an article ironically entitled 'A Kind of Settlement of Damages' (a term taken from the insurance industry), Habermas differentiated between legitimate historicization of the Third Reich and a revisionism driven by 'the impulse to *shake off* the mortgages of a happily de-moralized past'. Approaches of the former kind

> proceed from the view that the task of distantiating understanding liberates the power of a reflective remembrance and thereby extends the scope of an autonomous treatment of ambivalent traditions. The latter would like to use a revisionist history for the national-historical refurbishment of a conventional identity.[60]

In the acrimonious controversy, several historians and commentators adopted the same defensive and diversionary approach already mentioned, with much discussion of the fact that Habermas had run together two quotations (as I have just done above).

A second, more substantial example of critical theorists' engagement with the German past is Helmut Dubiel's book on West German parliamentary debates. In a preliminary presentation of this material, he had noted that 'In the immediate post-war period totalitarian domination and democracy were perceived by the Germans as unrelated historical phenomena.'[61] Dubiel's analysis is however guided by the idea, first formulated by the philosopher

Karl Jaspers in lectures at Heidelberg in 1945–46, that the reconstruction of German democracy was linked to a willingness to accept collective responsibility for Nazism. For Dubiel, in an approach which he has later applied to the European Union (EU), '. . . collective identity, the awareness of a shared social space, always arises only when the various groups in a society argue (*streiten*) over the shaping of its future and the interpretation of its past.'[62]

As Dubiel shows, an acceptance of guilt was astonishingly slow to develop in West Germany. (In the East, the issue was side-stepped in another way, with the argument that the German Democratic Republic (GDR) had emerged from the struggle *against* German fascism.) The West German federal republic, also established in 1949 with limited sovereignty, was conceived as a provisional state, pending future reunification of Germany, and also as the legal successor to the Third Reich. This status carried with it certain concrete obligations, such as reparation payments to Israel and to other victims of Nazism inside and outside Germany, but also a broader responsibility to confront the horror of the recent past. Yet as late as 1997, long *after* reunification, an exhibition of photographs of well-documented atrocities by the German armed forces in the Second World War caused a storm of protest, recalling earlier motifs of the West German discussion such as the projection of all responsibility onto Hitler and other fanatical Nazis for a catastrophe in which *all* Germans were presented as victims.[63]

The Bundestag's opening session in September 1949 echoes the evasions noted by the young Habermas and revived in the *Historikerstreit* of the 1980s. When the 'father of the House' (*Alterspräsident*), the SPD representative Paul Löbe, referred to the 24 social democratic representatives in the old Reichstag who had become victims of Nazism, members from other parties protested that some of *their* predecessors had also suffered, and the session degenerated into mutual recrimination. On the whole, the Nazi past seems to have been passed over in the 1950s, with an anti-totalitarian discourse stressing the difference between the Third Reich and the Federal Republic, and the continuation of dictatorship in the GDR. The 1960s saw a more substantial discussion in the context of the prosecution of Nazi crimes; the normal period after which prosecution was impossible was extended from 15 to 20 and then 30 years (and, at the end of the 1970s) indefinitely. In the 1970s, the panic over terrorism led to a revival of the critique of totalitarianism, with a number of more perceptive commentators pointing out the contribution of Fascism and Nazism to the violence of generational conflict in Italy and West Germany. The 1980s were marked by the clumsy attempts of Helmut Kohl and his advisor and speech-writer Michael Stürmer, along with right-wing parliamentarians such as Alfred Dregger, to draw a line under the past.[64] The Federal President, Richard von Weizsäcker, made an important counter-initiative in a speech on the 40th anniversary of the end of Nazism. As Dubiel comments, 'Never before in the history of the Federal Republic had one of its political representatives acknowledged with such force and rhetorical precision the specific responsibility of the Germans for their Nazi past.'[65] This broke with the longstanding tendency to identification either with the victims of the Third Reich or with the victors (particularly the *Western* allies) in the War.[66]

Yet, as we have seen, the conflicts over German history continued through the 1980s, until the frame changed again with the 1989 revolutions and the countdown to unification. Despite the flood of literature on the history of the German nation, one can, Dubiel suggests, see the beginnings of a reflective conception of post-national democratic identity which engages seriously with the darker sides of the past. This theme recurs on a larger stage, in the work of Dubiel and others, in relation to contemporary Europe and its own conflicted past of colonialism and war. Precisely because of the past, West Germans have been particularly keen to identify with Europe, and in his opening speech in the Bundestag Paul Löbe expressed the wish that a united Germany would be 'an upright and well-intentioned member of a united Europe'.[67] The *Grundgesetz* was reformulated in 1992 to give constitutional weight to the pursuit of European unity. Furthermore, the success of German federalism means that what in Britain is called the 'f-word' is not a source of anxiety. Once again, German political culture displays a dualism between the defensive nationalism of a kind which was prevalent in the post-war years and a more cosmopolitan strand, grounded in a reflective appropriation of historical memory.

What I have called the third response of critical theory to the Nazi catastrophe, the strengthening of defences against any revival of that kind of irrationalist nationalism, can be seen in some of the practical work of the Post-War Frankfurt School, in Habermas's early and continuing concern with the public sphere and, more broadly, in his rationalist approach to moral and political discussion. Axel Honneth's analysis of recognition and (dis) respect can also be seen as an attempt to provide a grounding for humanistic politics.

Once again, the stereotype of Adorno and Horkheimer as elitist mandarin intellectuals is belied by their active involvement in a broadly pedagogic project in post-war Germany. As Clemens Albrecht and his co-authors write in their rather critical account of the impact of the Frankfurt School, it was a crucial part of what they call the 'intellectual inauguration' of the Federal Republic in the late 1960s and early 1970s – a process closely linked to the theme of 'working through the past' from around 1959 onwards, and to which Adorno made a key contribution.[68] As early as 1942, the Institute produced a memorandum for the US State Department urging the need 'to study the question of combating post-War chauvinism in Germany'.[69] As Albrecht et al. note, citing the second-generation critical theorist Albrecht Wellmer, '. . . critical theory was the only position which made possible a radical break with fascism without breaking with one's own cultural identity.' In Wellmer's words, it was Adorno 'who liberated the authentic elements of German culture from reactionary contamination and made them available to . . . [the] . . . post-war generation.[70]

Elisabeth Noelle-Neumann, the doyenne of West German public opinion research, comments in a similar vein:

Only if one knows how hard it is to change people and societies can one discern how extraordinary was the achievement of Adorno and the Frankfurt School . . . the value-change and therefore the generation gap was much starker than in other countries.'[71]

The fact that the Institute returned to Frankfurt was an important element in its impact, as Horkheimer later noted.[72] The city and the state of Hessen also provided a favourable base for public engagement on radio and television. As Albrecht documents, Horkheimer and Adorno were much the most prominent figures in discussions of philosophy and sociology, and one of the peaks of newspaper coverage of the Frankfurt School coincides with the discussion of 'working through the past' at the end of the 1950s – the others being the years of its return to Frankfurt and 1967–68.[73]

The Institute's research projects were also centred around German political culture, broadly conceived. The two most substantial ones were the group experiment discussed above and, at the end of the 1950s, a survey of students and politics in which two post-war critical theorists, Habermas and Ludwig von Friedeburg, played a leading role. The study was set up in such a way as to problematize the relationship between formal and substantive democracy and the question whether political participation should be seen, as Habermas put it in his introduction, 'a value in itself'.

Habermas's account of the contemporary situation in West Germany and other Western European states prefigures that in his later book on the public sphere. With the partial resolution of the 'social question' in a welfare state with a fully democratic franchise, and with the decline of open class antagonism, the contradiction 'has changed its form: it now appears as the depoliticization of the masses coinciding with the progressive politicization [in the sense of party political and parliamentary incorporation] of society itself'. This society 'increasingly functionalizes its citizens for various public purposes, but it privatizes them in their consciousness'.[74] It is thus not surprising that a large proportion of students, even those who consider themselves to be 'good citizens', are relatively distanced from politics.

The results of the study, then, suggested a rather unpolitical student cohort, with a rather weak commitment to democracy. Almost as interesting as the results themselves were the divergent reactions of Horkheimer and Adorno. Horkheimer, predictably, was unhappy about publishing the study, fearing hostile publicity; it eventually appeared not in the Institute's book series but with a different publisher. Adorno defended the study in terms that were to recur later in the 1960s in relation to the student movement. In a letter to Horkheimer, one of the first exchanges reflecting their switch from the formal 'Sie' to the more intimate 'Du', he wrote:

> In the end our young people [literally 'colts and fillies'] have tried to do something which we always demanded of them: to bring theoretical motifs which they got from us . . . together with empirical material. I do not think we should reproach them for this.[75]

For Adorno, the results were not pessimistic enough: he suspected that they concealed latent tendencies to paranoia and authoritarianism behind what appeared on the surface as realism; the apparently uninvolved threatened to present themselves at some future time as a new charismatic elite.[76] The study had a massive impact, not least on the emerging socialist student movement, the Sozialistischer Deutscher Studentenbund (SDS).[77]

By now Horkheimer had retired to live in Switzerland, having prevented Habermas from submitting his Habilitation thesis at Frankfurt. This study, *The Structural Transformation of the Public Sphere,* was his first major work and, like the student study, had a major impact in Germany. In this book, Habermas's strategy was to relate the concept of public opinion back to its historical roots in the idea of public sphere or public domain (Öffentlichkeit) in the hope of 'attaining a systematic comprehension of our own society from the perspective of one of its central categories'.[78] Among the causes of the emergence of the eighteenth century bourgeois public, which took on a political role in the evaluation of contemporary affairs and, in particular, state policy, was a shift in the relationship between state and society which prefigures the later one described in *Student und Politik*. With the growth of trade and industry, state policy came to have an importance for the growing bourgeoisie which it had not had in a society of small-scale household production and retailing; hence the enormous growth in the newspaper market. In addition to any independent desire for greater democratic influence, people needed to know what the state was doing or failing to do and to influence it as far as they could.

Of course, Habermas admits, the idealized concept of public opinion as it was incorporated into constitutional theory was not at all fully realized; he notes, somewhat casually, the limitations of class and gender[79] and the tendencies to commercialization in the press.[80] The second of these processes forms part of what Habermas calls the transformation of the public sphere – a shift from publicity in the abstract sense of openness, to the modern sense of the term in journalism, advertising and politics.[81] In addition to these trends, there is the expansion of the state's role as it develops into a welfare state, and the growth of large private concerns with a 'quasi-political character'.[82] Private law, especially in relation to property rights, is transformed as it necessarily becomes relevant to public law, in, for example, labour law or the law of tenancy, or in increasingly frequent contracts between the public authorities and private individuals or corporations. This blurring of the distinction between public and private law corresponds to a changed relationship between state and society.[83]

In *Structural Transformation*, however, Habermas focuses on the role of publicity and public opinion in these changed conditions. The principle of critical publicity gets watered down as it expands into wider and wider areas of modern life. The reading public, which had prefigured the political public, also prefigures the latter's decline into 'minorities of specialists who put their reason to use publicly and the great mass of consumers whose receptiveness is public but uncritical'.[84] 'Whereas the press could previously merely mediate the reasoning process of the private people who had come together in public, this reasoning is now, conversely, only formed by the mass media' (p. 188). The same is true of the political process, split between a small number of party activists and a basically inactive mass electorate; public opinion ceases to be a source of critical judgement and checks, and becomes a social-psychological variable to be manipulated. The result is a 'gap between the constitutional fiction of public opinion and the social-psychological dissolution of its concept'.[85]

Habermas writes at times of a dialectic of Öffentlichkeit, evoking Horkheimer and Adorno's *Dialectic of Enlightenment*. Just as the enlightenment critique of myth turned into another myth, the principle of the bourgeois public sphere, the critical assessment of public policy in terms of rational discussion oriented to a concept of the public interest, turns into what Habermas calls a manipulated public sphere in which states and corporations use 'publicity' in the modern sense to secure for themselves a kind of plebiscitary acclamation. Habermas's version, however, is both more carefully grounded in the results of historical, sociological and political scientific research, and also somewhat less pessimistic in its conclusions. Habermas envisaged certain counter-tendencies to, and opportunities in, the process he described.

When the liberal constitutional state develops into a welfare state and thus massively extends the range of its activity, 'the requirement of publicity is extended from the organs of the state to all organizations acting in relation to the state'.[86] These organizations are thus opened up to scrutiny by, and dialogue with, a corresponding variety of interest groups which link together members of the public concerned with specific aspects of welfare state provision. Although the bureaucratization of administration may seem to remove the activity of specialists from rational control, it might yet be possible to create, by means of public communication within these organizations, 'an appropriate relation between bureaucratic decision and quasi-parliamentary deliberation'.[87] With these two books, Habermas had opened up issues of relevance both to contemporary Germany and to the West as a whole.[88] As Specter points out, *Structural Transformation* was in part the beginnings of a response to

> . . . the peculiarities of the West German intellectual field, which was structured by an empirical and positivist political science on the one hand, and a conservative statist constitutional theory on the other. What was missing was a combined Critical Theory of politics, the state, and law with a strong normative perspective.[89]

I have already discussed the work of Klaus Eder and Helmut Dubiel, representing a response to the authoritarian past by a third generation of critical theorists. Axel Honneth's focus on injustice, which shapes his work since as early as 1981, forms a link with earlier critical theory, as he notes in what is more or less the title essay of *Pathologien der Vernunft. Geschichte und Gegenwart der kritischen Theorie*. In this essay, 'A Social Pathology of Reason. On the intellectual heritage of critical theory', Honneth suggests that, although we are now a similar distance from the beginnings of critical theory as its protagonists were from the last representatives of classical idealism,[90] critical theory is still linked by its model of '. . . socially effective reason.' In Honneth's work, this involves a model of recognition, of respect and disrespect, but also a notion of social pathology which he locates in relation to 'processes of social development that can be viewed as misdevelopments . . .'.[91] The 'diagnosis of the times' becomes specifically a diagnosis of social pathology. Thus 'In order to be able to speak of a social pathology that is accessible to the medical model of diagnosis, we require a conception of normality related to social life as a whole.'[92] In what he calls 'a weak, formal, anthropology',[93] Honneth gestures towards 'an ethical conception of social normality tailored to conditions that enable human self-realization'.[94]

This important initiative makes explicit something which had been latent in much of critical theory. The theme of suffering, of misdevelopment and 'damaged life',[95] pervades the work of the first generation of critical theorists, and Habermas's reworking in *Theory of Communicative Action* of Marxist, Weberian and indeed Parsonian theory contains a substantial discussion of social pathologies. Honneth has however pushed this theme further, against the limits of the organic analogies and functionalist assumptions which he, like most of us these days, would find unacceptable.[96] And in the book based on his lectures on reification, having given a hostage to fortune with an example of his notion of 'reification as forgetting' as someone forgetting themselves in the heat of a sporting contest, Honneth clarifies in his 'Rejoinder' that his real starting point was reflection on industrialized mass murder.[97]

Notes

1 Helmut Dubiel, 'Ihre Zeit in Gedanken erfasst. Entwicklungsstufen kritischer Theorie', *Institut für Sozialforschung, Mitteilungen*, Heft 4, 1994, p. 6.

2 Institut für Sozialforschung, *Studien über Autorität und Familie*, Paris: Alcan, 1936.

3 Theodor W. Adorno et al., *The Authoritarian Personality*, New York: Harper and Row, 1950.

4 Max Horkheimer and Samuel Flowerman (eds), *Studies in Prejudice*, vols 1–5, New York: Harper and Brothers, 1949–50.

5 Friedrich Pollock (ed.), *Gruppenexperiment: Ein Studienbericht*, Frankfurt: Europäische Verlags-Anstalt, 1955.

6 David Smith, 'The Ambivalent Worker', *Social Thought and Research*, 21(1–2), 1998, pp. 35–83, traces the continuity from studies of workers by Max Weber and Adolf Levenstein (1912) through to critical theory.

7 Siegfried Kracauer, *The Salaried Masses: Duty and Distraction in Weimar Germany*, London: Verso, 1998, p. 88.

8 Ibid., p. 101.

9 Benjamin, 'An Outsider Attracts Attention', *The Salaried Masses*, p. 114.

10 Ibid., pp. 109–10.

11 Quoted by Inka Mülder-Bach, 'Introduction' to *The Salaried Masses*, p. 19, n. 9. Walter Benjamin's 'Theories of German Fascism', published in the same year, translated in *New German Critique*, 17, 1979, pp. 120–8, applies his own theory of political aesthetics to the proto-fascist writers he discusses.

12 Erich Fromm, *The Working Class in Weimar Germany*, Bonss, W. (ed.), Leamington Spa: Berg, 1984, p. 41.

13 Fromm, *The Working Class in Weimar Germany*, p. 44.

14 The survey was not representative of gender, with only 9 per cent women, and the young and old also under-represented.

15 The final stage was a half-hearted invitation to rejoin the Institute in Frankfurt in 1953–54, by which time Marcuse had accepted a post at Brandeis University in Massachusetts.

16 G. L. Ulmen, *The Science of Society. Toward an Understanding of the Life and Work of Karl August Wittfogel,* The Hague: Mouton, 1978, Chapter 5.

17 'Warum Hitler seine Konkurrenz zerschlug', *Der Rote Aufbau,* Nr. 13, 1932, reprinted in Kommunistischer Bund, *Kampf dem Faschismus,* Hamburg: J. Reents Verlag, 1973, pp. 217–21.

18 K. A. Wittfogel (Hans Petersen) (1932b) 'Wer finanziert Hitler?', *Der Rote Aufbau,* Nr. 13, 1932, reprinted in Kommunistischer Bund, *Kampf dem Faschismus,* Hamburg: J. Reents Verlag, 1973, pp. 222–5.

19 K. A. Wittfogel (1932c) 'Die Demagogie der Frühprogramme des Faschismus', *Der Rote Aufbau,* Nr. 16, 1932, reprinted in Kommunistischer Bund, *Kampf dem Faschismus,* Hamburg: J. Reents Verlag, 1973, pp. 245–56.

20 Franz Borkenau, *The Totalitarian Enemy,* London: Faber, 1940, p. 13.

21 Rolf Wiggershaus, *The Frankfurt School,* Cambridge: Polity, 1994, p. 125.

22 Ibid., p. 228.

23 Ibid., p. 286.

24 Ibid., p. 290.

25 Keith Tribe, 'Franz Neumann in der Emigration: 1933–1942', in Axel Honneth and Albrecht Wellmer (eds), *Die Frankfurter Schule und die Folgen,* Alexander von Humboldt-Stiftung Symposium 1984, Berlin: De Gruyter, 1986, pp. 259–74.

26 Georg Rusche and Otto Kirchheimer, *Punishment and Social Structure,* New York: Columbia University Press, 1939.

27 Otto Kirchheimer, 'Changes in the Structure of Political Compromise', *Studies in Philosophy and Social Science* 9(2), 1941, pp. 264–89. Reprinted in Andrew Arato and Eike Gebhardt (eds), *The Essential Frankfurt School Reader,* Oxford: Blackwell, 1978, pp. 49–70.

28 Honneth stresses the contribution of the 'outer circle' made up of Fromm, Benjamin, Neumann and Kirchheimer in his essay in Anthony Giddens and Jonathan Turner (eds), *Social Theory Today,* Cambridge: Polity Press, 1987.

29 Alfred Schmidt (1993: 27) notes however that they were a significant influence on the West German student movement. Horkheimer's critique of the socialist and communist parties in Germany interestingly echoes Kant's famous maxim that 'concepts without perceptions are empty: perceptions without concepts are blind'. For Horkheimer (1978: 63), the theoretical weakness of the socialists is contrasted with the conceptual dogmatism of the communists. On Horkheimer's early reflections on the Soviet Union, see Chapter 4, below.

30 Max Horkheimer, 'Die Juden und Europa', *Zeitschrift für Sozialforschung*, 8(1–2), 1939, p. 115.

31 Wiggershaus, *The Frankfurt School*, pp. 429–30.

32 Ibid., p. 441.

33 A. Demirović, *Der nonkonformistische Intellektuelle. Die Entwicklung der kritischen Theorie zur Frankfurter Schule*, Frankfurt: Suhrkamp, 1999, p. 361.

34 Pollock, *Gruppenexperiment*, pp. 278–9.

35 See Wiggershaus, *The Frankfurt School*, pp. 472–9; Demirović, *Der nonkonformistische Intellektuelle*, pp. 353–72.

36 P. 376. For more discussion of the 'stimulus', see pp. 42ff., 340 and 482.

37 Pollock, *Gruppenexperiment*, p. 11.

38 Ibid., p. 377.

39 Theodor W. Adorno, 'Die auferstandene Kultur', *Frankfurter Hefte* 5, May 1950, pp. 469–77. Reprinted in Adorno, *Gesammelte Schriften*, Frankfurt: Suhrkamp, 1986, 20.2, pp. 453–64.

40 Wiggershaus, *The Frankfurt School*, p. 257. See also Martin Jay, 'The Jews and the Frankfurt School: Critical Theory's Analysis of Anti-Semitism', *New German Critique*, 19, Winter 1980, pp. 17–149; reprinted in Jay, *Permanent Exiles. Essays on the Intellectual Migration from Germany to America*, New York: Columbia University Press, 1985, pp. 90–100.

41 'Vobemerkung' (sic), *Zeitschrift für Sozialforschung* III(2), 1934, p. 230, cited in Michael Robertson's translation in Wiggershaus, p. 142.

42 Wiggershaus, *The Frankfurt School*, p. 448.

43 Max Horkheimer, *Dämmerung*. Translated by Michael Shaw as *Dawn and Decline. Notes 1926–1931 and 1950–1969*, New York: Seabury, 1978, pp. 195–6. As the last surviving Nazi war criminals are sporadically apprehended in the present century, it is worth recalling that Eichmann was only 54 when he was captured in 1960.

44 Horkheimer wrote in 'The Jews and Europe' that 'those who can only play politics should stay clear of it'. (last page)

45 As Demirović notes (*Der nonkonformistische Intellektuelle*, pp. 367–71), they were also willing to discuss cooperating with the West German army in designing a process for screening recruits and advising the internal security agency, the Bundesamt für Verfassungsschutz, on issues to do with communism.

46 Ibid., p. 486.

47 Eder, *Geschichte als Lernprozess? Zur Pathogenese politischer Modernität in Deutschland*, Frankfurt: Suhrkamp, 1985, pp. 9, 14.

48 Ibid., pp. 57–62.

49 Ibid., p. 112.

50 Ibid., p. 119.

51 Ibid., pp. 289–90.

52 Ibid., p. 527, n. 119.

53 Hermann Korte, 'Norbert Elias', in Dirk Kaesler (ed.), *Klassiker der Soziologie 1. Von Auguste Comte bis Norbert Elias*. Munich: Beck, 2000, pp. 321–2.

54 Norbert Elias, *The Germans*, Cambridge: Polity, 1996, p. 14. The weakness of the German middle classes at national level did however combine with a stronger local presence. As Joachim Radkau (*Max Weber*, Cambridge: Polity, 2009, p. 57) notes in his biography of Max Weber, 'Those who speak of imperial Germany's fake parliamentarism and emphasize its civic deficit in comparison with the West usually overlook the fact that the German middle classes had a local field of political activity that was better developed than in Britain or France.' Weber's own fiercely nationalistic liberal politics is an example of many of the attitudes discussed by both Elias and Eder.

55 See Micael Björk, 'A Plea for Detached Involvement: Norbert Elias on Intellectuals and Political Imagination in Inter-war Germany', *History of the Human Sciences*, 18(2), 2005, pp. 43–61.

56 'The German Idealism of the Jewish Philosophers', in Jürgen Habermas, *Philosophical-Political Profiles*, London: Heinemann p. 41. See also Jürgen Habermas, *Autonomy and Solidarity*, Peter Dews (ed.), London: Verso, 1986; 2nd edn, London: Verso, 1992, pp. 77–8.

57 Habermas, *Philosophisch-Politische Profile*, p. 75.

58 Rolf Wiggershaus, *Jürgen Habermas*, Reinbek bei Hamburg: Rowohlt, 2004, p. 30.

59 Some of these themes are discussed in later chapters; see also my book on Habermas and further literature listed there.

60 Habermas, 'A Kind of Settlement of Damages (Apologetic Tendencies)', *New German Critique*, 44, Spring–Summer 1988, p. 37; translation modified.

61 *Merkur* 48, pp. 546–7, September–October 1994. The phrase is repeated in the introduction to the book, *Niemand ist frei von der Geschichte. Die nationalsozialistische Herrschaft in den Debatten des deutschen Bundestages*, Munich, Carl Hanser, 1999, p. 9.

62 Dubiel, op cit., p. 13.

63 As Dubiel notes (op cit., p. 74), the German word Opfer combines the notion of a *victim* of crime with a more mystical sense of a sacrificial victim.

64 See, for example, Helmut Dubiel and Günther Frankenberg, 'Entsorgung der Vergangenheit. Widerspruch gegen eine neokonservative Legende', *Die Zeit*, 18(3), 1983.

65 Dubiel, op cit., p. 208.

66 Ibid., p. 215.

67 Cited by Dubiel, op cit., p. 38.

68 Clemens Albrecht et al., Introduction, *Die intellektuelle Gründung der Bundesrepublik. Eine Wirkungsgeschichte der Frankfurter Schule*, Frankfurt p. 20; see also p. 96. As the authors note, Adorno was repeatedly cited, most recently just before the book's publication, in a speech of 1999 by the president of the Bundestag.

69 Cited in Albrecht, p. 120.

70 Albrecht, p. 570. The quotation from Wellmer is from p. 26 of his essay, 'Die Bedeutung der Frankfurter Schule Heute', in Axel Honneth and Albrecht Wellmer (eds), *Die Frankfurter Schule und die Folgen*, Berlin: De Gruyter, 1986, pp. 25–34.

71 Elisabeth Noelle-Neumann, 'Familie und Schule im Spannungsfeld gesellschaftlicher Umbrüche', *Pädagogische Welt*, 49(4) 1995, p. 191; cited by Demirović, *Der nonkonformistische Intellektuelle*, p. 10.

72 Horkheimer interview, cited by Demirović, p. 15. He and Adorno had written in the Introduction to the 1969 reprint of *Dialectic of Enlightenment* that they had returned to Germany believing that they 'could do more there than elsewhere' (Demirović, p. 42). At the end of the War, Horkheimer had canvassed the idea of an 'inter-European academy' (Demirović, pp. 105–6) – something eventually realized, at least for doctoral students, in the European University Institute in Florence.

73 See the tables in Albrecht et al., pp. 228–31.

74 Habermas, *Student und Politik*, p. 34.

75 Letter of 15 March 1960, cited by Demirović, *Der nonkonformistische Intellektuelle*, p. 253.

76 See Demirović, *Der nonkonformistische Intellektuelle*, pp. 253–7.

77 Ibid., pp. 258–63.

78 Jürgen Habermas, *The Structural Transformation of the Public Sphere*, Cambridge: Polity, 1989, p. 5.

79 Ibid., pp. 85ff.

80 Ibid., pp. 181ff.

81 Ibid., p. 140.

82 Ibid., p. 148.

83 See, for example ibid., pp. 151, 231.

84 Ibid., p. 175.

85 Ibid., p. 244; cf. section 24, pp. 236–44.

86 Ibid., p. 232.

87 Ibid., p. 234.

88 On the way in which this model of the public sphere is limited by a focus on the territorial national state, see the title essay of Jürgen Habermas, *The Postnational Constellation*, Cambridge: Polity, 2001 and Nancy Fraser, 'Transnationalizing the Public Sphere: On the Legitimacy and Efficacy of Public Opinion in a PostWestphalian World', in Seyla Benhabib, Ian Shapiro and Danilo Petranović (eds), *Identities, Affiliations, and Allegiances*, Cambridge: Cambridge University Press, 2007, pp. 45–66. See also Chapter 5, below.

89 Matthew Specter, *Habermas: An Intellectual Biography*, New York: Cambridge University Press, 2010, p. 60; cf. Habermas, *Structural Transformation*, p. xvii.

90 Axel Honneth, *Pathologien der Vernunft. Geschichte und Gegenwart der Kritischen Theorie*, Frankfurt: Suhrkamp, 2007, p. 28.

91 Honneth, *Pathologien der Vernunft*, p. 4.

92 Ibid., p. 34.

93 Ibid., p. 42. In the sense, of course, of philosophical anthropology (see Honneth and Joas, 1980).

94 Ibid., p. 36.

95 T. W. Adorno, *Minima Moralia. Reflections from Damaged Life,* Frankfurt: Suhrkamp, 1951, tr. London: Verso, 1974.

96 There is an excellent discussion of these issues by Christopher Zurn: 'Social Pathologies as Second-Order Disorders', in Danielle Petherbridge (ed.), *The Critical Theory of Axel Honneth*, Leiden: Brill. Zurn notes at the beginning of his article that it has received much less attention than the theme of recognition. I am grateful to Gordon Finlayson for drawing this to my attention. See also Zurn, 'Recognition, Redistribution, and Democracy: Dilemmas of Honneth's Critical Social Theory', *European Journal of Philosophy*, 13(1), 2005, pp. 89–126.

97 Axel Honneth, *Reification. A New Look at an Old Idea.* With Commentaries by Judith Butler, Raymond Geuss and Jonathan Lear. Edited and Introduced by Martin Jay. The Berkeley Tanner Lectures 2005, New York: Oxford University Press, 2008.

2

'Late' capitalism, from the post-war boom to the crises of the 1970s: the 1968 years and the *Tendenzwende*

The term 'late capitalism' (Spätkapitalismus), sometimes translated more neutrally as 'advanced capitalism', is now firmly associated with the 1960s, though it appears in the first volume of the *Zeitschrift für Sozialfoschung*, in a review by Gerhard Meyer of a pamphlet by Werner Sombart and other literature on the planned economy.[1] Adorno and Horkheimer had not had much to say about the post-war 'economic miracle' in West Germany or the related 'thirty glorious years' in Western Europe as a whole. They confined themselves to occasional dismissive comments about the 'Americanisation' of West Germany[2] and the culture industry. The key contribution came in fact from America, in the form of Marcuse's *One Dimensional Man*. This book developed motifs from Marcuse's earlier discussion of technology and culture in his pre-war essays and in *Eros and Civilization* (1955), and also forms a 'Western' counterpoint to his book on *Soviet Marxism* (1958). Like that book, it focuses particularly on ideology; it was originally sub-titled 'Studies in the Ideology of Industrial Society'. The critique of 'one-dimensional' thinking, which overlooks or excludes critical reflection on alternative possibilities in advanced capitalist societies, is grounded in a broadly sketched account of post-war affluence and an economy dominated by technology – the latter being a common feature of capitalist and communist societies. Although the illustrative examples are mainly North American, Marcuse, who had frequently taught in France in the late 1950s and early 1960s, drew substantially on contemporary French critiques of capitalism and technocracy, by François Perroux, Serge Mallet and others. In Perroux's formulation, 'The collusion of modern industry and territorial power is a vice which is more profoundly real than capitalist or communist institutions or structures . . .'[3]

What Marcuse did, then, was to bring together the critique of domination which he had shared with Adorno and Horkheimer at the time they were writing *Dialectic of Enlightenment* with a more developed analysis of the contemporary West. As Albrecht Wellmer noted, *Dialectic of Enlightenment* aimed 'to ground the critique of capitalist society so deeply in the philosophy of history that it touches both the liberal capitalism criticised by Marx and its state capitalist or state interventionist successors'.[4] As Johann Arnason notes, the same is true of *One Dimensional Man*.[5] He had also managed to present an uncompromisingly philosophical analysis of the contemporary world in a remarkably readable text which reached readers across Europe and America unaware of Adorno, Horkheimer or Habermas. The theme of technology was common to the Left and the Right in the mid-twentieth century, linking Heidegger, with whom Marcuse had studied in the early 1930s, the philosopher Arnold Gehlen, Helmut Schelsky, Germany's leading right-wing sociologist in the 1950s, and the young Habermas. In a 1960 article, Marcuse had written that 'technology has replaced ontology'. This convergence aroused the suspicion of a number of critics on the left, including Claus Offe. More substantively, Offe and a number of other critics pointed to the lack of a theory of capitalism which would explain *why* it had been technologised in this way. For Offe, this required an attention to 'concrete, *socially interpreted interests*': '. . . the technical universe should itself be traced back to the antagonism of interest which sustains it.[6]

Habermas took up the theme in the course of the 1960s, with a series of essays published together under the title *Technology and Science as Ideology*, of which the title essay was originally intended for the volume he edited on Marcuse.[7] Habermas was concerned more precisely with the critique of technocracy – the undermining of rational political discourse by arguments from ostensibly scientific authority. Already in 1963 he had addressed these issues in an essay in *Theory and Practice* entitled 'Dogmatism, Reason and Decision – on Theory and Practice in a Scientised Civilisation'. Here, he writes, the problem is not just that science has become 'a technical force', but that 'we can no longer distinguish between technical and practical [in the sense of moral or political] force'.[8] This had also been the main theme of his intervention in the 'positivism dispute' in the early 1960s, in which the 'Frankfurt School', as it was now coming to be called, upheld its conception of critical science against more empiricist and value-neutral ones. What came to be called the 'positivism dispute' began in 1961 with lectures to the German Sociological Association by Karl Popper, the Austrian philosopher of science based in London, and Adorno, and a comment by the liberal sociologist Ralf Dahrendorf; there was a second round between Habermas and the empiricist Hans Albert.

Marcuse's book, translated into German and Italian in 1967 and into French (by the feminist theorist Monique Wittig) in 1968, Europeanised the reception of critical theory. By now there were active student and youth protest movements across Western Europe, as well as in North America. For anyone looking for signs of the emergence of a common European culture, these movements are crucially important. The British slogan 'We shall fight and we shall win: London, Paris, Rome, Berlin' reversed the historical sequence of the movements' peaks, which was more like Berlin (and Frankfurt) 1967, Paris summer 1968, Rome and London 1968 onwards, but points up their internationalism. Daniel Cohn-Bendit, one of the leading figures in the French movement, symbolised this in his dual nationality. When a right-wing paper attacked him as a German and a Jew and the Communist Party leader Georges Marchais also called him a 'German anarchist', demonstrators shouted 'we are all German Jews'. Although there was no realistic prospect of revolution (though the Gaullist regime in France came close to collapsing), the Marxist critique of capitalism was solidly back on the agenda, with even Marcuse being rebuked by more orthodox Marxists for straying too far from the tradition. In Eastern Europe, of course, 1968 came to mean something very different: the extinction of the dream that communism could be liberalised.

Marcuse was seen everywhere as the godfather of the student revolt and was a prominent speaker in France and West Germany.[9] There, it was the 'Frankfurt School' which was seen as the intellectual backbone of the movement, with considerable justification. Habermas, Claus Offe, Oskar Negt (who was Habermas's assistant in Heidelberg from 1961 to 1964) and others were active around the SDS, and even Adorno, who had occasionally lectured at SDS meetings but was otherwise more reserved, joined in the protests against the murder of a Berlin student by a police officer.[10] Offe, in particular, Habermas's first assistant in sociology from 1965, had been one of the authors of a substantial pamphlet by the socialist student association, the SDS, in 1961 on the university in democracy, which was republished in expanded form as a book in 1965.[11] Ulrich Preuss, one of the authors of the book, later published a brilliant

discussion of 'the political mandate of the student body', in response to a decision in 1967 by the West Berlin Administrative Court condemning the Free
University students' association's support for the South Vietnamese National
Liberation Front.[12] Preuss argued that the students' 'freedom to learn' and thus
to participate in scholarly research necessarily included a right to reflect on the
social conditions of scientific (including social scientific) work.

*Questioning
Science*

A conception of scholarship which restricts itself to, on the one hand
individual reflection with the subjective purpose of discovering truth and
on the other to the strict demands of the modern sciences, overlooks a line
of development characterised by an interest in the enlightenment of the
practical consciousness of active human beings.[13]

An implication of a 'critical theory' of scholarship is that 'politics' has a
legitimate place in the University, not only as the discipline of 'political
science'.[14]

Wellmer and Habermas published a short statement in support of this position on the basis of their work in the philosophy of science.[15]

Habermas had been writing on university issues since the late 1950s
and his essays represent a major engagement with contemporary reality.
Although Habermas ended up taking a much more critical attitude to the
adventurism of the student movement, as Adorno had done from the beginning, and had always been sceptical about this aspect,[16] he wrote a good
deal on it and continued to see it as a crucial element in the modernization
of West German political culture. This, like the democratic reform of universities, he saw as entirely positive; what he attacked was what he called
'actionism' and an unrealistic revolutionary rhetoric. In particular, the 'disfunc-
tionalisation' of university teaching had no justification as a political tactic.[17]
But although the 'repression' criticised by the movement was not the same
as in the Third World, it appears in the more subtle forms of 'rigid orientations and prejudice'. '. . . The students have developed an unusual sensitivity
to just these repressions . . . to the costs for life histories of a society dominated by status competition, pressure to perform and bureaucratisation'.[18] As
Habermas put it in his 1969 introduction to his essays *Protestbewegung und
Hochschulreform*, 'the SDS [the Socialist Student Association] was the motor
of a "movement" which opened up an unforeseen political terrain and thus
the prospects of enlightenment for the purposes of a radical reformism.'[19]
Radical reformism remained his guiding political principle:

The twin categories 'reform' and 'revolution' were sharply differentiated
under other historical conditions. In industrially advanced societies this

contrast no longer discriminates between possible alternative strategies of change. The only way I see for the conscious structural transformation of an authoritarian welfare state social system is radical reformism.[20]

For his part, Adorno, in a major address to the German Sociological Association conference in 1968, took a more theoretical approach to the question of whether contemporary western societies should be seen as late capitalist or industrial (his answer was that they were both).[21] This conference, taking place at the height of a second wave of student protest, was an impressive attempt to address the issues of the time and represented, however problematically, a high-point of the influence of critical theory, which continued to shape the political culture of the '1968' generation of scholars, publicists and politicians now approaching retirement.[22]

After 1968, the movements diffused into an 'alternative' scene on the one hand and professional lives somewhat shaped by 'critical' or 'anti-authoritarian' practices on the other. The critique of capitalism remained however as a main focus of critical theory and other work in the social sciences throughout the following decades. The term 'industrial society', which had been so prominent in the 1950s and early 1960s, even in critical works such as Marcuse's *One Dimensional Man*, tended to be displaced by 'capitalism', just as 'modernity' later became the buzz-word of the last two decades of the twentieth century. In one of his first explicit reflections on earlier critical theory, Habermas noted that '. . . since the end of the 1930s its analytical attention was focussed not on the antagonisms of capitalism but the integration achieved by a transformed system.' This had shaped the reception of critical theory in Germany after the war and led to an attitude of resignation.[23] His own work and that of others in the 1970s put the emphasis back onto capitalism, which had of course always been present in his earlier critiques of scientism, technocracy, and consumerism.

Habermas moved in 1971 to Starnberg, near Munich, to co-direct the 'Max Planck Institute for the investigation of the Life-Conditions of the Scientific-Technical World'. Joining a group around the other Director, the physicist Friedrich von Weizsäcker,[24] Habermas was also able to choose up to 15 research associates, nicknamed the 'habermice', who included, as well as Klaus Eder and Helmut Dubiel, the philosopher Ernst Tugendhat and the sociologists Claus Offe, Rainer Döbert and Gertrud Nunner-Winkler. Habermas arrived with a major theoretical project in hand: the reformulation of his critical theory on the basis of a theory of language which he had outlined in his Christian Gauss lectures in 1971 and which eventually appeared in a different form in 1981 as his two-volume *Theory of Communicative Action*. He and his associates also worked on three project areas: the new forms taken by capitalist crises, the ways in which states attempted to contain them and their indirect offshoots in psychological and cultural processes. This was also an attempt to rethink critical theory's earlier analysis of economic, political and cultural processes in the changed conditions of the 1970s. The underlying model, as Habermas presented it in his 1973 book on 'problems of legitimation in late capitalism', was one in which the attempts by capitalist states to manage economic crises undermine their performance (rationality crises) and their legitimacy (legitimation crises), leading to motivational and cultural crises. This model had already been anticipated in Offe's contribution to *Die Linke antwortet Jürgen Habermas*,[25] and he presented it in an essay in 1973.[26]

Legitimation Crisis is a preparatory and tentative work, as indicated by Habermas's expression in the Preface of his concern 'that the clarification of very general structures of hypotheses not be confused with empirical results'.[27] As discussed below, the themes of the book have been carried further by a number of other writers, notably Claus Offe, whom Habermas cites early in the book in relation to the concept of 'late capitalism' and who coined the apt expression 'crises of crisis management', and Johannes Berger.[28]

It is the second part of the book which deals specifically with 'Crisis tendencies in advanced capitalism'. Habermas begins with the reference to late capitalism' in the original title of the book. 'To use the expression "late capitalism" is to put forward the hypothesis that, even in state-regulated capitalism, social developments involve "contradictions" or crises.'[29] In modern social theory, the term crisis involves a disturbance of both system and social integration:

> only when members of a society experience structural alterations as critical for continued existence and feel their social identity threatened can we speak of crises/Social integration refers to the socialization or, better, sociation (Vergesellschaftung) of acting subjects in symbolically structured lifeworlds; system integration to 'the specific steering performances of a self-regulated system.'[30]

Echoing his critique of Niklas Luhmann, Habermas insists that, whereas system theory reduces the former to the latter, an adequate theory must deal with the interconnection of both.[31]

More concretely, Habermas describes 'three universal properties of social systems'. Their 'exchange' with their environments involves both production and socialization, linked, it seems, to factual and normative statements respectively. Second:

> Change in the goal values of social systems is a function of the state of the forces of production and of the degree of system autonomy; but the

variation of goal values is limited by a logic of development of world-views
on which the imperatives of system integration have no influence.

In other words, the increasingly secular, rationalized, universalistic and reflexive character of belief systems is not a simple result of changes in the mode
of production on other system properties. Third, learning in both dimensions, production and socialization, 'determines the level of development of
a society'.[32] This learning theory model of social evolution, which I shall not
discuss here in more detail, is at the core of Habermas' 'reconstruction' of
historical materialism – a theme which he pursued in a number of substantial
essays in the 1970s and in *Theory of Communicative Action.*

Habermas distinguishes four types of social formation, their basic organizational principles and the types of crisis to which they are prone. In 'primitive' societies, based on age and sex roles institutionalized in kinship, change
comes mostly from demographic pressure, ecological effects or inter-ethnic
processes such as exchange and war. Traditional' social formations like the
European anciens régimes are based on political class rule and threatened by
crises arising from internal contradictions, generating problems both of system 'steering' and of the ideological legitimation of an unstable class structure. In liberal-capitalist social formations, whose organizational principle is
the relationship of wage labour and capital, the economic and political spheres
are 'uncoupled', and class exploitation and class rule become anonymous and
depoliticized. This in turn means that ideologies in liberal-capitalist societies
take on a universalistic form, appealing to the common interest embodied in
a system that appears to legitimate itself. In practice, the acquiescence of
the proletariat may owe more to traditionalism, fatalism and repression than
to the convincing force of bourgeois ideologies. 'This does not diminish the
socially integrative significance of this new type of ideology in a society that
no longer recognizes political domination in personal form.'[33]

Despite this qualification, expressed in terms very close to those of Max
Weber's discussion of legitimate domination, it is clear that Habermas, like
Weber, assigns crucial importance to the ways in which social orders are
legitimated. Ideology, in other words, is not simply one means among others by which societies are stabilized; it enters crucially at the level of social
integration into the constitution of societies seen in some way as reflexive
learning systems. This becomes clear when one looks more closely at the
crises characteristic of traditional societies in Habermas's model. In addition
to the 'crowding out' or undermining of the ancien régime state by the market
economy, and the functional weaknesses of the state machine, Habermas
emphasizes the ideological incoherence of traditional societies. 'The contradiction exists between validity claims of systems of norms and justifications

that cannot explicitly permit exploitation, and a class structure in which privileged appropriation of socially produced wealth is the rule.'[34]

As in more conventional forms of Marxism, however, everything depends on the mediating links between the abstract contradiction and empirical social conflicts. For Habermas, 'We can speak of the "fundamental contradiction" of a social formation when, and only when, its organizational principle necessitates that individuals and groups repeatedly confront one another with claims that are, in the long run, incompatible.'[35] In liberal capitalism, because it is the economic system that is primarily responsible for social integration, economic crises are also social crises: 'the dialectical contradiction between members of an interaction context comes to pass in terms of structurally insoluble system contradictions or steering problems.'[36] As Marx put it, rather more snappily, political economy is the anatomy of capitalist society. The question then arises whether this 'logic of crisis' also applies to advanced or 'organized' capitalism, characterized by oligopolistic corporations and state intervention to support or compensate for market mechanisms.[37] The interventionist welfare state, like the pre-capitalist state, again requires direct legitimation. This is provided by a system of formal representative democracy and a structurally depoliticized sphere, which secures mass loyalty but keeps participation below a level which 'would bring to consciousness the contradiction between administratively socialized production and the continued private appropriation and use of surplus value'.[38]

Compared to the analysis in *Structural Transformation of the Public Sphere*, the context is now more explicitly one of a 'processed and repressed system crisis', in which economic tendencies may be displaced on to the political and sociocultural systems.[39] This continues a process characteristic of the classical bourgeois state, in which economically based class conflicts came to be 'channelled into the political system as an institutionalized struggle over distribution'.[40] When this system is instituted, we have the modern welfare state. Now, however, the economic and political systems are recoupled; the politicians are held responsible for the performance of the economic system. Crises become increasingly, in Claus Offe's phrase, crises of crisis management.[41]

Forty years on, it is interesting to look back at this book which was written in the aftermath of the events of May 1968, before the first oil price shock and the neo-conservative turn known in West Germany as the Tendenzwende. Many early readers of the book, especially in countries like the United Kingdom whose economies were already in a very shaky state, questioned the notion that cyclical crises of capitalism could be deflected in the way Habermas suggested, and stuck to more orthodoxly Marxist prognoses of an eventual final crisis. This has of course not materialized, even with the financial crisis of 2008. On the other hand, the more traditional Keynesian methods of eco-nomic crisis management suffered a long period of eclipse, and remain in an uneasy coexistence with more neoliberal and monetarist approaches. More relevant in this context, the neo-Marxist analysis of the fiscal crisis of the state and the other limitations on the welfare state was echoed by the big battalions of the New Right.[42]

What stands out most sharply, perhaps, is the instability of the original conceptual relation between legitimation and 'mass loyalty'. While conceding that there are all kinds of loose ends in the book, Habermas has never really responded to the charge that a normative conception of legitimacy is relatively unimportant for the factual stability of real societies. In a reply to W. Fach, he simply restates his belief in the value of a conception of legitimation grounded in discourse 'for the investigation of critiques of legitimacy and the resul-tant transformations of systems of domination.'[43] As David Held pointed out, Habermas's theory suffers from 'a problematic emphasis on the centrality of shared norms and values in social integration and on the importance of "internalization" in the genesis of individual identity and social order'.[44] But, as Michael Mann, Anthony Giddens and others have also noted, ideologies are much less systematic than intellectuals, including social theorists, tend to assume.[45] And a normative consensus on the legitimacy of a regime may be less crucial than what critical theory tends to brush aside as a residual category of 'mass loyalty'.

In a related line of criticism, Axel Honneth brings out the complexity of the ideas of natural justice and relatively unarticulated critiques of social injustice which may go along with a pragmatic or fatalistic acceptance of it.[46] The con-trast between legitimation and 'mass loyalty' seems much too simple to do justice to this complexity. There is also the question, discussed in the next chapter, of legitimacy in state socialist societies; the long survival, and incred-ibly rapid collapse, of the state socialist dictatorships in Eastern Europe and the USSR are a reminder of the practical difficulties of analyses of this kind. Here too, the applicability of the model has been questioned but it has been an important element in many of the best studies. As Frank Nullmeier notes, the financial crisis of 2008 gives a new relevance to Habermas's account of crises, 'even if, or just because . . . [his] . . . basic thesis of the dampening down and recuperation of economic crises through politics may have mas-sively declined in plausibility'.[47]

Claus Offe, who had been Habermas' assistent in Frankfurt and had been writing about capitalism since 1968, did most to develop this line of analysis in the 1970s and 1980s. Offe's interests had been more precisely focussed on the political sociology of capitalist labour markets and state administra-tion, and his work supplies some at least of the empirical basis called for in

Legitimation Crisis. In Offe's model of late capitalism, the welfare state is the central focus. The main problem becomes that of

> preventing the regulatory processes of *administrative power* (which are 'foreign to capital' and yet upon whose permanent expansion the monopolistic sphere of the economy is dependent) from becoming autonomous and controlling private exchange relationships, either by paralysing them or by subverting them in revolutionary ways . . . As means which deal with the problems generated by capitalist exchange processes, the 'flanking subsystems' (normative structures and state power) become increasingly important.[48]

This is not so much a crisis model, as in Habermas' version, as a structural model of permanent crisis tendencies. As Offe points out, this 'Left' analysis of welfare states overlaps with that from the neoliberal Right, though '. . . for obvious reasons these similarities are not emphasized by either side'.[49] The difference is in the proposed remedies: whereas the Right response to what it calls the problem of 'ungovernability' is to protect capitalism from democratic interventions by reducing welfare provision and expectations, for the Left, following a strategy whose intellectual foundation was best formulated at the end of the Second World War by Karl Polanyi, it is the capitalist '. . . imperatives themselves that must be curbed and rendered capable of subordination to political-normative rules'.[50] This involves, in particular, a strategy of 'de-commodification', contrasted with the right-wing attempt to 're-commodify' health services, education etc.

Offe's analysis stands out from other analyses of capitalist welfare states in its theoretical range and sophistication[51] In an interview conducted in 1982, he spells out his relation to critical theory as a whole. Like Habermas, he acknowledges the historical importance of early critical theory

> for understanding an explaining both fascism and the post-fascist period of political normalization . . . [but] . . . these analyses are less relevant for the contemporary period. Classical critical theory is evidently a species of victimization theory, in that it represents the populations of welfare state countries as objects of near-total administration. This thesis is nowadays misleading and perhaps dangerous, and must in my view be questioned.[52]

Habermas was right, he continues, to insist on the need to rethink Marxist assumptions which 'the Frankfurt tradition' had tended to adopt uncritically. Habermas shares, however, with earlier critical theory an emphasis on the importance of '"superstructural" elements as the decisive level of social dynamics.'[53] What is here presented in neutral or positive terms as something which Offe learned from Habermas appears a little later in a somewhat more critical light when Offe agrees, in response to a question from David Held and John Keane, that his own earlier analyses have perhaps used the term legitimacy in too normative and rationalistic a manner. He now prefers to analyse these issues in terms of a wide spread of dissatisfactions with the output of advanced capitalist societies, as well as a broadening of the scope of political and social critique. 'The existing repertoire of values and practices ceases to be "natural" – it is now subject to political criticism and determination.'[54] Here one can see Offe both distancing himself from the model of *Legitimation Crisis* and at the same time taking on board, in a more substantive focus, Habermas's (and, later, Ulrich Beck's) stress on postconventional morality and normative commitments. He also echoes Habermas's critique, in *Theory of Communicative Action,* of the 'colonisation' of the life-world by monetary and bureaucratic systems: the 'exchange-like, rational-calculating mode of relating to incentives that itself undermines the process of informal interaction regulated by intersubjectively shared (if often repressive) norms.'[55]

This volume of Offe's essays and the companion volume *Disorganized Capitalism'* document the transition in the later 1970s from a period in which social democratic reformism was influential to one where it was eclipsed by economic neoliberalism and social conservatism. Offe's work concentrated on the more structural conditions and consequences of this transition in an analysis which converges, as he notes, with that of Scott Lash in the United Kingdom.[56] In a book published in 1996 but containing a number of essays from the late 1980s, Offe takes this analysis further in asking what states can do in conditions of what he calls, borrowing Habermas's phrase, a new obscurity and, as Daniel Bell put it in 1960, 'the exhaustion of political ideas'.

> . . . the formal similarity which exists between Western European social democracy, Eastern European party communism, Anglo-Saxon liberalism, and the politically significant new social movements is that, in a state of more or less open perplexity, they attempt to synthesize or achieve a precarious balance between entirely heterogeneous principles of political and social order.[57]

In a complementary essay, 'Democracy Against the Welfare State?', he argues that this is not just a matter of neoliberal populism of the kind associated with Thatcher in England.[58] 'Even a country relatively unaffected by changes in growth rates and governments, namely West Germany, showed a sharp decline in the proportion of social policy legislation implying increases in benefits or coverage.' At the same time, demographic changes such as the increase in single households, combined with trends towards higher unemployment, have increased the level of need. Furthermore, he agrees with Habermas that the utopian energy has drained out of the welfare state project:

> . . . on the one side, it is met with distrust by core working-class and upwardly mobile social categories who defect from collectivist ideas, and on the other, by those who, while recognizing the welfare state's accomplishment of a measure of social justice, are aware of its built-in contradiction between state power and lifeworld, or between the welfare state's method and its goal.[59]

What this means is that the process described by T.H. Marshall in the 1950s, by which political citizenship develops into social citizenship in welfare states, has gone into reverse. Marshall assumed that this process, emerging out of solidarities forged in the Second World War and a perceived need for change,[60] would then sustain itself in the political action of large social collectivities, but these are becoming both structurally and ideologically fragmented. In other words, politics produces welfare states, whereas their 'decline' results from economic pressures.

> While the rise of a welfare state requires mass mobilization and large political coalitions as a sufficient condition, its demise is mediated through economic imperatives as well as the silent and inconspicuous defection of voters, groups, and corporate actors whose heterogeneous structure, perceptions, and responses stand in the way of the formation of an effective defensive alliance.[61]

Soon after Offe published this gloomy prognosis for the capitalist welfare state, its communist counterpart was engulfed in the collapse of the political dictatorships which had presided over it. His subsequent work on social policy, prefigured by an essay of 1993 reprinted in *Modernity and the State*, reflects this change and the new focus of his work, discussed in more detail in Chapter 4.

The collection of essays which Habermas edited for Suhrkamp's 1,000th volume is substantially retrospective,[62] including an important essay on responses to the West German terrorism of the 1970s by Albrecht Wellmer, but also addressed the rise of the New Right. Critical theory was accused of inspiring the terrorism of the Red Army Fraction, as it had been in relation to the 1968 movement. Its response was relatively muted, perhaps in order not to further inflame a rather hysterical backlash. As Habermas wrote in a letter to the centre-right political scientist Kurt Sontheimer, who had led the attack on critical theory in the 'association for the freedom of science' (Bund Freiheit der Wissenschaft), 'If the attempt to de-dramatise terror, to live with terror *as if* it were a normal crime, does not succeed, the battle against terrorism will itself build the stage on which terrorism can develop and preserve itself.'[63] Wellmer's brilliant essay combines a trenchant rejection of the current terrorism, 'the senseless acts of violence by German urban guerillas',[64] with a spirited denial that critical theory was in any way responsible for it.

> If the earlier critical theory, beginning with Dialectic of Enlightenment, can be reproached for anything in conjunction with the question of terrorism, it would have to be the fact that . . . it hardly permits the envisaging of forms of emancipatory praxis that are not already infected by the irrationality of the system against which they are directed.[65]

More than this is 'to use a form of violent criminality understood as "leftist" and "social-critical" as the pretext for the criminalization of leftist and social-critical positions' – something which was easy 'in view of the weakness of republican traditions in Germany'.[66] And as he notes, it is no accident that the terrorism of the RAF and the Red Brigades emerged in former fascist societies.

More positively, Wellmer outlines an explanation of terrorism in terms of a 'loss of ethical life generated by the reproductive process of industrial systems . . . '.[67] He identifies a number of consequences, including notably the reduction of moral-practical questions to technical ones, a 'regression' to a 'preuniversalist' morality founded in group solidarity against a world simplistically and dogmatically defined as totally evil and a 'cult of immediacy' and actionism.[68] When western societies are again over-reacting to terrorism, Wellmer's article remains highly relevant.

The award of the Adorno Prize of the City of Frankfurt to Habermas in 1980 marked a return to a more normal climate of discussion of critical theory,[69] which continues to benefit from a certain amount of local civic pride.[70] The more specifically political critique of neoconservatism was also pursued by Habermas a little later, notably in a series of essays of the early 1980s published in 1985 as *The New Obscurity*, and by Helmut Dubiel in 1985, in *Was ist Neokonservatismus?* Dubiel's book focussed more on the US origins of neoconservatism than on its German offshoots, while noting that the German neoconservatives tended to emerge not from leftist or liberal backgrounds, as was the case in the United States, but from 'a specifically anti-liberal conservatism'.[71]

Critical theory's response to neoconservatism became curiously imbricated with a simultaneous critical response, particularly by Habermas, to postmodernism and what in the English-speaking world came to be called post-structuralism. There were of course some partial connections: when Lyotard announced the end of 'grand narratives' he was thinking in particular of the Marxism to which he had earlier been attached, as well as to the classical liberalism which Marxism had radicalized in its critique of it. Habermas however seems to have misunderstood the ironical French critique of enlightenment rationality, admittedly prone to rhetorical overstatement, as a revival of the more sinister currents of the *German* counter-Enlightenment. In a characteristically pugnacious spirit, he took his Frankfurt lecture series to the Collège de France in Paris, as well as to universities in the United States. Here perhaps was an opening to another European culture in the negative form of a dialogue of the deaf; at the end of one acrimonious conference bringing together the two sides a French observer commented that 'the Germans were grotesque and the French were crap' (nuls). Albrecht Wellmer adopted a calmer and more flexible approach, as did Manfred Frank, in a book on Lyotard and Habermas, and Axel Honneth in his early work bringing together Habermas and Foucault. Habermas himself came to realise that he was not so far apart from Foucault as he had initially thought, and became a close friend of Derrida in his last years. And as Seyla Benhabib notes, many of these issues returned in a different form in postcolonial theory and in the revival of normative political theory in the 1990s. They are also continued in Honneth and Nancy Fraser's discussion of power, in feminist theory by Fraser, Judith Butler, Amy Allen and herself, in the philosophy of science and language by Thomas McCarthy and James Bohman, in aesthetics by Wellmer, Jay M. Bernstein and others.[72] She also points to democratic theory, which I discuss in more detail in Chapter 4.

1968 had provoked a neoconservative backlash as well as a demobilisation of the Marxist or anarchist left, leaving however an important legacy in 'alternative' and 'new' social movements. Critical theorists, notably Klaus Eder, joined in the theorisation of these movements and this continues to be a principal focus of his work on movements of both Left and Right.[73] Peace movements became increasingly important in the 1980s, especially in Germany for obvious historical and geopolitical reasons. (In East Germany, independent peace movements were one of the few arenas of semi-tolerated dissent.) The peace movements in both West and East Germany provided the impetus for Hans Joas' work on war and peace;[74] he was one of a number of sociologists, such as Anthony Giddens and Martin Shaw in the United Kingdom and Michael Mann in the United States, taking up such issues which for a long time had not been prominent in sociology. The political and constitutional

15 'Zur politischen Verantwortung der Wissenschaftler', in Preuss, *Das politische Mandat der Studentenschaft*, pp. 133–8. Another supportive statement was provided by the East German scientist and dissident Robert Havemann.

16 As Oskar Negt noted in *Die Linke antwortet Jürgen Habermas*, Frankfurt: Europäische Verlagsanstalt, p. 30.

17 Jürgen Habermas, *Protestbewegung und Hochschulreform*, Frankfurt: Suhrkamp, 1969, p. 45

18 Ibid., p. 183.

19 Ibid., p. 9.

20 Ibid., p. 49.

21 For a brilliant analysis of the background to Adorno's analyses of capitalism, see Axel Honneth, 'A Physiognomy of the Capitalist Form of Life: A Sketch of Adorno's Social Theory', *Constellations*, 12(1), 2005, pp. 50–64. Helmut Dubiel has stressed the influence on Adorno of Pollock's model of state capitalism 'Die Aktualität der Gesellschaftstheorie Adornos', in Ludwig von Friedeburg and Jürgen Habermas (eds), *Adorno-Konferenz 1983*, Frankfurt: Suhrkamp, 1983, pp. 293–313, here p. 296.

22 See, for example, my essay 'When Did 1968 End?', in Gurminder K. Bhambra and Ipek Demir (eds), *1968 in Retrospect. History, Theory, Alterity*, Basingstoke: Palgrave, 2009, pp. 175–83. For a critique of '1968' and a discussion of the alarm it caused, see Götz Aly, *Unser Kampf 1968: Ein Irritierter Blick Zurück*, Berlin: Fischer, 2008; also Riccardo Bavaj, '"Western Civilization" and the Acceleration of Time. Richard Löwenthal's Reflections of a Crisis of "the West" in the Aftermath of the Student Revolt of "1968"', in *Themenportal Europäische Geschichte*, 2010 http://www.europa.clio-online.de/2010/Article=435.

23 Habermas, *Protestbewegung und Hochschulreform*, p. 41.

24 Von Weizsäcker was the inventor of the term 'Weltinnenpolitik' (world domestic policy) which has been taken up by Habermas and other theorists of cosmopolitan democracy; see Ulrich Bartosch and Klaudius Gansczyk (eds), *Weltinnenpolitik für das 21. Jahrhundert: Carl-Friedrich von Weizsäcker verpflichtet*, Hamburg and London: Lit, 2008.

25 Claus Offe, *Die Linke antwortet Jürgen Habermas*, p. 110.

26 Offe, 'Crises of Crisis Mangagement', reprinted in his *Contradictions of the Welfare State*, pp. 48–51.

27 Jürgen Habermas, 'Preface', *Legitimation Crisis*, London: Heinemann, 1976 p. xxv. This should be read in conjunction with 'Legitimation Problems in the Modern State', ch. 5 of *Communication and the Evolution of Society*. The article 'What does a Crisis Mean Today?', reprinted in Connerton (ed.), *Critical Sociology*, Harmondsworth: Penguin, 1976 and Connolly (ed.), *Legitimacy and the State*, is a summary version of *Legitimation Crisis*.

28 Berger has since moved more substantially into economic sociology and the sociology of development, specifically issues of international inequalities; see 'Warum sind einige Länder so viel reicher als andere? Zur institutionellen

Erklärung von Entwicklungsunterschieden', *Zeitschrift für Soziologie*, 36(1), February 2007, pp. 5–24. He also contributed an essay, 'Expandierende Märkte, schrumpfende Solidarität', to Jens Beckert, Julia Eckert, Martin Kohli and Wolfgang Streeck (eds), *Transnationale Solidarität. Chancen und Grenzen*, Frankfurt: Campus, 2004, pp. 246–61. See also Berger, 'Social institutions, Technological Progress and Economic Performance', in Max Miller (ed.), *Worlds of Capitalism. Institutions, Governance and Economic Change in the Era of Globalization*. London: Routledge, 2005, pp. 33–56.

29   Habermas, *Legitimation Crisis*, p. 1. Cf. Adorno, 'Spätkapitalismus oder Industriegesellschaft?'

30   Habermas, *Legitimation Crisis*, pp. 3–4.

31   Ibid., p. 7. Cf. Habermas, Jürgen and Luhmann, Niklas, *Theorie der Gesellschaft oder Sozialtechnologie: Was leistet die Systemforschung?*, Frankfurt: Suhrkamp, 1971.

32   Habermas, *Legitimation Crisis*, p. 8. Habermas suggests that two features of this learning process are central: whether learning is reflexive, that is, involves the discursive thematization of validity-claims, and whether theoretical and moral-practical questions are, as they usually are in the modern period, differentiated (ibid., p. 15).

33   Ibid., p. 22. The fourth type of society he describes as 'post-capitalist *class* societies', 'in view of the political elite control of the means of production'. He also alludes to an emergent 'postmodern' type of society, coming after the class societies just as primitive or 'pre-high-cultural societies' precede them. This 'historically new principle of organisation' is not explored further.

34   Ibid., p. 20.

35   Ibid., p. 27.

36   Ibid., p. 30.

37   Ibid., p. 33.

38   Ibid., p. 36.

39   Ibid., p. 40.

40   The concept of motivation crisis, which Habermas now sees as misleadingly broad in its formulation, spans such diverse phenomena as the withdrawal of motivation from the occupational system, for example, a decline of the work ethic, and individual psychopathology on the other. (Cf. Thompson and Held (eds), *Habermas*, pp. 280–1).

41   Larry Ray, in *Rethinking Critical Theory. Emancipation in the Age of Global Social Movements*, London: Sage, 1993, applied this model in a global context, looking in particular at crises in three peripheral state forms, the USSR and the communist bloc (see Chapter 3 below), Iran under the Shah and apartheid South Africa. The book is an important and rare attempt to counter the focus of critical theory as a whole, and Habermas' work in particular, on Western Europe. See also, more recently, Max Pensky (ed.), *Globalizing Critical Theory*, Lanham and Oxford: Rowman and Littlefield, 2005.

42 Claus Offe, in particular, has traced these convergences in theories of the welfare state, 'ungovernability', etc. See, for example, 'Ungovernability: On the Renaissance of Conservative Theories of Crisis', and 'Some Contradictions in the Modern Welfare State', pp. 219–29; Berger, 'Changing Crisis-types', pp. 230–9. For recent discussions, see Chris Pierson, *Beyond the Welfare State?*, Cambridge: Polity, 1991 and Ulrich Beck, *Risk Society*, London: Sage, 1992.

43 'Stichworte zum Legitimationsbegriff – eine Replik', in Habermas, *Zur Rekonstruktion des historischen Materialismus*, p. 336.

44 Held, 'Crisis Tendencies, Legitimation and the State', in Thompson and Held (eds), *Habermas*, ch. 10, p. 188. This theme is also raised in the interview with Claus Offe discussed below.

45 Mann, 'The ideology of intellectuals and other people in the development of capitalism'.

46 Honneth, 'Moral Consciousness and Class Domination'; pp. 12–24. See also Honneth, *The Struggle for Recognition*.

47 Frank Nullmeier, 'Spätkapitalismus und Legitimation', in Hauke Brunkhorst, Regina Kreide and Cristina Lafont (eds), *Habermas-Handbuch*. Stuttgart: Verlag J.B. Metzler, 2009.

48 Offe, *Contradictions*, pp. 48–9.

49 Ibid., p. 65; see also p. 243.

50 Ibid., p. 84.

51 The same is true of his geographical range. Although his empirical work was largely confined to West Germany, it was informed by a wide reading of literature from and on Western societies as a whole. More recently, of course, he turned his attention to post-communist transition. For an excellent discussion of Offe's state theory in the German context, see Martin Carnoy, *The State and Political Theory*, Princeton University Press, 1984, chapter 5.

52 Offe, *Contradictions*, p. 255.

53 Ibid., p. 256.

54 Ibid., pp. 269–70.

55 Ibid., p. 281. For a later discussion by Offe of the model of *Legitimation Crisis*, see his 'Rote Faden und lose Enden', in Geis and Strecker (eds), *Blockaden*, Frankfurt and New York: Campus, 2005, pp. 245–77. The theme of legitimacy has also been central to critical theorists' analysis of state socialism, discussed below (chapter 3).

56 Claus Offe, *Disorganized Capitalism*, Cambridge: Polity, 1985, Introduction, note 1, p. 317. One of the most important of these structural conditions was the mutation of the 'work society' of post-war capitalism into a forming which informal work and state benefits become more important for growing numbers of citizens; see his essay of 1986, 'Beyond the Labour Market' (with Rolf Heinze, reprinted in Offe, *Modernity and the State*, Cambridge: Polity, 1996, pp. 121–46).

57 'State Action and Collective Will Formation', in Offe, *Modernity and the State*, p. 116.

58 I say England rather than Britain, since Thatcherism had little appeal in Wales and Scotland, nor for that matter in most of northern England.

59 Offe, *Modernity and the State*, p. 159. Cf. Habermas, *Die neue Unübersichtlichkeit*, pp. 149–62.

60 This was reflected in the electoral defeat of Britain's Conservative wartime leader, Winston Churchill, and in the remarkably progressive policies initially proposed by the emergent Christian Democratic parties in continental Europe. Marshall's influential essay, 'Citizenship and Social Class', was published in 1949.

61 Offe, *Modernity and the State*, p. 175.

62 The essay by Karl Heinz Bohrer discusses cultural change across Western Europe since 1968.

63 Quoted by Stefan Müller-Doohm, *Jürgen Habermas*, Frankfurt: Suhrkam, 2008, p. 42.

64 'Terrorism and the Critique of Society', in Habermas, *Observations,on the Spiritual Situation of the Age*, Cambridge, MA: MIT Press, 1984, p. 301.

65 Ibid., pp. 294–5.

66 Ibid., p. 291.

67 Ibid., p. 298.

68 Ibid., p. 299. The term 'actionism' is of course one which Habermas had frequently used in his critique of the 1968 movements.

69 Wiggershaus, *The Frankfurt School*, p. 657; Wiggershaus, *Jürgen Habermas*, p. 45.

70 I was struck by this when speaking to the Anglo-German society there in 1997.

71 Helmut Dubiel, *Was ist Neokonservatismus?*, Frankfurt: Suhrkamp, 1985, p. 27.

72 Seyla Benhabib, 'Verteidigung der Moderne', in Hauke Brunkhorst et al. (eds), *Habermas-Handbuch*, pp. 251–2.

73 Eder, Klaus, *The New Politics of Class: Social Movements and Cultural Dynamics in Advanced Societies*, London: Sage, 1993. See also Larry Ray, *Rethinking Critical Theory*.

74 See Joas, 'A Pragmatist from Germany', in Alan Sica and Stephen Turner (eds), *The Disobedient Generation. Social Theorists in the Sixties*, Chicago: Chicago University Press, 2005, pp. 169–70. Joas comments in the same memoir (p. 163) that he chose to study in West Berlin rather than Frankfurt 'because Berlin promised to be more pluralistic than the Frankfurt School that I had always associated with bourgeois pride of place. . . .' He edited a book with an East German colleague, Helmut Steiner, in 1989, something which, as they say in their introduction, was not by any means an everyday occurrence (Joas and Steiner (eds), *Machtpolitischer Realismus und pazifistische Utopie*, Frankfurt: Suhrkamp, 1989, p. 8). Joas' book on *War and Modernity* was published in German in 2000 and in English in 2003.

75 Ulrich Preuss, *Politische Verantwortung und Bürgerloyalität: Von den Grenzen der Verfassung und des Gehorsams in der Demokratie*, Frankfurt: Fischer, 1984, p. 191. In this book Preuss anticipates later theories of cosmopolitan democracy, in an early use (p. 211) of the term 'world domestic policy' (Weltinnenpolitik), coined in 1963 by Habermas's future colleague at Starnberg, the physicist Carl Friedrich von Weizsäcker. (See note 24, above.)

76 Paul Statham, for example, who has worked substantially with Eder, showed how three environmental movements focussed their styles of political action in a kind of informal division of labour oriented to media impact.

77 Ulrich Beck (ed.), *Sozialforschung und Praxis*.

78 Ulrich Beck, *Gegengifte*, Frankfurt: Suhrkamp, 1988; *Ecological Politics in an Age of Risk*, Cambridge: Polity, 1995; *Politik in der Risikogesellschaft*, Frankfurt: Suhrkamp, 1991; *Ecological Enlightenment*, Humanities Press, 1995; *Die Erfindung des Politischen*, Frankfurt: Suhrkamp, 1993; *The Reinvention of Politics*, Cambridge: Polity, 1997.

3

State socialism and its crises

The Institute had been in at the beginning in the analysis of the Soviet Union, with one of its core members from the pre-Horkheimer period specialising in the economics of the planned economy. Friedrich Pollock's book of 1929 on the beginnings of Soviet economic planning is a sympathetic though by no means uncritical discussion of the economy and the political context; a promised sequel on a 'theoretical evaluation' never appeared.[1] The book was favourably reviewed in the Soviet Union, though criticised for its focus on technical and statistical issues rather than the big picture of social change.[2]

It is therefore all the more surprising that the *Zeitschrift* contains no substantial discussion of the Soviet Union, especially as a series of articles by Kurt Mandelbaum (who also wrote under the name Kurt Baumann) and Gerhard Meyer discussed literature on the planned economy. The first in the series[3] promises a future article on the Soviet planned economy, but this never materialises. A substantive article by Mandelbaum and Mayer begins with a note that it will not discuss Russia[4], while another review article by Mandelbaum merely mentions that one of the books discussed, on industrial planning in the Soviet Union, draws on Pollock's earlier study.[5] The Webbs' book receives a favourable review from the London School of Economics labour historian H.L. Beales,[6] but this is one of very few reviews of books on the Soviet Union, in a journal whose coverage of current literature in philosophy, history and social science is otherwise so impressive. Even Wiggershaus, usually so quick to point to lacunae in the Institute's work, has made only a brief mention of Pollock's book.[7]

It is hard not to conclude that there was a conscious effort at the Institute not to speak ill of the Red. For Horkheimer, at least, the Soviet Union had been a touchstone for people's attitudes and even their 'moral character'. As he wrote in his *Notizen*,

In 1930, the attitude toward Russia casts light on people's thinking. It is extremely difficult to say what conditions are like there. I do not claim to know where the country is going; there is undoubtedly much misery. But those among the educated who don't even perceive a hint of the effort being made there, adopt a cavalier attitude and dismiss the need to reflect, are pathetic comrades. Their company is unprofitable. The senseless injustice of the imperialist world can certainly not be explained by technological inadequacy. Anyone who has the eyes to see will view events in Russia as the continuing painful attempt to overcome this terrible social injustice. At the very least, he will ask with a throbbing heart whether it is still under way.[8]

The first substantial discussion of the Soviet Union came in a series of three review articles at the end of the 1930s by the German communist and later Glasgow professor Rudolf Schlesinger.[9]

Andrew Arato argued in 1984 that critical theory's pre-war analysis of state socialism can be divided into the following periods: 'backward socialism' from 1932 or 1929 to 1937; 'deformed socialism' from 1939 and 'authoritarian convergence or "state capitalism"' in 1940–41. Of these, he suggested, only the third escapes from 'more or less concealed [Marxist] orthodoxy' though this shares the defects of later theories of totalitarianism. (He identifies two further periods, discussed below: that of Marcuse's 'immanent critique' in his *Soviet Marxism* and that developed by Habermas and his associates at Starnberg in the 1970s.)[10] After their essays of 1940–41, he writes,

Neither Pollock nor Horkheimer ever again concerned themselves with Soviet society, and the reason is evident. It was simply too hateful for them to reflect on the possibility of the unlimited survival of such a form of society, while to criticise it could clearly only reinforce the most conservative and warlike elements in Western societies, without making a contribution to the liberation of any human being.[11]

Before returning to Frankfurt, Adorno and Horkheimer had been particularly careful to distance themselves from any perceived sympathy for the Soviet Union and its new European satellites. In December 1949 Adorno had drafted an unpublished declaration of his and Horkheimer's position.

We reject as strongly as possible any interpretation of our work as being an apology for Russia, and we believe that the potential for a better society is more faithfully preserved where the existing one is allowed to be analyzed than where the idea of a better society has been corrupted in order to defend the bad one that exists.[12]

After the return to Frankfurt, Adorno wrote in discussion of the project published as *Student und Politik* that the absence of any concrete imagination of socialism was explained not only by the 'Americanisation' of German society 'but above all because the ghastly dictatorship in the Soviet Union so compromises the idea of socialism – and not just in a human sense but also with immediate relevance to the standard of living . . .'[13] He and Horkheimer had been sufficiently nervous about the risk of Soviet expansionism to reject the idea that the Institute might locate in West Berlin.

As in the case of *One Dimensional Man*, it was Marcuse who first directly addressed contemporary realities, taking up the issue of state socialism in his earlier book *Soviet Marxism*.[14] This rather curious book is a critical discussion of both what the German translation calls more precisely the social theory of Soviet Marxism[15] and the society which generated that theory. As Marcuse puts it, 'The critique employs the conceptual instruments of its object, namely, Marxism, in order to clarify the actual function of Marxism in Soviet society and its historical direction.'[16] Whereas

A critique of Soviet Marxism "from without" must either discard its theoretical efforts as "propaganda" or take them at face values, namely, as philosophy or sociology . . . an immanent critique . . . could reveal the political intention which is their real content.[17]

Lest anyone should think that this was just a roundabout way of presenting a Marxist account of the USSR and its social theory, Marcuse identifies his approach as a Hegelian one and then presents Marxism as following Hegel in its conception of historical laws.[18] Marcuse's discussion is shaped by an emphasis on technology which one can relate to Heidegger or to Marx or, more plausibly, both.[19] Even the qualitative break which Marcuse identifies between Leninism and Stalinism is explained by the technological, economic and geopolitical context in the USSR and the world as a whole.

The 'retardation' of the revolution in the West and the stabilization of capitalism made for qualitative changes in the structure of Soviet society. Lenin tried to counter the isolation of the revolution in a backward country by establishing the priority of industrialization over socialist liberation . . . Stalin accelerated the program of 'civilization' which Lenin had made the prerequisite for the preservation of the Soviet system.[20]

This also explains his relatively optimistic prognosis for Soviet society, despite his merciless criticism of its current state.

> The Soviet bureaucracy . . . does not seem to possess a basis for the effective perpetuation of special interests against the overriding general requirements of the social system on which it lives. The bureaucracy constitutes a separate class which controls the underlying population through control of the economic, political and military establishments, and exercise of this control engenders a variety of special interests which assert themselves in the control; however, they must compromise and ultimately succumb to the general policy which none of the special interests can change by virtue of its special power? Does this mean that the bureaucracy represents the common interest of society as a whole?[21]

This is of course one of the crucial questions in both Marxist and non-Marxist analyses of Soviet-type societies. Marcuse however frames it in a particular way which recalls both his earlier book on psychoanalysis and his later one focussed largely on industrial *capitalism*. As in *Eros and Civilization*, there is a notion in *Soviet Marxism* of a kind of 'surplus repression' – terror, punishing both economic failure and political deviance, which goes beyond the requirements of the system as a whole and derives from its current pathological state. This is not to equate sexual repression in the Freudian sense with Soviet terror – merely to indicate their structural similarity in Marcuse's analysis. As Johann Arnason pointed out in an early book which remains one of the most incisive discussions of Marcuse's work,

> Critical theory had already come to similar conclusions in the analysis of late capitalism: its dynamic seemed to be determined less by privileged minorities than by a repressive global system based on a symbiosis of domination and technology and no longer tolerating resistance in the sphere of the social structure but only in isolated realms of social consciousness.[22]

There is also a parallel in the underlying contradiction of both capitalist and state socialist systems: the drive towards technological progress, whether for the sake of capitalist profit or for the development of a backward society, is limited by the value relation in capitalism and the unavoidable dysfunctions of bureaucratic planning in socialism. However, '. . . in soviet society there seem to be no *inherent* forces which resist accelerated and extensive automation – either on the part of management or on the part of labour.'[23]

As Johann Arnason noted, it was clear already in the late 1960s that the Soviet Union was lagging behind the West in technological developments.[24] More fundamentally, what is missing in all this is attention to the social dimension and in particular to the dynamics of social conflicts. This neglect '. . . leads on the one hand to an over-emphasis on the objective logic of the system, and on the other to an excessive trust in the emancipatory content of the [official] ideology.'[25] The details of Marcuse's account are now of merely historical interest, and Arnason does not mention it in his own later book on the Soviet Union, discussed below.[26] Of more interest is the demonstration of another area in which early critical theory tends to combine a deterministic account of an objective process and its distorting effects on consciousness with a surprising neglect of the possibilities of conflict and contestation which so impressed Marcuse, as well as Habermas and other members of the post-war generation, in the later 1960s.

Marcuse's book went into a second edition, and was eventually published by Penguin, but its impact on the field of Soviet Studies was relatively slight. Marcuse himself never returned to the theme, except indirectly in comparative remarks in *One Dimensional Man*. He responded however with great enthusiasm to a book of 1977 by an East German dissident, Rudolf Bahro.[27] Bahro probably had no knowledge of Marcuse's book, but his own analysis parallels Marcuse's at a number of points, notably his stress on technology and on the production both of an attitude of 'subalternity' (Subalternität) and of a 'surplus consciousness' which has the potential to undermine the 'quasi-theocratic state' of actually existing socialism.[28] His proposed remedy, a 'cultural revolution' inspired by 'a truly communist party, a new League of Communists'[29] was coolly received by other critics of state socialism[30] but it appealed to Marcuse, who had always had a rather vanguardist conception of the role of intellectuals. Marcuse, as the title of his review indicates, was however mainly concerned to stress the parallels between capitalism and state social-ism, tending to accept Bahro's conception of the historical achievements of socialism introduced under difficult conditions. The Hungarian dissident Ivan Szelényi, whose own book of 1979 had just appeared and pushed him, like Bahro, into exile, put his finger on the issue:

. . . Bahro's definition of 'actually existing socialism' is somewhat ambiguous. When he is confronted with the ideologies of Soviet Marxism, then he refers back to the empirical realities of Eastern Europe. From this vantage point Eastern Europe is viewed as *'actually existing socialism'*, while the ideologies of Soviet Marxists exist only in their heads. Yet, when he confronts the realities of Eastern Europe with his own ideological vision of communism, then this reality suddenly becomes 'proto-socialism' . . .[31]

This is more than just the theoretical disagreement over whether state socialist societies should be seen as embryonic or distorted forms of a socialism which was still understood as an advance over capitalism, or as something else altogether – an issue which divided in particular, the already small clusters of Western Trotskyists. It marks the dividing line between an internal and an external critique of state socialism, and it is in the second form, which became dominant in the 1980s, that critical theory developed a distinctive perspective.[32]

Horkheimer and Adorno, following their return to Frankfurt, were already extremely distant from these concerns, and from earlier associates such as Ernst Bloch who had clung to communism. More importantly, critical theory had developed a perspective which, whatever its sociological weaknesses in identifying lines of conflict in modern societies, enabled it to side-step the fixation with forms of production and distribution which hamstrung much of the more orthodox Marxist analysis. In retrospect, questions about whether enterprises in Soviet-type societies produced value seem as much a side-issue as whether domestic labour did. An approach which focussed more upon power and domination as relatively independent of economic relations proved to be more fruitful in analysing the later stages of state socialism. As Andrew Arato wrote of Habermas,

> . . . from the very beginning his reconstruction of Marxism has sought to make possible a thoroughly autonomous treatment of what was previously relegated to the superstructure (politics and culture), with the unintended consequence that the two other major factors necessary for the genesis and reproduction of Soviet society (the heritage of the bureaucratic state and of cultural traditionalism) could now become accessible to analysis. This means *in principle* a break with those elements of classical Marxist theory which confront the Soviet Union with the bad alternative of unintended apology and theoretical impotence.[33]

Habermas, as we saw in the previous chapter, had a place in the model of *Legitimation Crisis* for state socialist societies, though not much more than that.[34] There, he described them as 'post-capitalist *class* societies', 'in view of the political elite control of the means of production'. In a slightly later essay, 'Toward a Reconstruction of Historical Materialism', he poses the question: 'Is bureaucratic socialism, compared to developed capitalism, in any sense an evolutionarily higher social formation; or are the two merely variants of the same stage of development?'[35]

Arato is sceptical about this antithesis:

While the two societies undoubtedly share an enormous number of common characteristics as industrial-urbanised societies and welfare-warfare states, the theoretical grounds for treating them as two expressions of the same stage of development are doubtful. I am thinking of their specifically different institutional systems, and even more of their entirely 'non-simultaneous levels of legal development.'[36]

Instead, he takes up the prior question 'of the principle of organisation of this social formation'.[37]

Within the domain of critical sociology, Habermas and Offe present us with two alternatives.

1   According to Habermas, state socialism is a political-elitist class rule over a politically constituted but industrial system of social labour. This definition focuses on the fundamental relation of class domination and implies a juridical relationship different from that of capitalism: the absence of 'free' labour. . .

2   . . . Offe gives us a three-term typology that allows us to locate 'state socialism', as well as late capitalism, among industrial societies . . . Given the possibility of the functional primacy of three social spheres, exchange (economy), coercive relationships (bureaucracy) and poliical choice (normative structures), Offe defines capitalism as the primacy of exchange economy over bureaucracy and the normative sphere; presumably he would not object if one defined state socialism as the primacy of an administratively or bureaucratically conceived political domain over both the economy and the normative-cultural sphere.[38]

Building on Offe's model and on a number of recent critical accounts of state socialism, Arato brilliantly outlines the rationality crises and crises of crisis management characteristic of state socialism. The basic dilemma, which also shapes much of the subsequent critical literature on state socialism, is that between social differentiation, the independent development of subsystems such as the economy or the educational sector, and central control by the party-state, which Arato represents in Ernst Fraenkel's terms as a preroga-tive state (Massnahmenstaat), which intervenes unchecked in all areas of society. The party-state, to put it crudely, cannot live without these relatively independent institutional subsystems, but nor can it live *with* their tendencies to develop in ways which are perceived to threaten the system. 'With the road back to Stalinism foreclosed, full *positive subordination* of society to politics became very difficult to achieve.'[39] The crisis of crisis management thus becomes, paradigmatically, one in which the party-state intervenes to remedy a sectoral crisis and thereby makes matters worse. Nor, as Gorbachev learned, can it withdraw from intervening, except under special conditions such as those which obtained in Yugoslavia at the time Arato was writing (or those which we have seen in China in the past two decades).

> The party's claim of being the agent of both substantive justice and *total* social welfare originally rested on its supposed *global* knowledge of all society, and its supposed representation of the *general* (national, popular or working-class) interest. With the partial abandonment of the commanding heights of the central plan . . . and the tacit admission of selective sectoral lobbies into the party-state itself, these foundations would be decisively weakened; and the weakening of the legitimacy of the party endangers the legitimacy of the patronage state.[40]

In his very substantial 'Reply', Habermas reformulates his account of crisis in terms of his new model of the 'colonisation of the life-world'. In capitalism,

> . . . economic imperatives intrude deeply into the communicatively structured life-world of employees and consumers. The overextension of the medium of legal-administrative power [in state socialism] results in a similar intrusion of systemic mechanisms into the life-world. The points of incursion are not private households, but politically relevant memberships. Here, too, a sphere relying on social integration, namely the political public sphere, is transferred over to system-integrative mechanisms. But the effects are different; instead of the reification of communicative relations we find the shamming of communicative relations in bureaucratically dessicated, forcibly 'humanized' domains of pseudo-democratic will-formation . . . The life-world is not assimilated to the system, to formally organised domains of action subject to law; rather, the systematically independent organisations of the state are fictively transposed back into the horizon of the life-world: the system is draped out as a coercively integrated life-world.

One of the key critical accounts of state socialism which Arato cites is that by three members of the so-called 'Budapest School' associated with Georg Lukács.[41] *Dictatorship Over Needs*, by Fehér, Heller and Márkus was probably the watershed in studies of state socialism, bringing a new critical and analytic approach to bear on the socialist system. The authors were sympathetic to critical theory, rather than directly associated with it.[42] In bringing together an economic and cultural category, needs, with a political one, dictatorship, they develop however a characteristically Frankfurtian style of analysis:

> . . . disposition over, and appropriation of, the social surplus exercised and realized by the apparatus as a corporate entity constitutes only the material foundation and economic component of a monopolistic expropriation by it of all means of social organization and intercourse. Its social domination over the whole society rests upon the fact that no social group outside it has either the opportunity or the right to articulate and to attempt to realize its own particular interests either *vis-à-vis* the apparatus itself or in relation to other social groups.[43]

The book closes with a discussion of the types of conflict characteristic of this system. First, there is the critique of the irrationality of the planning system and its failure to provide everyday commodities. Second, 'the need for free cultural activity and cultural consumption.' Third, 'the campaigns for the free unfolding of civil society', notably in demands for human rights. Finally, 'The supreme type of all possible conflicts is rebellion as an expression of need for collective autonomy . . . the economic, social and political autonomy of social groups, for workers' control over factory affairs, a nuclear form of self-management movement, an explicit need for free trade unions, outbursts of the universal need for self-organization and coalition.[44]

The authors declined to offer any predictions:

> Of course, no one possesses prophetic capacities and the highly covert, fetishistic processes of life in Eastern European societies make even normally predictive assessments very difficult. The possibility of a revolution . . . can never be totally excluded, but precisely because of the mysterious character of gestation of any revolution, it is anybody's guess and not a matter of sociological consideration whether it will come or not.[45]

Completing their book in the aftermath of the repression of Solidarity in Poland, they suggested that this kind of opposition and the regimes' authoritarian responses will probably '. . . be the way of life of most Eastern European countries in the next decade, with the possible upshot that all this could contribute to the inner erosion of the Soviet centre of domination itself'.[46]

Dictatorship Over Needs marked something of a sea-change in the Western discussion of state socialism, as the term 'totalitarianism' ceased to be seen as a prerogative of the antisocialist Right and dissident literature became more widely diffused in the West. The year 1984 provided a convenient peg on which to hang analyses of the persistence of totalitarian aspirations in the post-Stalinist dictatorships.[47]

Marcuse's *Soviet Marxism*, which had given special emphasis to ethics in the Soviet Union,[48] had another echo in 1984, with a book by a Swiss diplomat, Tim Guldimann, who had worked for three years on a scholarship with Habermas and his colleagues at Starnberg. Guldimann's book combines a memoir of his time in the Soviet Union in the 1970s and early 1980s with a more analytic attempt to conceptualise Soviet morality in terms of Kohlberg's stage model. Kohlberg's model posits a gradual advance at an individual level, with the societal context appearing only as the 'domain of validity' of what eventually become moral principles; Habermas maps the advance from conventional to post-conventional morality onto an evolutionary sequence which can include both individual and societal learning: 'Only at the level of a universal ethics of speech (*Sprachethik*) can need interpretations themselves – that is, what each individual thinks he should understand and represent as his "true" interests – also become the object of a practical discourse.'[49] Habermas' reformulation is most clearly expressed in the version presented by McCarthy.

Guldimann suggests, in an argument that deserved more attention than it has received, that, whereas in Western society a largely conventional private morality coexists with post-conventional norms at the level of constitutional theory, the Soviet Union is more solidly fixed at the fourth, conventional, stage, dominated by a law-and-order orientation and making the political community the reference-point for the application of moral principles.

> At the fourth stage the socio-moral order is limited to the members of ones own community or society. The alien (der Fremde) is a potential enemy or scapegoat. The socio-moral order of the fifth stage, by contrast, includes all participants in the legal system: the alien is a potential partner in a contract . . .
>
> The advance of the fourth stage over the third is that moral judgement is removed from personal connections and becomes valid for all members of the community, whose interests are raised to a moral measuring standard. The advance of the fifth stage over the fourth is the . . . possibility of testing norms against principles and as a result the ability of the system to renew itself constantly and to adapt itself to changed conditions.[50]

The law-and-order orientation reflects both the all-pervasive state and its regulations and the domain of everyday life: 'A Soviet parents' evening is not concerned with the accountability of the teacher to the parents but with disciplining parents for the misbehaviour of their children in the school.'[51]

The Starnberg institute included two other members who made a name for themselves in the study of state socialism. Mikhail Vozlensky came as a guest from the Academy of Sciences of the Soviet Union; his book *Nomenklatura. The Ruling Class of the USSR* was a considerable success in German, French and English translations. It was impossible for him to return to the USSR and he eventually acquired Austrian citizenship.[52] The other was Sigrid Meuschel, who worked at Starnberg as Habermas' personal assistant and then moved to the GDR studies institute at the Free University in West Berlin. She had already made a name in GDR studies by 1989, and she contributed to a lecture series at the Institute for Social Research in 1989–90 and the resultant book edited by Dubiel and other Frankfurt colleagues.[53] Meuschel's article, 'Wandel durch Auflehnung. Thesen zum Verfall bürokratischer Herrschaft in der DDR', was shortly followed by her major book, *Legitimation und Parteiherrschaft: Zum Paradox von Stabilität und Revolution in der DDR, 1945–1989*, Frankfurt, Suhrkamp, 1992. In both, she traces the strategies by which the SED regime legitimated itself or at least secured the, mass loyalty' of the population. In an earlier article, she had distanced herself from more normative conceptions of legitimation, arguing that, despite the basic illegitimacy of party rule, it remained possible and worthwhile to examine the attempts by socialist regimes to legitimate themselves.[54] In the case of the GDR, she suggests, this took place in three phases. The first, an, anti-fascist' phase of Stalinism which remained an important ideological element long afterwards; second, an era of (largely technocratic) reform in the late 1950s (after the suppression of the only substantial protest movement in 1953) and 1960s, and finally a phase of post-utopian consolidation or stagnation, oriented around the slogans of developed socialist society and, actually existing socialism'.

The GDR differed from the other state socialist societies in several ways. First, the, anti-fascist' theme, which had parallels only in states like Yugoslavia and Albania, where communism had emerged out of partisan movements, and of course the Soviet Union, where the, Great Patriotic War' (though not of course the Nazi–Soviet pact which had preceded it) was an important theme of offical ideology. Meuschel quotes the leading GDR novelist Christa Wolf:

> My generation identified itself early with the society which was arising, because here in the forties we were forced to confront the fascist past intensively and radically, more sharply than was the case in the Federal Republic. That created a strong attachment to this society which had been

constructed by anti-fascists. This attachment was lasting because we saw no alternative.[55]

Germany's Nazi past also made both German states more docile members of their respective blocs and, in the GDR case, more careful to repress dissent. More importantly, the open border in Berlin till 1961 enabled the export of those opposed to the regime, and even after the building of the Berlin Wall oppositionsts were often allowed, encouraged or even forced to leave. As a result, opposition was most often channelled through the offical structures or through the relatively free churches. As Meuschel puts it,

> Precisely because offensive opposition to the dominant system was relatively weak, the potentials for a practice of resistance came together only in the moment of the revolution . . . There was a great potential of social discontent, but . . . an absence of recognised new elites or of the beginnings of a cultural and political restructuring of society.[56]

This fundamental ambiguity, 'the paradox of stability and revolution,'[57] was particularly stark in the GDR but it bedevilled not just predictions of the collapse of state socialism but, more fundamentally, contemporary and subsequent analysis of communist systems.[58] Meuschel, whose analysis was strongly influenced by that in *Dictatorship Over Needs*, defended the use of the term totalitarianism in relation to the state socialist regimes,[59] while noting the parallels between Marxism–Leninism and Western technocratic ideologies.

> The central thesis of the theory of technocracy, that technocratic power-claims and their social foundation are increasingly . . . based on knowledge, contains an almost startling potential for the analysis of post-Stalinism. The argument that politics should be determined not by interests but by knowledge, that expertise should be the only legitimate basis of political decision-making, that conflicts derive from inadequate information or a lack of knowledge, is structurally similar to the standard justification for the power-claims of a Marxist–Leninist party.[60]

The Institute's book which emerged from the 1989–90 lecture series, *Demokratischer Umbruch in Osteuropa*, also contained three important articles by East Germans: Wolfgang Engler, whose book *Die ungewollte Moderne* came out in 1995, Hans-Peter Krüger, who had written on Habermas, and an industrial manager, Lutz Marz. There were also contributions, both retrospective and forward-looking, from leading scholars and activists from East

Central Europe, including Adam Michnik and Jadwiga Staniszkis from Poland and László Varga from Hungary. A further volume on the end of the GDR, edited by Hans Joas and Martin Kohli, two critical sociologists who had long had intellectual and personal, rather than institutional, connections with the Institute, came out in 1993 but included earlier contributions, including one from Claus Offe, whose work on post-communism will be discussed in detail in the next chapter.

Along with Meuschel's book, the other major retrospective analysis of state socialism, focussing on the Soviet Union itself, was Johann Arnason's *The Future that Failed. Origins and Destinies of the Soviet Model.*[61] Arnason, an Icelander who himself had studied in Prague between 1960 and 1966, presents Soviet socialism as a variant of modernity.

> Recent interpretations, both neo-Marxist and non-Marxist, have tended toward the view that . . . ['Soviet-type societies'] . . . represent a distinctive pattern of modernity rather than a deviant path or transitional phase of modernization; the difference between Parsonian and Habermasian approaches to this question exemplifies the shift.[62]

In this analysis, Russia displays a 'reactive pattern' to Western modernity: 'we might provisionally describe it as both the least Western offshoot of the West and the most Western of the non-Western alternatives.'[63] Like Meuschel, Arnason defends the relevance of the concept of totalitarianism, while recognising at the same time 'the extreme fragility of the Soviet model . . .'

> It is not on the basis of its economic institutions as such that the Soviet model can be described as a counter-paradigm of modernity. In this sphere, it deviated from the capitalist pattern but failed to transcend it. But the economic structures were . . . embedded in a broader institutional complex and subordinated to its distinctive organizational principles. The concept of totalitarianism can be applied – and must be adapted – to this overall framework.[64]

On the questions of what Meuschel called the paradox of stability and revolution, or more crudely, did the regimes fall or were they pushed?, Arnason, with his Soviet focus, plumps for internal collapse.

> The reform which resulted in the collapse of the regime and the ruin of the empire was not a response to the demands or pressures of rising social forces; rather, it revealed the predicament of a political centre in search of a new social basis for its modernizing strategy, and the absence of any

social actors that could have sustained a progressive radicalization of the reform project.

The impact of movements emanating from and oriented to 'civil society' has, he suggests, been over-stated, even in relation to East Central Europe.

> The Polish situation was . . . unique in that a mass movement of industrial workers found an ally in the Catholic establishment and became a vehicle for national aspirations. A conjunction of class, church and nation can hardly be regarded as an embodiment of the ideals that have traditionally been linked to the concept of civil society . . .[65]

Arnason's comment may seem a little severe in relation to a movement which attracted support from almost the whole of Polish society for a wide variety of reasons, but it is hard to disagree with his claim that 'The precondition for the demise of the Soviet model in Eastern Europe was a stalemate in the Soviet leadership.'[66] The theme of civil society has been at the centre of critical theory (in a broader sense) and oppositional practice in communist Europe in the 1980s and in post-communist Europe through to the present. The most substantial defender of the concept, both in general and in its application in the context of communist Europe, is Andrew Arato. The theoretical background goes back to Marx's critique of Hegel. In Hegel's *Philosophy of Right*, civil society (bürgerliche Gesellschaft) appears as an intermediate category and developmental stage between the selfish privatism of the family and the reconciliation of social antagonisms in the state. For Hegel, civil society as a realm of market exchange is an advance beyond the family but still antagonistic: the relevant chapter in his earlier *Phenomenology of Spirit* is headed 'the spiritual animal kingdom and deception'. For Marx, bürgerliche Gesellschaft is *bourgeois,* the capitalist society presided over by the bourgeoisie, and the defence of the associational life of society against the state, associated with radicals like Thomas Paine in England, France and the United States, is necessarily incomplete without the overthrow of capitalism. Bourgeois revolutions, of which the French is the paradigm, cannot carry through their programmes of liberty, equality and fraternity or of political and legal equality and rights; these slogans all become ideological defences of the status quo where they do not point to the need for a communist revolution.

In a brilliant book of 1983 Jean Cohen, Arato's partner and later co-author, criticised the reductionism of Marx's model and argued for the relevance of the concept of civil society. This, rather than class, was at the centre of the post-1968 social movements in the West on which she had also written.[67] Meanwhile in the East, the concept of civil society, which Arato claims was introduced by the Polish dissident Jacek Kuron,[68] had become important for practitioners as well as for outside observers. For Arato, writing in the early 1990s, 'the idea of the "self-limiting revolution", internally linked to the project of the reconstruction of civil society, represents one of the major contributions of recent East European thought and action to political philosophy.'[69]

Larry Ray, in *Rethinking Critical Theory. Emancipation in the Age of Global Social Movements*, London, Sage, 1993, in a sense combines Arnason's emphasis on the reactive character of Soviet modernity and Cohen and Arato's focus on social movements. Chapter 6 of the book, on 'The Crisis of State Socialism', argues that

> The collapse of state socialism serves as a paradigm of crisis in peripheral regulatory systems. In the context of Russian history, Stalinism could be understood as a wave in a long cycle of modernization through revolution from above, beginning with the Petrine reforms (1682–1725) and continuing through the nineteenth century, each of which attempted to redress Russian underdevelopment through enhancing the centralized power of the state.[70]

This charismatic-bureaucratic mode of legitimation, which of course looked more convincing in the USSR than in more developed countries like Czechoslovakia or East Germany, gradually ran out of steam, leading to crises of reform which either got out of hand, as in Czechoslovakia in 1968, or were abandoned in case they did (or ran out of steam themselves, in increasingly gerontocratic regimes). In the end it was a final attempt at reform from above by Gorbachev which brought down the system by reinforcing anticommunist opposition elsewhere in the Empire as well as more far-reaching internal reform movements. The failure of 'regulatory strategies' led to a choice of one or more 'exit routes' which were all emergency exits.

With the virtual extinction of European communism in 1989, critical theory had come full circle. It had emerged in the 1920s as a response to the failure of communism in the West and its highly ambiguous 'success' in Russia. It now confronted the definitive failure of the Eastern experiment. Two critical theorists who responded rapidly to this situation were Habermas and Offe. Offe was first off the mark, with an article in *Die Zeit* in December 1989 in a series entitled 'Is socialism over?' He presented a series of antitheses represented by the capitalist democracies of the West and 'actually existing socialism', notably one much cited in later literature that in the former there are queues in front of the labour exchanges and in the latter in front of the butchers. Capitalist societies 'combine industrial micro-planning with economic macro-anarchy', while state socialist macro planning is unable to control micro-anarchy in the enterprises. Capitalism makes economic life independent of popular support, yet tends to enjoy this support, whereas state socialism depends on active and enthusiastic participation yet 'systematically discourages it'. Capitalist democracies display dynamic change without making this an agreed social purpose: state socialism does set this as a goal but instead produces stagnation. Traditionally communist aims might however be well worth pursuing, even if the previously existing communist route was no longer viable.

> As the image of actually existing socialism becomes more and more sad and hopeless, we all become 'communists' in so far as we are unable finally to get rid of our concern about public affairs and our horror at the possibility of catastrophic developments in global society.[71]

Habermas, in a wide-ranging essay published in the following year, offered one of the fundamental responses to 1989 – the notion of a 'catching-up' or rectifying revolution which had not contributed substantial new ideas to European critical thinking.[72] For Habermas, one of whose formative experiences had been the restoration of democracy in Western Germany in the 1940s and of economic prosperity soon afterwards, the GDR and the other socialist countries were essentially 'scrolling back' to repeat what they had missed at that time.[73] In a related argument, Hans Joas suggested that explanations of the 'collapse' of the GDR and other socialist systems should not be sought in the mere fact that they failed to make the transition to more modern forms of economic production or to respond to political pressures, 'but *why* they were incapable of doing so, that is to say, why their institutional repertoire was so disastrously restricted'.[74]

In a curious mirror image of Germany's precipitate rush to unification,[75] of which he rapidly became a severe critic, Habermas moved briskly on from the revolutions themselves to the implications for the contemporary Western left. In West Germany, 'The non-communist left has no reason to don sackcloth and ashes, but equally it cannot act as if nothing had happened.'[76] In particular, he writes, in a formulation which shapes his later discussions of socialism, we must acknowledge that markets cannot be replaced by administrative planning 'without jeopardizing the level of differentiation achieved in modern societies'.[77] The idea that they could be so replaced was one of the elements in Marxism which, along with a productivist emphasis on the emancipatory possibilities of technology and human labour and of the basis of social conflict, combined with an evolutionary teleology of history, explain 'how Marxism, in the form in which it was codified by Stalin, could degenerate into an ideology which legitimated a simply inhuman practice'.[78] Social democracy, too, was wrong to believe that it could use state power as a neutral instrument of emancipation.[79] Despite all this, Habermas concludes,

> The challenges of the twenty-first century will be of an order and magnitude that demand answers from Western societies which cannot be arrived at, nor put into practice, without a radical-democratic universalization of interests through institutions for the formation of public opinion and political will. The socialist Left still has a place and political role to play in this arena.[80]

Habermas, in the final essay in *The Rectifying Revolution* and in subsequent political writings, continued, like Günter Grass and others of his generation, to worry about the way in which German unification was pursued. Not only did the unification process lack legitimacy, since it was achieved by the fast-and-dirty route of creating five new states out of the GDR and having them accede to the Federal Republic, rather than replacing the provisional Federal constitution of 1949 with a new one to be placed before the whole German population,[81] but West Germany also missed the opportunity to pioneer a 'coordinated European economic aid programme *for all* the transformation countries in Central and Eastern Europe'.[82] If Habermas, like Offe and many others, seems in retrospect to have been too worried about the reanimation of German nationalism in the euphoria of reunification, his argument about the other missed opportunity, that of a coordinated European response to the aftermath of communism, remains highly relevant.[83] Offe, who soon moved to a post at Humboldt University in what had been East Berlin, turned to work more systematically on the process of post-communist transition both in Germany and in the rest of Europe. The next chapter focuses on his work and that of his collaborators.

Notes

1 Friedrich Pollock, *Die planwirtschaftlichen Versuche in der Sowjetunion 1917–1927*, Leipzig: Hirschfeld, 1929. Reprinted in *Archiv sozialistischer Literatur*, 21, Frankfurt: Verlag Neue Kritik, 1971. This phrase is from the preface, p. v. Pollock notes on the following page that '. . . economic policy is discussed in the Soviet Russian literature and in the party conferences very openly and incisively. However the publications of the Communist International often bear the mark of political propaganda.'

2 Two reviews in specialist Soviet journals are cited by Renate Schmucker in her introduction to the reprint, pp. v and vi.

3 *Zeitschrift* I, 3, 1932, p. 377n.

4 *Zeitschrift* III, 2, 1934, p. 230n.

5 *Zeitschrift* IV, 1, 1935, p. 85.

6 *Zeitschrift* V, 2, 1936, pp. 310–12.

7 Wiggershaus, *The Frankfurt School*, pp. 61–4.

8 Horkheimer, *Dawn and Decline. Notes 1926–1931 and 1950–1969*, New York: Seabury, 1978, p. 72.

9 'Neue sowjetrussische Literatur zur Sozialforschung', *Zeitschrift*, VII (1–2), VII (3), 1938; VIII (1–2), 1939–40. For a discussion of Schlesinger, see Stephanie J. McKendry, *The Scholar Advocate: Rudolf Schlesinger's Writings on Marxism and Soviet Historiography*. PhD Thesis, University of Glasgow 2008 (available online).

10 Arato, 'Autoritärer Sozialismus und die Frankfurter Schule', in Axel Honneth and Albrecht Wellmer (eds), *Die Frankfurter Schule und die Folgen*, Alexander von Humboldt-Stiftung: Symposium 1984, Berlin: De Gruyter, 1986, pp. 193–4.

11 Ibid., p. 202.

12 Quoted by Wiggershaus, p. 405.

13 Memorandum of 18 September 1958, cited by Demirović, *Der nonkonformistische Intellektuelle*, p. 255.

14 Herbert Marcuse, *Soviet Marxism: A Critical Analysis*, New York: Columbia University Press.

15 *Die Gesellschaftslehre des sowjetischen Marxismus*, Berlin and Neuwied: Luchterhand, 1964.

16 Marcuse, *Soviet Marxism*, p. 1. For Arato, this masks a return to Marxist orthodoxy ('Autoritärer Sozialismus', p. 193).

17 Marcuse, *Soviet Marxism*, pp. 10–11.

18 Marcuse, *Soviet Marxism*, p. 2. Marcuse had earlier analysed Hegel's place in 'The Rise of Social Theory' in *Reason and Revolution*.

19 See John Abromeit, 'Left Heideggerianism or Phenomenological Marxism? Reconsidering Herbert Marcuse's Critical Theory of Technology', *Constellations* 17(1), 2010, pp. 87–106.

20 Marcuse, *Soviet Marxism*, pp. 74–5.

21 Ibid., 116.

22 Johann Arnason, *Von Marcuse zu Marx*, Frankfurt: Suhrkamp, 1971, p. 194; my translation.

23 Marcuse, *Soviet Marxism*, p. 256.

24 Arnason, *Von Marcuse zu Marx*, p. 203.

25 Ibid., p. 205.

26 Johann Arnason, *The Future that Failed. Origins and Destinies of the Soviet Model*, London and New York: Routledge, 1993. For an overview of Western sovietology, see William Outhwaite and Larry Ray, 'Prediction and Prophecy in Communist Studies', special number of *Comparative Sociology*, 10(5), 2011, pp. 691–709.

27 Rudolf Bahro, *The Alternative in Eastern Europe*, London: NLB, 1978. Original edition 1977. See Kellner, *Herbert Marcuse*, pp. 307ff. Marcuse's review, 'Protosocialism and Late Capitalism: Toward a Theoretical Synthesis Based on Bahro's Analysis', is reprinted in Ulf Wolter (ed.), *Rudolf Bahro: Critical Responses*, White Plains, NY: M.E. Sharpe, pp. 24–48. The German title is more explicit in referring not just to 'Theory' but to a theory of revolution.

28 Bahro, p. 13. The term 'realer Sozialismus', usually translated as 'actually existing socialism', was invented by the regime in the GDR to stress the difference between their 'developed socialist society' (with all its faults) and utopian fantasies found in the West. See also Bahro, p. 17.

29 Bahro, p. 14.

30 See, for example, the critiques by Ivan Szelényi and by Andrew Arato and Mihaly Vajda in *New German Critique*, nos. 20 and 21.

31 Szelényi, 'Whose Alternative?', *New German Critique*, no. 20, p. 122. This is arguably the same contradiction which prevented earlier critical theory from providing an adequate analysis of state socialism.

32 Bahro of course developed his analysis independently of critical theory, though after his expulsion to the Federal Republic he studied for a doctorate with Oskar Negt.

33 A. Arato, 'Critical Sociology and Authoritarian State Socialism', in J. B. Thompson and D. Held (eds), *Habermas: Critical Debates,* London: Macmillan, 1982, p. 197. Arato had earlier co-translated Konrád and Szelényi's book *The Intellectuals on the Road to Class Power*, Brighton: Harvester, 1979. His later books on *Civil Society, Constitution and Legitimacy*, Lanham, MD: Rowman and Littlefield, 2000 and with Jean Cohen, on *Civil Society and Democratic Theory*, Cambridge: MIT Press, 1992, were substantially shaped by their long involvement with oppositionists in Hungary and elsewhere. His work on constitutional theory and practice is discussed in the next chapter.

34 Arato rightly criticises 'an almost incomprehensible lack of interest'. ('Autoritärer Sozialismus', p. 193), given his assumption that at that time 'no macro-theory of the modern world can be taken seriously which cannot in principle, or for political reasons, undertake a adequate determination of authoritarian state socialism' (p. 193). The neglect of state socialism by both Marxist and non-Marxist social and political theory and, in particular, state theory is a topic in itself. That it is not just a matter of political correctness or what the Sovietologist Alfred Meyer called 'anti-anti-communism'is shown, as we shall see in chapter four below, that it persists in the neglect of post-communist societies. It is still possible to find analyses of 'comparative European capitalisms' confined purely to *western* Europe.

35 Jürgen Habermas, 'Toward the Reconstruction of Historical Materialism', in Habermas, *Communication and the Evolution of Society,* Cambridge: Polity, 1991, p. 152.

36 Arato, p. 200. Though Habermas does not spell this out, it is clear that for the same reasons he would reject the idea that state socialism might be a 'higher' stage.

37 Ibid. Habermas elsewhere noted the continuity with the analyses of Pollock and Horkheimer. See Habermas, *Theory of Communicative Action*, vol. 2, pp. 378–83; Arato, 'Autoritärer Sozialismus', p. 202.

38 Arato. Autoritärer Sozialismus, p. 202.

39 Ibid., p. 206.

40 Ibid., p. 210.

41 See, for example, André Tosel, 'Le dernier Lukács et l'école de Budapest', in Jacques Bidet and Eustache Kouvélakis (eds), *Dictionnaire Marx contemporain*, Paris: Presses Universitaires de France, 2001, pp. 159–69.

42 See, for example, Agnes Heller's friendly but critical discussion of 'Habermas and Marxism' in *Habermas. Critical Debates*, pp. 21–41.

43 F. Fehér, A. Heller and G. Márkus, *Dictatorship Over Needs*, Oxford: Blackwell, 1983, p. 131.

44 Ibid., pp. 284–6.

45 Ibid., p. 297.

46 Ibid., p. 297.

47 I should own up to having been on the 1984 bandwagon, with my 'Newspeak Est-Ouest', published in *Sociolinguistics*, vol. XVI, no. 2, December 1986, pp. 45–50 (English version (abridged) in *Aspects*, 1986).

48 See Part II, 'Ethical Tenets', chapters 9–13.

49 Habermas, *Communication and the Evolution of Society*, p. 90. See also the table in Habermas, *Communication and the Evolution of Society*, p. 81 and Habermas's reformulation in the version presented by McCarthy: see Outhwaite, *Habermas*, 2nd edn p. 51 and (Ray, figure 6.2 (p. 123).

50 Tim Guldimann, *Moral und Herrschaft in der Sowjetunion*, Frankfurt: Suhrkamp, 1984, pp. 218–19, 223.

51 Ibid., p. 221.

52 M. Vozlensky, (1985) *Nomenklatura. The Ruling Class of the USSR*, London: Overseas Publishing House. see also Drieschner, 'Verantwortung der Wissenschaft', n. 20.

53 Rainer Deppe, Helmut Dubiel and Ulrich Rödel (eds), *Demokratischer Umbruch in Osteuropa*, Frankfurt: Suhrkamp, 1991. Sigrid Meuschel's article, 'Wandel durch Auflehnung. Thesen zum Verfall bürokratischer Herrschaft in der DDR', was shortly followed by her major book, *Legitimation und Parteiherrschaft: Zum Paradox von Stabilität und Revolution in der DDR, 1945–1989*, Frankfurt: Suhrkamp, 1992.

54 Meuschel, 'Integration durch Legitimation? Zum Problem der Sozialintegration in der DDR', in Ilse Spittmann-Ruhe and Gisela Helwig (eds), *Ideologie und gesellschaftliche Entwicklung in der DDR. Achtzehnte Tagung zum Stand der DDR-Forschung in der Bundesrepublik Deutschland, 28 bis 31 Mai 1985*, Köln, Edition Deutschland-Archiv, 1985, pp. 15ff. See also Sigrid Meuschel, *Legitimation und Parteiherrschaft*, p. 22 and n. 83.

55 Christa Wolf, *Im Dialog. Aktuelle Texte*, Frankfurt: Luchterhand, 1990, pp. 134ff. Cited by Meuschel, *Legitimation und Parteiherrschaft*, p. 28. My translation.

56 Meuschel, *Legitimation und Parteiherrschaft*, p. 9.

57 Meuschel was writing specifically about Germany, but with reference to the broader context of 'the disastrous effects of socialism of the Soviet type in general' (Meuschel, *Legitimation und Parteiherrschaft*, p. 7).

58 See Outhwaite and Ray, 'Prediction and Prophecy'; also the superb book by Alexei Yurchak, *Everything Was Forever, Until It Was No More. The Last Soviet Generation*, Princeton and Oxford: Princeton University Press, 2006.

59 Meuschel, *Legitimation und Parteiherrschaft*, pp. 84ff.

60 Ibid., p. 130. See also pp. 130–4 and note 17 on the relation between totalitarianism and technocracy.

61 Johann Arnason, *The Future that Failed. Origins and Destinies of the Soviet Model*, London: Routledge, 1993.

62 Arnason, *The Future that Failed*, p. ix. See also pp. 5–6 and Arnason's earlier essay, 'Modernity as Project and as Field of Tensions', in *Communicative Action*, A. Honneth and H. Joas (eds), Cambridge: Polity, 1991, pp. 181–213.

63 Arnason, *The Future that Failed*, p. 17. Arnason notes however (p. 138) that, despite the importance for communism of traditional Russian statism and imperialism, 'the fortunes of domestic Communist movements did not depend primarily on the relative strength or weakness of statist traditions: Communism was strongest in Czechoslovakia, the most Westernized country of the region.'

64 Arnason, *The Future that Failed*, p. 90. See also p. 100: 'Economic transformation and ideological adaptation served the purposes of state- and empire-building.'

65 Arnason, *The Future that Failed*, p. 188.

66 Ibid., p. 188.

67 Jean Cohen, *Class and Civil Society*, London: Martin Robertson, 1983; Cohen, Telos. See also Klaus Eder, *The New Politics of Class: Social Movements and Cultural Dynamics in Advanced Societies*, London: Sage, 1993.

68 'Revolution, Restoration, and Legitimation', in Arato, *Civil Society, Constitution, and Legitimacy*, Lanham, MD: Rowman and Littlefield, 2000, p. 277, n. 3. See also 'Revolution, Civil Society and Democracy' in Arato, *From Neo-Marxism to Democratic Theory*, Armonk, New York: M. E. Sharpe, 1993, pp. 296–312.

69 Arato, 'Revolution, Restoration, and Legitimation', p. 81.

70 Larry Ray, *Rethinking Critical Theory*, p. 108. One of Lenin's slogans was of course that communism was 'electrification plus Soviet power'.

71 Claus Offe, 'Kommunistischer Kapitalismus', *Die Zeit*, 8 December 1989.

72 Jürgen Habermas, *Die postnationale Konstellation*, Frankfurt: Suhrkamp, 1998. Translated as *The Postnational Constellation*, Cambridge: Polity, 2001. The title essay, 'What does Socialism Mean Today? The Rectifying Revolution and the Need for New Thinking on the Left', appeared earlier in *New Left Review*, 183, 1990; references below are to this version. Habermas' label was criticised by Offe (see below) and more severely by Arato; see his *Civil Society, Constitution, and Legitimacy*, pp. 10–11.

73 Habermas, *The Rectifying Revolution*, pp. 4–5. In a sympathetic discussion of liberal interpretations such as those by Daniel Bell and Ralf Dahrendorf, he notes that even if one does not adhere to the theory of totalitarianism and takes care to distinguish between national socialist, Stalinist and post-Stalinist regimes, one can still still 'recognize their similarities in the mirror of Western democracies' (p. 8).

74 Joas, *War and Modernity*, p. 108.

75 The best account of this, by Chancellor Kohl's foreign policy advisor who was one of its main protagonists, is Horst Teltschik, *329 Tage*, Berlin: Siedler, 1991. See also Timothy Garton Ash, *In Europe's Name. Germany and the Divided Continent*, London: Jonathan Cape, 1993, and Konrad Jarausch, *The Rush to German Unity*, New York: Oxford University Press, 1994.

76 Habermas, *The Rectifying Revolution*, p. 10.

77 Ibid., p. 11. Sigrid Meuschel's analysis of the GDR and by implication of other state socialist societies focuses on the theme of a lack of institutional and social differentiation. Differentiation, which had a central place as a category in Niklas Luhmann's system theory, is used in a more modest (or differentiated!) way in critical theory, notably by Claus Offe.

78 Habermas, *The Rectifying Revolution*, p. 12.

79 Ibid., p. 13.

80 Ibid., p. 21.

81 For a recent discussion of this issue, see Ulrich Preuss, 'German Unification: Expectations and Outcomes', Hertie School of Governance – Working Papers No. 48, November 2009. Preuss was an advisor to the constitutional commission.

82 Habermas, 'Nochmals: Zur Identität der Deutschen. Ein einig Volk von aufgebrachten Wirtschaftsbürgern?', p. 211. This, the first of his articles, appeared in *Die nachholende Revolution* immediately after the title essay.

83 It has recently been made in an important book by Mary Sarotte, *1989. The Struggle to Create Post-Cold-War Europe*, Princeton: Princeton University Press, 2009.

4

Critical theory and post-communist transition

Offe had already written, in the volume edited by Joas and Kohli on the collapse of the GDR, that although it was 'too early even to speculate about the driving forces and the consequences of the dissolution of communism as a whole, on the other hand in the autumn of 1990 it is already too late to describe the change as a unitary one taking a similar course in all the countries of "real socialism"'.[1] He was concerned both with the peculiarities of the German situation and with the former communist bloc as a whole. In both cases, the massive nature of the transformation made Habermas's notion of a mere 'catching-up' or rectifying revolution inadequate.[2] Offe coined what became one of the dominant motifs of the literature on post-communism: the notion of a 'triple transition' involving the territorial shape and/or ethnic composition of the states concerned, controversies over their constitutional form and finally their other political characteristics, '. . . the "normal politics" of the allocation and distribution of positive rights and resources through legislatures and executives'.[3] Germany was of course one of the countries experiencing a territorial transition; another was Czechoslovakia, which split into the Czech and Slovak Republics at the beginning of 1993. The Soviet Union and Yugoslavia also split apart, with less violence than expected in the former and drastically more in the latter.[4] The sizeable Hungarian minority in Romania remains a destabilizing factor in both states, while in the three Baltic states ethnic issues – essentially concerning the Russian minorities – have played an important part; the Russian exclave of the Kaliningrad region is an anomaly on the eastern borders of the EU.

With hindsight, the territorial transitions may not have been as substantial as they threatened to be,[5] but Offe was undoubtedly right to point to the way in which such territorial and constitutional issues interwove with other aspects of politics. This was not just a matter of choices between presidential or parliamentary regimes or between voting systems. There were major issues of property, including of course privatization and reprivatization but also, and relatedly, those concerning restitution and the availability of remedies for what were now perceived as injustices of the communist regimes.[6] Offe joined with Ulrich Preuss, the legal and political theorist who had defended the student movement in 1967, in studying these new developments. Preuss, who had been writing on constitutional and democratic politics throughout the 1980s,[7] had immediately become involved in work on a commission drafting a proposal for a new German constitution and analysing the 1989 revolutions and their outcome.[8] He emphasized in particular the fact that although '. . . in the years since 1989 the European continent has undergone social and political changes which are hardly less radical and far-reaching than those in the last quarter of the eighteenth century',[9]

> . . . the elimination of the communist regimes and the erection of profoundly new economic, social, and political structures happened, with few exceptions, within the framework of the existing constitution of the respective country. Before the revolutionaries overturned the old regimes, they amended the communist constitutions according to the amendment procedures of those very constitutions. Thus, for example, the leading role of the Communist Party, which in fact meant the dictatorship of the *nomenklatura*, or the category of the people's property were not abolished until the pertinent articles of the constitution had been repealed. Having been forced to listen to hypocritical revolutionary phraseology and having experienced a all-pervasive legal nihilism for the preceding forty years, the anticommunist opposition wanted to be nether revolutionary nor negligent of the rule of law.[10]

Preuss notes that initially what occurred throughout the bloc was:

> . . . a process of repeated amendment of the old constitutions according to the prescribed procedures by majorities of the people's deputies elected under the old system. Even the removal of the old elite from office in East Germany took place as provided for by Article 57, Paragraph 2, which stated that elected representatives could be dismissed 'by the voters' if they committed gross abuses; it was on this basis that the parliament voted to remove top party functionaries from the government on 17 November 1989.[11]

There is a parallel here with the process of government, as described by President Havel in a volume of memoirs:

> There was not a lot that was specifically communistic in what you call the 'technology of power' once the leading role of the Communist Party no longer applied, and things were no longer decided first in the Politburo. The government simply meets on certain days; there's an agenda, there are procedural rules, the ministers have to receive their briefing materials in time, and so on . . .[12]

In the early 1990s Offe and Preuss worked with the Norwegian political theorist Jon Elster and others on a major project on transformation based at Bremen, resulting in a book published in 1998.[13] The focus on constitutional politics[14] reflects Elster's earlier work on constitutionalism and democratic transition and on the 'Round Table Talks' which were a feature of almost all the transitions, as well as the interests of all three senior authors.[15] The book traces the details behind the creation of formal constitutions in the four countries studied (Hungary, Bulgaria and what became the Czech and Slovak Republics), since 'the choices which the relevant actors – the *pouvoir constituant* – make are likely to have long-lasting effects'.[16] The authors conclude:

> . . . it appears that it is the formative impact of new institutions – i.e. their capacity to shape the frames, habits, routines, and expectations (and even memories) of citizens in convergent ways and thereby to render inherited fears, hostilities, and suspicions groundless – that is the critical determination of consolidation.[17]

Meanwhile in New York, Andrew Arato who, as we saw in the previous chapter, had been extremely active writing on and with the Hungarian opposition in the 1980s,[18] was completing, with Jean Cohen, their major theoretical study of *Civil Society and Political Theory*, which came out in 1992, the same year as Habermas's similarly massive *Faktizität und Geltung*, translated as *Between Facts and Norms*.[19]

Both book have a primarily theoretical and historical focus, but *Civil Society and Political Theory* includes some analysis of the rise of civil society in Eastern Europe and elsewhere in the 1980s and some prescient comments on its decline at the beginning of the 1990s.

> . . . the turn to political society has as its pathology the demobilization of civil society and the failure to replace its mobilized forms by institutionalized ones, This is a serious matter in Eastern Europe, where atomization and

the disruption of social ties, solidarities, and associations far surpassed anything under even the recent bureaucratic-authoritarian regimes . . .

There is a danger that populism, which has strong roots in Eastern Europe, will be the response to elitism on the part of demobilized or undeveloped, semiatomized, unsolidaristic civil societies.[20]

Arato was also becoming more closely concerned with constitutional theory and the practice of constitution-making in the post-communist context. In a retrospective postscript to a volume of essays from the 1990s, he writes of the eclipse of civil society:

Recognizing the empirical phenomena of the depoliticization of civic initiatives and social movements at the time of the Round Tables and the first competitive elections, I was nevertheless deeply concerned about the neglect of autonomous associations and publics in the emerging political designs and in the policy process. I came to the conclusion . . . that civil society had to be securely institutionalized before becoming a key terrain of participatory politics in the long term . . .

I have always stressed fundamental civil and political rights as the necessary conditions for the institutionalization of a modern civil society. These rights, however, could be established only in a setting that satisfies the demands of liberal constitutionalism. This is how I can explain my shift in interest to the study of constitution making, constitutional adjudication, and constitutional politics.[21]

The outcomes in most of post-communist Eastern Europe, 'where formerly legal nihilism and paper constitutions were the rule',[22] demonstrate this.

I cannot prove with any rigor that democratic and liberal forms of constitutional legitimacy are necessary conditions of democratic consolidation. Nevertheless, I strongly believe this is the case . . . Even radical economic deprivation and dislocation; the emergence of second revolutionary, counterrevolutionary, and nationalist rhetoric; and, in . . . Bulgaria and Romania, total international disinterest, have not led to the weakening of democratic institutions. . . .[23]

Like Preuss, who took up his earlier stress on the 'self-limiting' character of the 1989 revolutions and their constitutional aftermath, Arato considers '. . . the efforts of Central European constitution makers, especially the archi-tects of Round Tables, to postulate the fiction of legal continuity with a past

without legality . . . highly innovative and worthy of imitation.[24] The political ideas at the back of 'self-limiting' opposition movements of civil society
and their continuation by others in the post-communist transition to genuine
constitutionalism mean that Arato was irritated by Habermas's 'catching-up'
notion and also with Habermas's and with Offe's claim that 1989 failed to
produce any theoretical programme. What, he asks, does he want: '. . . *State
and Revolution? What is the Third Estate?* or some imagined piece of social
science?'.[25] As he wrote in an earlier essay, 'None of [these] interpretations
. . . really grasp the meaning of what is potentially new in the transformation
of the East, the option of a self-democratizing civil society.'[26] As he notes
later in the same article, civil society theory experiences '. . . a distinct innovation when thinkers like Jacek Kuron, Adam Michnik, Claude Lefort, and Alain
Touraine begin to include social movements in the concept.' The concept of
civil society is of course used in a variety of ways.

> For some, including myself, the goal is finding new loci of the potential
> democratization of really existing democracies, new ways to revitalize
> the public space of these societies. Others, however, are interested in
> agendas as diverse as the reconstruction of the supposedly communal
> presuppositions of society and the radical liberation of market rationality
> from political regulation and social constraint. The concept of civil society
> has been used to justify all of these potentially incompatible strategies.
> But it cannot be denied that all the perspectives mentioned can find their
> progenitors during the course of the initial revival in Central Europe.[27]

Over the period of the Bremen project Offe also produced one of the definitive
books on post-communist transition, with the ironic title of 'the tunnel at the
end of the light'.[28] While rejecting, as we saw in the last chapter, Habermas's
notion of a 'catching-up' revolution, he noted the

> 'a-theoretical' character of the upheaval. . . . Where the social theorists
> express themselves at all, they do so not in the form of global interpretations
> of the events and their driving dynamics, but rather in more modest
> descriptions of single aspects . . .[29]

Offe concentrates, therefore, on specific aspects of transition, though his
comparative focus and his theoretical reference-points make his work more
wide-ranging than this suggests. Having identified the 'triple transition', he
addresses national and ethnic issues, legal and constitutional questions, particularly in relation to restitution of property, and thirdly the, for him, more
familiar territory of the politics of social policy.

The 'return of nationalism' was one of the main themes rapidly identified in 1989 and with the break-up of the Soviet Union in 1991. First, of course, for most of the region, to escape from the tutelage of the now moribund USSR was to experience full state sovereignty for the first time since the late 1940s and to reopen issues of national history such as the Katyn massacre in Poland or 1956 and 1968 in Hungary and Czechoslovakia. As Offe notes, a nationalist emphasis is a good way for new elites (and for re-badged old elites) to distance themselves from communism. Second, the taboo was lifted off ethnic politics, both for minorities and for states which opposed them, as in the persecution of Turks by late communist Bulgaria or of Roma by a number of states,[30] or acted as external sponsors. And if the core idea of nationalism, self-rule by 'ourselves alone' (sinn fein in Irish), is a simple one, it unpacks into two main variants. The first involves escape from a larger entity seen as holding one back, as in the case of Slovenian, Baltic and Czech separatism, and the second a more defensive and backward-looking nationalism, illustrated by, for example, Serbia, Russia and more recently 'Eurosceptical' nationalism across the EU. This is probably a more important division than the more familiar one between 'civic' and 'ethnic' nationalism, which is of course often used at the expense of Eastern Europe.

As Offe notes, 'Large parts of the Western public in general and liberal intellectuals in particular are dismayed by the outbursts of national and ethnic politics and ethnic strife that have emerged in post-communist societies.'[31] Rather than bewailing this, as both liberal and Marxist commentators had tended to do, Offe is concerned to demonstrate the 'rationality' of ethnic politics and hence the difficulty of attempts to displace it in favour of something more promising. In the short term, fighting over the cake may make more sense than waiting for it to grow larger. He cites Judy Batt: 'Nationalism has the potential to breathe life into the new democracies by mobilizing dispirited and apathetic electorates, but at the same time relieving the pressure of popular material demands which the economy cannot satisfy.'[32] In the specific case of social policy, Offe points out that in the West ethnic homogeneity has been shown to be a determinant of readiness to support welfare schemes.[33]

There is of course a kind of ethnic politics which is relatively harmless and is found in the more benign areas of US politics, where political candidates from one ethnic group form alliances with running-mates from another in order to harvest ethnically based support. Offe is however rightly concerned with the more problematic and dysfunctional forms of ethnic politics found in post-communist Europe.

The problem that designers of institutional cures to the ills of ethnic politics would, have to face is clear enough. The task is to reconstruct by legal and constitutional means the measure of unity, integration and peace that has prevailed in the area under Communist rule and that has been due in the past . . . to repression and military force.[34]

Constitutional issues arise not only because the rules of the post-communist political game are in any case being set, but because ethnic politics quintessentially foregrounds issues of *who* should be taking decisions. This creates problems for solutions relying on participatory rights, whether or not they also invoke human rights and whether or not these approaches are reinforced by external pressures.[35] Territorial boundary-drawing or re-drawing is also no solution in the European context of dispersed populations. Offe is reduced to hoping for 'evolutionary' solutions: learning from the experience of the past or from horror stories elsewhere (Yugoslavia, Russia . . .), the emergence of class politics as an alternative focus and, thirdly, the growth of multiple identities of which ethnicity becomes only one, whose relative importance is up to the individual.[36] Preuss had also warned at an early stage of the dangers of giving a narrowly ethnic reading to the notion of the people.

> I do not mean to discredit the feelings of national identity which we find in almost every country of the world. But the idea of modern constitutionalism is the separation of fellow-feelings of a nation from the structure of government and the rights of individuals given from the constitution.'[37]

This was also a major focus of an article he published in the same year, which concludes with some anxious remarks on 'The Predominance of "Communitarian" Concepts of Citizenship in East and Central Europe.'[38] It is no accident that it was in West Germany, a segment of the former country institutionalized under international supervision by a new democratic constitution (albeit a provisional one), that the concept of 'constitutional patriotism', introduced by Dolf Sternberger in 1979 and taken up by Habermas in 1986, had considerable resonance. Habermas, who had displayed a certain suspicion of constitutions in his critique of Luhmann and in *Legitimation Crisis*,[39] and had criticized the excessive 'juridification' (Verrechtlichung) of social processes in the modern state in *Theory of Communicative Action*,[40] picked up Sternberger's term in an essay forming part of the *Historikerstreit* (which, as discussed in Chapter 1 above, had begun with an attempt by right-wing publicists to revalorize a concept of national pride).

> The unreserved opening of the Federal Republic to the political culture of the West is the great intellectual achievement of the postwar period . . .

The only patriotism which does not estrange us from the West is a constitutional patriotism. Unfortunately, it was only after – and through – Auschwitz that an attachment to universalistic constitutional principles anchored in convictions was able to develop in the cultural nation of the Germans.[41]

Here the concept of the constitution appears as a symbol of a procedural consensus rather than a substantive consensus on values, even if this is of course located in a specific political culture.[42] In the later 1980s and early 1990s, as we shall see in the next chapter, Habermas focused more on constitutional theory itself. Constitutional issues took on a peculiar form in Germany, where the reinterpretation and modification of the GDR constitution was rapidly overtaken by the prospect of reunification.

Even when it became clear that reunification was going to happen, however, there remained the question of *how* it would be accomplished. The West German 'Basic Law' (Grundgesetz) had explicitly not been called a constitution, and Article 146 envisaged that it would cease to exist if and when the German people as a whole freely adopted a constitution for a united country. Over the years reunification had come to seem a less and less realistic prospect,[43] until the implosion of the GDR regime suddenly put it again on the agenda. Now however Chancellor Kohl chose the fast and dirty alternative strategy of unification according to Article 23, which provided for territories outside the Federal Republic to join it. (The Saarland, initially occupied by France, had done this after a plebiscite in 1956.) Five new states were rapidly cobbled together out of East German districts and they acceded to the Federal Republic, as did the former East Berlin. As Offe puts it, the GDR 'has, as it were, relocated without leaving a forwarding address.' This meant that under the umbrella of constitutional unity two radically different social and economic systems were slammed together like particles in a CERN experiment. The completely different abortion regimes in the two countries were only one striking example of the mismatch – resolved in this case by a temporary compromise between the liberal Eastern regime and the Catholic-influenced one in the West.

The German fast-track transition was therefore both easier and more difficult than that in comparable countries. It was much quicker, with a complete legal and economic regime (including membership of the EU, for which the other states had to wait more than a decade) put in place overnight,[44] and lubricated by massive transfers of funds. As Offe neatly puts it, in a play on the subtitle of the Bremen book, the other countries 'had to repair their sinking ships while still at sea, whereas the GDR was retrofitted in the FRG dry dock'.[45] On the other hand, the monetary union which had preceded unification destroyed the East German economy and many East Germans felt they had become 'a colony in their own country'.[46] In a useful typology of six post-communist states, Offe locates the GDR, along with Czechoslovakia, as the two most productive, with weak anti-communist opposition and a rapid transition following the collapse of the old regime. These similarities make the GDR not so much an exception as more a 'special case' within this pair. It operates as a test case for three issues, the impact of the East on the West, the attraction or otherwise of the Western model for the East, and whether, if it *is* perceived as attractive, it can be implemented with aid from the West. The first of these issues, 'whether Western democracies . . . will be able to avoid becoming infected, as it were, by the structural and moral shortcomings of the collapsed system'[47] is one which had received some attention in Germany but not much outside. In the German case, Offe writes,

> The political system in the old FRG was characterized by a great degree of cooperation and consensus between the agents of the central state, the parties, the judiciary, regional authorities and functional bodies representing specific interests . . . This system relied on self-administration, consultation and continuing compromises, and can hardly be extended in the short term to apply to conditions in East Germany . . . Hitherto valid procedural rules and customs have clearly been dented in the process. In the face of this observers from East [sic?] Germany have been prompted to diagnose an 'Easternisation' of the practices of the German state, in other words the approximation of German government to the largely opaque development of state powers and attempts at steering that were typical of the state socialist system.

The impact on Europe of massive inequalities between East and West, the parallel (and, I would say, largely independent) development of forms of populist politics in the two halves of Europe, and the difficulties of reshaping a not yet fully embedded system of EU governance is a topic which I shall discuss in the next chapter in relation to the more recent work of Habermas, Offe, Brunkhorst, Benhabib and others. It is however to Offe's credit that he pointed to such issues at an early stage. The second and third issues have been more or less resolved. Post-communist citizens, despite all disillusionment and 'Ostalgie', the German slogan for nostalgia for the communist past, have opted firmly for western-style capitalism and democracy, though not without nationalist and fundamentalist counter-currents, and the slow and ungenerous aid ultimately provided has produced, for much of the region, an impressive advance in living standards.

The German prelude however remains ambiguous. In another chapter, comparing West Germany after the War with East Germany after 1989/90, Offe draws the following conclusion:

> The paradox . . . is that the East German case, which is much less dramatic and catastrophic in its initial (moral, economic, military) conditions, does not turn out, as one might expect, to be the case in which the problems of transformation and reconstruction are more easily overcome in 'objective' terms and at the same time experienced as being more easily manageable. The depth of the abyss would seem to allow for a steeper and more sustained way out, with a clearer and much less contested direction.[48]

Another main section of *Varieties of Transition* is concerned with questions of restitution and retribution. Once again, as in 1989, the question is not so much 'What is to be done?' but 'Should/can *anything* be done?'[49] Whatever one thinks of the rather simple slogan that these just were 'regimes of injustice' it is clear that they made possible and even required all sorts of individual and collective acts of injustice against all sorts of individual and collective victims. One response is to say that because everyone was both a victim of and to some degree complicit with the past regimes it is pointless and/or unjust to single out only some perpetrators of abuses. Something like this seems to have been President Havel's view, though he claims he also always insisted that 'crimes must be punished'[50] and recalls that 'We talked a lot . . . about setting up a kind of "ethical tribunal" to render a verdict on the moral and political responsibility for conditions under the previous regime, but there obviously wasn't the appetite, or even the energy, for that.'[51] Offe cites a paper by Elster which argues: 'Because nobody is innocent, nobody should be put on trial. Because everybody suffered, nobody should be compensated . . . One might imagine a kind of public autodafé of the procommunist property records as well as the archives of the secret police and those of the Communist Party.'[52] But this, Offe comments, would involve 'a sweeping disregard for matters of degree'. Nevertheless, it can be argued that informal retribution might be preferred and would be less costly. Perhaps more importantly, retroactive justice focuses on violations of rights but not on other damage such as 'the ruined economy, the spoiled environment or broken and aliented personalities'.[53]

It was in fact in Germany that the most thorough attempts were made to remedy injustices and to expose and, in some cases, punish those responsible. In particular, anyone who had a state security file on them is entitled to see it (if it still exists), though not before the names of other victims or third parties are removed for the sake of their privacy.[54] As Offe points out, '. . . it is only Germany that is in command of the political resources to effectively enforce whatever rules and principles have been derived from the intense theoretical and moral debate about how to come to terms with the past . . .[55] The three relevant options, which he says usually need to be combined, are disqualification (deprivation of jobs or individual or collective resources), retribution via the criminal law and restitution (or compensation).

> Disqualification cannot be excluded because there are many functionaries whose acts made up the old regime and whose further presence in, or access to, important positions in society is therefore unlikely to be tolerated . . . even though they have not committed criminal acts according to the laws of the old regime . . .

> Retribution also cannot be excluded, as key protagonists in the old regime seem to have regularly violated their own legality in the service of the regime . . . And nor can restitution be excluded, as victims of the old regime will generate pressure for re-privatization and compensation.[56]

Offe brilliantly analyzes the practical (including legal and moral) difficulties with all these measures and the ways in which Germany and other post-communist states have handled them. Given these complexities, he favours an approach which, as he put it in the chapter mentioned earlier, '. . . keeps in focus the similarity of problems in the individual countries as well as the presence of social and cultural traditions, not to mention institutional and economic resources, typical only for particular nations'.[57] In practice, this amounts to an emphasis on restitution (the topic of his chapter 6), where diverse local conditions determine, for example, the dates of expropriations for which compensation can be sought.[58] Even here, however, Offe addresses the 'suspicion . . . that underneath the proclamation of lofty principles of justice all kinds of arbitrary interests, privileges and resentments govern the actual practice of restitution'.[59]

In the final chapter of *Varieties of Transition*, Offe considers the prospects for 'The Left after the West's Victory', in the context of the historical development of Western social policy and, after the 'Sputnik shock' of 1957 (when the USSR launched the first satellite), educational and science policy. '[West] German social policy in the fifties would not have taken the dynamic and "progressive" form it did had it not been for the challenge of the opposing system behind the Iron Curtain . . . the thrust of the Cold War fuelled the fires of socio-political progress.'[60] More generally, '. . . state socialism formed the "exoskeleton" of Western democracies: its presence enabled them to process challenges of social and technological policy productively and in so doing to demonstrate that they were economically, militarily and, moreover, morally "better" than the only other operative counter-model for an industrial society, namely the state socialist variant.'[61] In the West, then,

> The problems we were spared by the automatic side-effects of state socialism, that is, the problems of shoring up peace in Central and Eastern Europe, the problems of economic underdevelopment and of migration due to poverty, are problems we are now having to solve with our own means, namely those of the capitalist market economy and of liberal democracies. We benefited far more from the functioning of the Second World than from exploiting the Third World, and we must now substitute these advantages with means drawn from our own system.[62]

Offe addressed the issue of social policy more directly in an article of 1993 in *Social Research*, reprinted in *Modernity and the State*. The crisis results from the fact that it is squeezed between a massive increase in demand, as firms collapse and workers are dismissed, and the need to create new systems of supply, partly to make up for the disappearance of workplace-based systems. He neatly summarizes the positive and negative aspects of state socialist policy:

> State socialism . . . provided a free and universal system of health, education, and vocational training to its citizens;

> it also provided heavily subsidized housing, which, however, remained scarce and qualitatively deficient in most places;

> formal unemployment was virtually unknown, an accomplishment that was paid for in terms of vast inefficiencies of production . . .

> childcare services were generously provided in order to free female labour for employment, and also in order to maximize state control over the political socialization of children;

> many mass consumption items were heavily subsidized, again causing vast inefficiencies;

> income inequality was significantly lower than in market societies, but disposable income was also lower;

> but many quality consumption items were unavailable in the market or excessively highly priced . . .

> retirement incomes were extremely low by most Western standards;

> health and other services were of poor quality in many places;

> enforcement of positive rights and claims was difficult . . . [63]

Given the scale of the task of constructing a social policy system to fill so many different gaps in provision after the collapse of the socialist system, the time pressure of transition and the absence of civil society organizations able to participate in designing new structures and policies, Offe concludes pessimistically that he expects to see '. . . a pattern of the politics of social policy that remains – beyond the initial period of emergency measures – erratic, shifting, fragmented, clientelistic, and based on the bits and pieces of state power that derive from transient parliamentary majorities or presidential rights to issue decrees.'[64]

Policy was certainly erratic,[65] and the situation in much of the post-communist world was indeed dire: most of the former Soviet Union shared with Iraq, Afghanistan and much of sub-Saharan Africa the distinction of *falling* rates of life expectancy between 1990 and 2006.[66] If provision did not unravel quite as disastrously as Offe had expected (and the chapter on social policy in *Institutional Design in Post-Communist Societies*, drafted by Ulrike Goetting, is remarkably upbeat), it is probably largely because of the sort of stickiness of social provision which also surprised observers of the neo-liberal attack on the welfare state in the United Kingdom and elsewhere in the 1980s. In a recent 'Epilogue' to an edited volume, he notes that '. . . the vanished state socialist institutional system had nurtured, during its rule of roughly 40 years, expectations and notions of social justice that persisted after its demise'.[67] In Germany, he notes, Easterners are much more likely than Westerners to believe that the state is responsible for reducing unemployment or that it should control the banks.[68]

Social and political theorists with a background in critical theory[69] have, then, made a leading contribution to the analysis of post-communist transition – notably to issues of constitutional politics and the politics of welfare. Preuss and Offe continue to work together, currently at the Hertie School of Governance in Berlin. Larry Ray, who had done some research in Hungary and Bulgaria in the late 1980s, included in his book of 1993, *Rethinking Critical Theory*,[70] a chapter on 'The Crisis of State Socialism' and some analysis of the emerging contours of post-communism; we pursued this further in our joint book of 2005, *Social Theory and Postcommunism*,[71] and in other work jointly or separately.[72]

The concept of civil society remains controversial in relation to post-communist Europe. Arato remains a powerful advocate, while others deplore the inflationary and moralizing use to which it has sometimes been put, and the way in which international interventions have often undermined local political structures in the name of civil society and in favour of NGOs.[73] There would however be substantial agreement with the sort of model outlined by Habermas in *Between Facts and Norms*, in which public sphere, civil society and formal political structures mutually reinforce one another in the formation of political will under modern conditions. The same issues return in the reflections by Habermas and others on politics at the level of Europe as a whole, as discussed in the next chapter.

Notes

1 Offe, 'Wohlstand, Nation, Republik. Aspekte des deutschen Sonderweges vom Sozialismus zum Kapitalismus', in Hans Joas and Martin Kohli (eds), *Der Zusammenbruch der DDR*, p. 282. Expanded English version in Offe, *Varieties of Transition. The East European and East German Experience*, Cambridge: Polity Press, 1996, p. 10.

2 'Capitalism by Democratic Design? Democratic Theory Facing the Triple Transition in East Central Europe', in Offe, *Varieties of Transition*, p. 32.

3 Offe, *Varieties of Transition*, p. 34. On ethnic cleavages, see also chapter 7, drafted by Offe, of J. Elster, C. Offe and U. Preuss with Frank Boenker, Ulrike Goetting and Friedbert W. Rueb. *Institutional Design In Post-Communist Societies: Rebuilding The Ship At Sea*, Cambridge: Cambridge University Press, 1998, on 'Consolidation and the Cleavages of Ideology and Identity'.

4 Chapter One of *Institutional Design in Post-Communist Societies*, drafted by Offe, notes 'the inversion of the familiar sequence: world wars did not trigger regime transformations and transitions to democracy, but regime transformations (and subsequent regime decompositions) triggered local wars' (p. 11).

5 Andrew Arato suggested that the transitions in Poland, Hungary, Romania and Bulgaria (like the earlier one in Spain) were double rather than triple. Arato, *Civil Society, Constitution, and Legitimacy*, p. 263, n. 53. This may be true, but of course Hungary and Romania have territorial concerns over Transylvania; Spain is also hardly an uncontested territorial state. More to the point is perhaps the question whether triple transitions are necessarily more problematic than double or single ones; Arato makes the similar point that the 'greater structural challenge' in Eastern Europe as opposed to Latin America may not be a disadvantage 'from the point of view of the patience of the population that is asked to sacrifice.' See also Arato's comments (p. 40) on Preuss's view of double transition.

6 As Arato noted, 'normal politics could not fully commence until such issues were decided at least provisionally . . .' Arato, *Civil Society, Constitution, and Legitimacy*, p. 8. He comments in the footnote (p. 259) that 'In Hungary, the only functioning constitutional court in the region has rightly insisted on the constitutional nature of the initial decisions.'

7 See in particular Preuss, *Politische Verantwortung und Bürgerloyalität: Von den Grenzen der Verfassung und des Gehorsams in der Demokratie*, Frankfurt: Fischer, 1984. Preuss was particularly concerned in the essays reprinted in this book with the tendency in West Germany to use the constitution to restrict oppositional activity, with some commentators suggesting that the

critique of capitalism amounted to rejection of the free political order (p. 240). This, he suggested, makes the constitution into an instrument of 'political-moral exclusion' (Ausbürgerung) (p. 238).

8   Ulrich Preuss, 'Constitutional Powermaking for the New Polity: Some Deliberations on the Relations between Constituent Power and the Constitution', *Cardozo Law Review*, 14, 1992–93, pp. 639–60; Ulrich Preuss, *Constitutional Revolution. The Link between Constitutionalism and Progress*, Atlantic Highlands, NJ: Humanities Press, 1995. Earlier version published as *Revolution, Fortschritt und Verfassung*, Klaus Wagenbach, 1990; 'Patterns of Constitutional Evolution and Change in Eastern Europe', in Joachim Jens Hesse and Nevil Johnson (eds), *Constitutional Policy and Change in Europe*, Oxford: Oxford University Press, 1995, pp. 95–126.

9   Preuss, *Constitutional Revolution*, p. 3.

10 Preuss, *Constitutional Revolution*, p. 8. See also chapter 5, pp. 91–107.

11 Ibid., p. 94. He notes that, although some West German legal scholars suggested that the communist constitutions had 'simply become obsolete as a result of the revolution', this view was not accepted in the GDR or the other states in the bloc.

12 Václav Havel, *To the Castle and Back*, London: Portobello Books, 2008, p. 72.

13 Elster et al., *Institutional Design in Post-Communist Societies: Rebuilding The Ship At Sea*, Cambridge: Cambridge University Press, 1998. Boenker co-edited with Hellmut Wolmann and Helmut Wiesenthal a special issue of the journal Leviathan: *Transformation sozialistischer Gesellschaften: Am Ende des Anfangs*, *Leviathan* Sonderheft, 15, Opladen: Westdeutscher Verlag, 1995, and later, with Klaus Müller and Andreas Pickel, *Postcommunist Transformation and the Social Sciences*, Lanham, MD: Rowman and Littlefield, 2002.

14 The running head of the book is 'Constitutional Politics and Economic Transformation', suggesting that this may have been an earlier title.

15 Jon Elster and Rune Slagstad (eds), *Constitutionalism and Democracy*, 1986; Elster (ed.), *The Round Table Talks and the Breakdown of Communism*, Chicago and London: Chicago University Press; 'Constitutionalism in Eastern Europe: An Introduction', *University of Chicago Law Review*, 58(2), Spring 1991, pp. 447–82. Elster worked at, and became Director of, the Centre for the Study of Constitutionalism in Eastern Europe, set up in 1989 at the University of Chicago Law School, which played an important part in analysing and advising on the production of new constitutions. (The other major institutional resource was the *East European Constitutional Review*, published by the New York University School of Law from 1992 to 2003, and its rubric Constitutional Watch.) Elster's background is in rational choice theory rather than critical theory, but in this fully co-authored book none of the authors is concerned to fly a theoretical flag. Offe has always been open-minded in relation to system theory and, like Habermas, has used it himself in various ways, and he notes in the essay on capitalist welfare states cited in the previous chapter that in the loss of enthusiasm for the welfare state, 'the behavioural consequences . . . are best captured and predicted by rational

choice theory' ('Democracy Against the Welfare State?' in Offe, *Modernity and the State*, p. 172).

16 Elster et al., *Institutional Design in Post-Communist Societies*, p. 63.

17 Ibid., p. 296.

18 See also Andrew Arato and Ferenc Feher (eds), *Gorbachev: The Debate*, Cambridge: Polity Press, 1989; Ferenc Feher and Andrew Arato (eds), *Crisis and Reform in Eastern Europe*, New York: Transaction Books, 1991.

19 Cohen, Jean and Arato, Andrew, *Civil Society and Political Theory*, Cambridge, MA, MIT Press, 1992; Habermas, Jürgen, *Faktizität und Geltung*, Frankfurt: Suhrkamp, 1992. Translated as *Between Facts and Norms*, Cambridge: Polity, 1996. Because no doubt of the greater speed of book production in Germany than in the United States, Habermas was able to comment on Cohen and Arato's book.

20 Cohen et al., *Civil Society and Political Theory*, pp. 68–9.

21 Arato, *Civil Society, Constitution, and Legitimacy*, pp. ix–x. See also chapter 5, p. 168.

22 Ibid., p. x.

23 Ibid., p. xiii.

24 Ibid., p. xiv.

25 Ibid., pp. 271–2.

26 Ibid., p. 4. See also p. 260, n. 23.

27 Ibid., p. 44. On the rejection of the concept of civil society, see p. 68.

28 Claus Offe, *Der Tunnel Am Ende des Lichts. Erkundungen der politischen Transformation im neuen Osten*, Frankfurt: Campus, 1994. Part translated in Offe, *Varieties of Transition*.

29 Offe, *Varieties of Transition*, p. 31. See also the introductory remark in *Institutional Design in Post-Communist Societies*, p. ix, that the authors' 'interest in Central East European transformations has been relatively recent, and they therefore had to operate ... without the benefit of the comprehensive experience, expertise, and linguistic competence that has normally been accumulated throughout a career by "area specialists"'.

30 Offe notes that, because Gypsy minorities are so poorly integrated into political structures, 'the (arguably) most blatant case of massive discrimination in the region is at the same time the most inconspicuous case in tems of political conflict and collective action'. *Varieties of Transition*, p. 59.

31 Offe, *Varieties of Transition*, p. 50.

32 Ibid., p. 72.

33 Ibid., p. 72. On this issue, which of course has disturbing implications for European social policy, see Chapter 5, below; also the work of Philippe van Parijs.

34 Offe, *Varieties of Transition*, p. 73.

35 Prospective membership first of the Council of Europe and then of the EU has of course been a major impetus to minority rights in post-communist Europe;

see, in particular, the work of Geoffrey Pridham and Milada Anna Vahudova. For a recent overview, see Frank Schimmelfennig and Hanno Scholtz, 'Legacies and Leverage: EU Political Conditionality and Democracy Promotion in Historical Perspective', *Europe-Asia Studies*, 62(3), pp. 443–60.

36　Offe, *Varieties of Transition*, pp. 80–1.

37　Ulrich Preuss, 'Constitutional Powermaking for the New Polity', p. 660.

38　'Patterns of Constitutional Evolution and Change in Eastern Europe', in Joachim Jens Hesse and Nevil Johnson (eds), *Constitutional Policy and Change in Europe*, Oxford: Oxford University Press, 1995, pp. 114–19.

39　Jürgen Habermas and Luhmann, Niklas, *Theorie der Gesellschaft oder Sozialtechnologie: Was leistet die Systemforschung?*, Frankfurt: Suhrkamp, 1971, pp. 243f.; Jürgen Habermas, *Legitimationsprobleme im Spatkapitalismus*, Frankfurt: Suhrkamp, 1973, pp. 138–9; *Legitimation Crisis*, London: Heinemann, 1976. See also Rainer Nickel, 'Verfassungspatriotismus', in Brunkhorst, Hauke, Regina Kreide and Cristina Lafont (eds), *Habermas-Handbuch*, Stuttgart and Weimar: Metzler, 2009, pp. 377–9.

40　Jürgen Habermas, *The Theory of Communicative Action*, vol. 2, Cambridge: Polity, 1987, pp. 356–73.

41　'A Kind of Settlement of Damages (Apologetic Tendencies)', *New German Critique*, 44 (Spring–Summer, 1988), p. 39 (translation modified). First published in *Die Zeit*, 11 July 1986. On constitutional patriotism, see Jan-Werner Müller, *Constitutional Patriotism*, Princeton, NJ: Princeton University Press, 2007 and, with specific reference to Europe, Patrizia Nanz, *Europolis. Constitutional Patriotism Beyond the Nation-State*, Manchester University Press, 2006.

42　See his essay on 'Struggles for Recognition in the Democratic Constitutional State' in Amy Gutmann (ed.), *Multiculturalism and the Politics of Recognition*, Princeton, NJ: Princeton University Press, 1993, pp. 107–48.

43　Adam Michnik recalls interestingly that the Polish opposition believed 'that a united Germany was only natural. It may not have been discussed publicly, but that is what we thought. For me it was obvious that under the normal conditions of democratic competition it would not be possible to maintain the division of Germany . . . The East German opposition thought differently.' Michnik, 'Verteidigung der Freiheit. Reflexionen über 1989', *Osteuropa*, 2–3, 2009.

44　Although the legal switchover was instantaneous, the preparation was substantial. The unification treaty (Einigungsvertrag) is over 500 pages long (Offe, *Varieties of Transition*, p. 213, n. 22).

45　Offe, *Varieties of Transition*, p. 151.

46　A book with this title by Peter Christ and Ralf Neubauer, *Kolonie im eigenen Lande. Die Treuhand, Bonn und die Wirtschaftskatastrophe der fünf neuen Länder*, Neuwied: Rowohlt, 1991, describes the sell-off of East German resources by the Federal state agency, the Treuhand-Anstalt, set up for this purpose. Offe estimates the unemployment rate in the former GDR as late as 1995 at 30%–40% (Offe, *Varieties of Transition*, pp. 94, 153). Official rates rose from 15% in 1995 to around 20% and are now back around 15%, with Bremen the only Western state with a similar figure to those in the East.

47 Offe, *Varieties of Transition*, p. 161.

48 Ibid., p. 184.

49 See the Introduction to *Institutional Design in Post-Communist Societies*, p. 25 on the *'tabula rasa of 1989'*: 'As the "leading role of the party" was stricken from the rulebook, nothing was on hand to fill the leading role – or to generate actors to do so. The question of the moment was not "What is to be done?" but "Is there anyone who might be able to do anything – including defining what is to be done . . .?"'

50 Havel, *To the Castle and Back*, p. 60.

51 Ibid., p. 61.

52 Offe, *Varieties of Transition*, p. 210, n. 1. Havel recalls that he 'pushed hard to have all the [secret police] archives sealed at once', while pointing out the practical impossibility: 'You can seal something only if you know where it is and what you're meant to be sealing.' Havel, *To the Castle and Back*, p. 106.

53 Offe, *Varieties of Transition*, p. 84.

54 See Timothy Garton Ash, *The File. A Personal History*, New York: Vintage Books, 1998. Garton Ash, whose book is based on his own file, notes the paradox: 'Probably no dictatorship in modern history has had such an extensive and fanatically thorough secret police as East Germany did. No democracy in modern history has done more to expose the legacy of the preceding dictatorship than the new Germany has' (p. 21).

55 Offe, *Varieties of Transition*, p. 86.

56 Ibid., p. 89.

57 Ibid., p. 138.

58 In Germany, for example, you can be compensated for expropriations carried out by the GDR after 1949, but not for those in the previous years of the Soviet occupation which had included not just reparations but a major land reform programme. In Hungary and Czechoslovakia, the dates were set to include communist expropriations but not those of property owned by Germans in the immediate post-war years. In some countries only land is considered; sometimes only citizens and residents are eligible for compensation. Backward-looking questions of justice intersect with more practical concerns about the likely use of restituted resources.

59 Offe, *Varieties of Transition*, p. 125.

60 Ibid., p. 194.

61 Ibid., p. 196. This argument may work better for West Germany than for countries like France and the UK, where military competition arguably diverted resources from more productive uses.

62 Offe, *Varieties of Transition*, p. 202.

63 Offe, *Modernity and the State*, pp. 237–8.

64 Ibid., pp. 239–40.

65 See, for example, Béla Tomka, 'The Politics of Institutionalized Volatility: Lessons from East Central European Welfare Reforms', Woodrow Wilson International Centre, 2005.

66 See, for example, the striking map in *Le Monde Diplomatique*, February 2010, p. 15. On Russia, see Claire Wallace and Pamela Abbott, 'The Consequences for Health of System Disintegration and Social Disintegration in the Commonwealth of Independent States', forthcoming.

67 Offe, 'Epilogue: Lessons Learnt and Open Questions' in Alfio Cerami and Pieter Vanhuysse (eds), *Post-Communist Welfare Pathways: Theorizing Social Policy Transformations in Central and Eastern Europe,* Basingstoke: Palgrave Macmillan, 2009, pp. 237–247.

68 As he notes, however, these expectations may not be met, especially given the economic crisis which was just breaking.

69 Arato describes himself as having moved *From Neo-Marxism to Democratic Theory,* but I think still within a critical theory framework.

70 Ray, *Rethinking Critical Theory.*

71 William Outhwaite and Larry Ray, *Social Theory and Postcommunism,* Oxford: Blackwell, 2005.

72 This is perhaps an appropriate place to mention someone who combined critical theory with a political career: Zoran Djindjic, a philosopher who studied with Habermas, became Prime Minister of Serbia and was assassinated in 2003.

73 See, for example, William Outhwaite and Larry Ray, *Social Theory and Postcommunism*; John Hall (ed.), *Civil Society – Theory, History, Comparison,* Oxford: Polity.

5

Critical theory at the turn of the twenty-first century

In the late 1980s and early 1990s, as we saw in the previous chapter, Habermas was working on a major collective project arising out of his Tanner lectures of 1986 on 'Law and Morality' and published in 1992 as *Faktizität und Geltung*.[1] The book is essentially a development of implications of Habermas's theories of communicative action and discourse ethics. To put it very briefly, post-conventional morality relies on rational consensus; we need law to give teeth to generally shared moral norms and this in turn can only be legitimated under modern conditions by political democracy. Thus what seems, and indeed is, a rather dry and formal line of argument (and one which is notably less critical of the law than *Theory of Communicative Action*) also directly confronts issues of contemporary democratic politics and the public sphere.

As he put it in the Tanner Lectures,

The rational quality of political legislation does not only depend on how elected majorities and protected minorities work within parliaments. It also depends on the level of participation and school education, the degree of information and the precision with which controversial issues are articulated – in short, on the discursive character of non-institutionalized opinion formation in the political public sphere.[2] (p. 570)

A legal system is autonomous only to the extent that the procedures institutionalized for legislation and legal decision guarantee a non-partisan formation of opinion and will and thereby give moral procedural rationality access, as it were, to law and politics. No autonomous law without the realization of democracy. (p. 599)[3]

It is impossible to apply discourse ethics or a simple concept of discourse directly to democratic politics. Following an earlier essay 'On the pragmatic, ethical and moral use of practical reason',[4] Habermas distinguishes in *Between Facts and Norms* between pragmatic discourses, relating individual or collective choices to given preferences, ethical-political discourses concerned with the implementation of broader collective ideals and moral discourses cast in universal terms. 'Ethically relevant' issues include environmental and animal protection, urban planning, immigration policy, the protection of minorities and 'generally issues of political culture'; morally relevant issues would be, for example, abortion law, statutes of limitations of criminal responsibility, or matters of social policy affecting 'the distribution of social wealth and of life or survival chances in general'.[5]

In many cases, however, there will be a pragmatic choice to be made between alternatives, opening the way to negotiation and compromise and leading hopefully to an accommodation (*Vereinbarung*) which balances out conflicting interests. (The *fairness* of such negotiations and compromises is however a *moral* question.) The complex relations between these various levels of discourse include 'at least' a 'process model of rational political will-formation' in which pragmatic discourses lead via regulated negotiations and/or ethical-political discourses to moral discourses and finally legal discourses; the latter are concerned essentially with the compatibility of new proposals with established laws and rights.[6] This reconstruction allows for familiar institutions such as parliamentary assemblies and majority voting.[7] Parliaments are however seen, not as simply expressing or discovering a hypothetical general interest but as structurally linked with 'the informal formation of opinion in culturally mobilized publics'.[8]

Habermas therefore focuses in chapter 8 on civil society and the public sphere, (*Öffentlichkeit*), which is not a fixed institution or organization but is best understood as 'a network for the communication of contents and the expression of attitudes, *i.e. of opinions,* in which the flows of communication are filtered and synthesized in such a way that they condense into *public* opinions clustered according to topics'.[9]

Civil society and the movements arising from it are a complement rather than an alternative to formally constituted politics; they are 'self-limiting'.[10] Conversely, the formal political system is not just one of several social subsystems, since it is enmeshed both with other legally regulated (e.g. administrative) systems and with the public sphere.

In this context Habermas offers a brief reformulation of his well-known model of legitimation crisis.[11] In the original version of the model, as we saw in Chapter 2, economic crisis tendencies give rise to rationality crises in state outputs and legitimation crises threatening the withdrawal of popular support. In the new version, Habermas characterizes rationality and legitimation crises in rather more precise terms. The political system's regulatory efficiency is threatened when its instructions are not obeyed, or when they lead to disorganization, or when they overstretch the capacity of the legal system and undermine the normative foundations of the political system itself. The combination of these three problems can lead to what Habermas calls a 'regulatory trilemma'. In its other aspect, the political system can fail to preserve social integration if its decisions, however effective, emerge from the independent operation of administrative systems and commercial corporations rather than from a functioning public sphere.

> The independent establishment of illegitimate power and the weakness of civil society and the political public sphere can come to a head in a 'legitimatory dilemma' which can in certain circumstances combine with a steering trilemma into vicious circle. Then the political system is sucked into mutually reinforcing legitimacy and steering deficits.[12]

These problems are not inevitable results of an overstretched welfare state but the lack of a 'social basis for the realization of the system of rights [which] is made up of neither the forces of a spontaneously operating market society, nor the measures of an intentionally operating welfare state, but rather the communication flows and mediatized influences which emerge from civil society, via democratic processes, into communicative power'.[13] Behind the varying forms of constitutions lies a single form of practice: the self-determination of free and equal citizens. Starting from their own current activities, participants can achieve an understanding of this general form of democratic practice.[14]

With this book Habermas completed his theoretical 'system'. Among the many responses to *Faktizität und Geltung*, one of the most useful was a review symposium in the *Deutsche Zeitschrift für Philosophie*.[15] The most fundamental issue, raised there by the British philosopher Peter Dews, concerns the place of law itself in relation to questions of mutual respect, recognition and solidarity. Habermas sees the law in a welfare state as steering a difficult path between a negatively discriminatory approach, which ignores the way factual inequalities limit the freedom of individuals, and a paternalism which overlooks the limits to freedom resulting from state action undertaken to compensate for these same inequalities.[16] What is lacking here as elsewhere,

Dews notes, is a more critical assessment of law itself, and in particular of the ways in which it isolates individuals and destroys rather than underpins social integration in the lifeworld.[17] We need to ask also what forms of social solidarity can be developed, in an increasingly globalized yet fragmented world in which people are both brought together and held apart by the operations of the mass media.[18]

The relationship with law remains an extremely uncomfortable one. Critical legal studies and deconstructionist legal theory converge in their scorn for Habermas's assimilation of more orthodox theories of law. And it is odd, to say the least, that someone whose main critical theme for over a decade had been the denunciation of the hollowing-out and colonization of the lifeworld by market and administrative systems should now be so much more sanguine about what he and others had analysed as the pathologies of juridification.

Sociologists in particular have tended to take a rather hostile view of law, and have rarely drawn on it as a resource in their theorizing as they have on other bodies of theoretical literature.[19] There was something of a shift in the 1980s, as revolutionary projects of social reconstruction came to seem less viable, and what Marx called the 'narrow horizon of bourgeois right' came to seem rather more attractive than the continuing arbitrariness of post-Stalinist rule.[20] Habermas, it should be stressed, never joined in the repudiation of law, either theoretically or practically, but he was perhaps partly trying to counter its residues among those likely to appreciate the underlying radical-democratic thrust of the book.

There was in fact a much more positive response to this new direction in Habermas's thought in democratic theory, and in particular what has come to be called deliberative, discursive or dialogical democracy. The US philosopher James Bohman, who had spent a year working with Habermas and his research group in Frankfurt, wrote:

> Why do social critics from Dewey and Mill to Horkheimer and Habermas so closely tie the reform of democratic institutions to improvements in deliberation? The simple answer is that such discussions of deliberation concern the way in which the practical reasoning of agents enters into political decision making. The call for more deliberation is . . . a demand for a more rational political order in which decision making at least involves the public use of reason. According to this position, the legitimacy of decisions must be determined by the critical judgement of free and equal citizens.[21]

Bohman had begun his career as one of a number of scholars on both sides of the Atlantic who had engaged with Habermas's thought. Thomas McCarthy, who had written the definitive guide to Habermas's earlier work,[22] set up a book series on Contemporary German Social Thought which published both translations of Habermas, Wellmer, Offe and other German critical theorists and much of the English-language work. Two books from the mid-1980s should be mentioned in particular: Axel Honneth's *Critique of Power* and Seyla Benhabib's *Critique, Norm and Utopia*.[23] At a time when Habermas had just published his critique of Foucault in *The Philosophical Discourse of Modernity*, Honneth argued that both could be read as offering alternative but complementary responses to the lack of an adequate social theory in first-generation critical theory. Benhabib similarly traces the theme of emancipatory critique from Kant and Hegel through to Habermas and outlines what is gained but also lost in the shift to more formal and reconstructive arguments. These, she argues, '. . . obscure some of the essential insights that the paradigm shift to communicative reason and action bring with them, namely, the emphasis on human *plurality*; the *narrative* and *interpretive* structure of action; the utopian hopes of a communicative access to need interpretations, and the vision of a community of *justice* that fosters a community of *solidarity*.'[24] Benhabib also defended a model of deliberative democracy in her contribution to a volume of essays, based on a conference held in 1993: *Democracy and Difference*.[25] As she notes, this contrasts with a more agonistic model of democracy represented in this volume by Chantal Mouffe and others. Deliberative democracy, she stresses, '. . . is not a theory in search of a practice; rather it is a theory that claims to elucidate some aspects of the logic of existing democratic practices better than others'.[26]

In an early essay, 'Moral Consciousness and Class Domination', originally presented at the legendary Dubrovnik Centre[27] in 1981, Honneth sets the substantive focus for subsequent work. He is not yet using the term recognition, but his focus on injustice contains the basic theme of his next major book. Habermas, he suggests, has escaped the pessimistic trap of earlier critical theory by his notion developed in his 'reconstruction' of historical materialism, of a process of moral evolution complementary to the evolution of the productive forces. But Habermas's model, he suggests, 'is constructed in such a way that it must systematically ignore all forms of existing social critique not recognized by the political-hegemonic public sphere'.[28] Honneth, in other words, is concerned with 'all those potentialities for moral action which have not reached the level of elaborated value judgements, but which are nonetheless persistently embodied in culturally coded acts of collective protest, or even in mere silent "moral disapproval"'.[29] Honneth writes in the Introduction to *The Struggle for Recognition* (p. 1) that he had reached the conclusion in *Critique of Power* that

any attempt to integrate the social-theoretical insights of Foucault's historical work within the theory of communicative action has to rely on a concept of morally motivated struggle. And there is no better source of inspiration for developing such a concept than Hegel's early, 'Jena' writings, with their notion of a comprehensive 'struggle for recognition'.[30]

The concept of recognition has become massively influential in critical social theory and the focus of numerous books. To put it very briefly, Honneth ranges over developmental psychology and object relations theory, Mead, Marx, Sorel and Sartre (among others), distinguishing three variants or domains in which recognition is in play: love, rights and self-esteem grounded in solidarity. As he summarized the theory in his inaugural lecture at Berlin, delivered shortly after the book was published,

> I distinguished three forms of social recognition which can be regarded as the communicative presuppositions of a successful formation of identity: emotional concern in an intimate social relationship such as love or friendship, rights-based recognition as a morally accountable member of society and, finally, the social esteem of individual accomplishments and abilities.[31]

Recognition is contrasted with disrespect, seen as the motor and idiom of social conflicts. As the *Internationale* goes, 'nous ne sommes rien, soyons tout', or at least let us be acknowledged for what we are.

It cannot I think be denied that this concept captures a good deal of the notions of natural justice which motivate many social movements of exploited or suppressed people. Strikes, notoriously, often begin with an apparently trivial violation of some perceived right rather than the broader context of ongoing exploitation. Critics of the concept have however argued, with more or less emphasis, that there is something flimsy about it. If Habermas is thought, in a typical caricature of his theory of communication, to reduce moral and political conflict to a seminar discussion, perhaps Honneth is reducing it to the senior common room or *salle des professeurs*, with its petty slights and interminable resentments. Nancy Fraser, in particular, has argued for the importance of issues of redistribution, in a friendly critique of Honneth's emphasis on recognition.[32]

The range of current social conflicts with which Honneth engages in his own work and in that which he encourages at Frankfurt[33] is enough to refute charges that the concept of recognition is in some way narcissistic and insubstantial, but it may be partly with these criticisms in mind that he tackled, in his Tanner Lectures at Berkeley in 2005, the grand Marxist theme of reification.[34] Critical theory, for Honneth, is alive and well as resuscitated by Habermas; it needs to be tweaked back into a direction which one could call post-Marxist, if the term had not been attached to rather different intellectual and political projects, and which also recalls Marx's early concern with a wide variety of social conflicts.[35] Two aspects of Honneth's work should be mentioned here: his bold rehabilitation of a strong notion of social pathology and his emphasis on 'diagnoses of the times'.

The term social pathology which has tended to be confined to political and journalistic phrases about our 'sick' or 'broken' societies. For Honneth, the 'diagnosis of the times', a term introduced into Britain by Karl Mannheim, becomes specifically a diagnosis of social pathology.[36] Thus 'In order to be able to speak of a social pathology that is accessible to the medical model of diagnosis, we require a conception of normality related to social life as a whole'[37] (p. 34). In what he calls 'a weak, formal, anthropology',[38] Honneth gestures towards 'an ethical conception of social normality tailored to conditions that enable human self-realization'.[39]

This important initiative makes explicit something which had been latent in much of critical theory. The theme of suffering of misdevelopment and 'damaged life'[40] pervades the work of the first generation of critical theorists, and Habermas's reworking in *Theory of Communicative Action* of Marxist, Weberian and indeed Parsonian theory contains a substantial discussion of social pathologies.[41] Honneth has however pushed this theme further. In another essay, 'A Social Pathology of Reason. On the intellectual heritage of critical theory', Honneth suggests that, although we are now a similar distance from the beginnings of critical theory as its protagonists were from the last representatives of classical idealism,[42] critical theory is still linked by its model of '. . . socially effective reason: The historical past is to be understood as a developmental process whose pathological malformation by capitalism can be overcome only by a process of enlightenment carried out by those affected'.[43]

In the conclusion to *Between Facts and Norms*, Habermas added a new theme, that the democratization of state power must go beyond the limits of the nation-state and its sovereignty in the context of the development of a 'world public sphere'.[44] For him, the turn announced here towards cosmopolitan democracy, something urged on him for a long time by David Held and others but pushed into the background by his theorization of the territorially based Rechtsstaat, has essentially meant a focus on the emergent political and social structures of contemporary Europe. This is also a major theme in the work of a number of contemporary critical theorists, notably Offe, Benhabib, Eder, Dubiel and Hauke Brunkhorst, as discussed below.

In 1996 Habermas published a volume of essays written since *Faktizität und Geltung*. *The Inclusion of the Other* can in part be seen as a belated acknowledgement of aspects of the postmodern critique and Honneth's more sympathetic response to it. Respect for difference has been always one of Habermas's core values, though necessarily in some tension with his rationalistic and universalistic programme. (For Habermas, it is actually *because of* particularistic irrationalism, as exemplified most horrifically by Nazism, that we require universalistic forms of reasoning.) *The Inclusion of the Other*[45] does not go as far in the direction of a greater openness to difference as the title perhaps suggests. It does however contain a discussion of group rights in multicultural societies. This essay is substantially shaped by Honneth's model, as indicated by its title ('Struggle for Recognition in the Democratic State') and by Charles Taylor's analysis of multiculturalism and recognition. Although this essay starts from Taylor's defence of language policy in Quebec, it leads on to a discussion of immigration in Western Europe and prefigures some of Habermas's later thinking on religiously defined communities. For Habermas, Taylor's defence of collective rights, in this case of the French-speaking majority in Quebec to support the use of the French language by legal restrictions on the use of English, is too 'communitarian' (Preface). A more individualistic conception of rights should be understood, Habermas argues, to include a 'politics of recognition which also protects the integrity of the individual in the life-contexts which form his or her identity'.[46] But 'the protection of identity-forming ways of life and traditions is intended ultimately to serve the recognition of their members; it in no way means an administrative protection of species diversity. The ecological approach to species conservation cannot be extended to cultures'[47] (tr.p. 222). Similarly, in the case of immigration, a state can require immigrants to acquiesce in the constitutional principles which make up the *political* culture of the state in which they settle, but not to abandon their culture of origin.[48] If this, to borrow for a moment the language of the political right, means the 'dilution' of the dominant culture, so be it.

The Inclusion of the Other also presents the beginnings of Habermas's analysis of what he came to call the post-national constellation.[49] As he writes in the preface, he is concerned with the implications of 'republican principles . . . for pluralist societies in which multicultural conflicts become sharper, for national states which combine into supranational entities and for the citizens of a world society who have been unwittingly and unwillingly united into a community of risk'. He describes the national state in functional terms as taking up the task of social integration after the dissolution of pre-modern forms of integration. More precisely, rather than distinguishing between ethnic and civic principles, as theorists of nationalism tend to do, Habermas stresses their combination. 'Whereas the willed nation of citizens is the source of democratic legitimation, the inborn nation of fellow people provides for social integration.' The national state embodies 'the tension between the universalism of an egalitarian legal community and the particularism of a historical community of fate'[50] (Habermas, 1996: 139).

Nationalism is essentially the effacement of the former by the latter, providing a kind of false concreteness to the question why the political community has the boundaries it does. (For nationalists, as it were, God or nature coloured in the political map of the world.) In a modern multicultural society, the emphasis has to shift in the other direction, from the imagined national community to 'the real nation of citizens' (144).[51] The question is whether this more civic conception of self-determination can be sustained in these more abstract terms, such as an orientation to a constitution and the associated political culture. Analyses of 'post-democracy' suggest that this may be difficult.[52] Secondly, if the national state is increasingly being undermined by globalization and superseded, as in Europe, by transnational political formations, the question becomes whether democracy can be sustained at a transnational level. Although the two issues are distinct, it is, not surprisingly, the same thinkers who play up the national at the expense of the civic who are the loudest critics of European political integration. No transnational democracy without a demos; no European democracy without a European 'people'. Against this 'substantialistic' (p. 181) conception of popular sovereignty, Habermas argues that Europeans *are* linked by a historical memory, notably that of two world wars, demonstrating the need to transcend nationalistic forms of exclusion.[53] The integration and democratization of European national states shows the importance of 'the communication circuits of a political public sphere, developed on the basis of civic/bourgeois forms of association and via the medium of the mass press'[54] (pp. 183–4). Similarly, European integration depends 'not on the substrate of some 'European people' but on the communicative web of a Europe-wide political public sphere'[55] (184). Hence, he argues, Europe needs a constitution, not so much to cement an existing political community as to set the foundations for its development.

In the title essay of *The Postnational Constellation*, which makes up a good third of the book, Habermas offers an extremely interesting political sociology of attitudes to European integration, which he sees as deriving from prior economic and political attitudes. The approaches to integration which he distinguishes are the familiar ones: 'Eurosceptics', who resist or regret the introduction of the common currency, 'market Europeans', who accept the euro but reject further political integration, 'Eurofederalists' and, finally, cosmopolitans who see a federal Europe as the starting point for a world cosmopolitan order emerging, as the EU did, from international treaties but establishing a 'world domestic policy' (Weltinnenpolitik). Intersecting with and underpinning these positions are, he suggests, four basic issues: the future of employment, the relation between market efficiency and social justice, the capacity of the EU to substitute for the national state in areas such as social policy and, relatedly, the possibility of transnational identity and post-national democracy.

On the first of these, it can be plausibly argued that the reconfiguration of employment in ways which, for example, share out available and necessary work more equitably between classes and generations is only practicable, if at all, at a supranational level. The second issue tends to generate an opposition between market liberals, who favour a single market and perhaps a common currency, but without further political integration, and social democrats pursuing greater political control at national or supranational levels.[56] Social democrats have often been suspicious of the European integration project, but are increasingly reconciled to it. European social policy, however, so far exists largely in the indirect forms of agricultural and regional policy; a more substantial European social policy depends, as Habermas argues, citing Wolfgang Streeck, on 'whether Europe as a political system can summon the necessary political resources to impose redistributive duties on powerful participants in the market'. This, Habermas concludes, requires democratization of the EU: 'positively redistribution policies must be borne (getragen) by a Europe-wide democratic will-formation, and this cannot happen without a basis of solidarity' (p. 99).[57]

This sounds a bit like a chicken-and-egg problem, and Habermas concedes that 'The next steps toward a European Federation involve extraordinary risks . . . (p. 99)'.[58] On the other hand, he points out, the construction of *national* consciousness in Europe also took place in a number of different ways, involving a variety of political and cultural contingencies, notably the press. '. . . precisely the artificial conditions in which national consciousness arose argue against the defeatist assumption that a form of civic solidarity among strangers can only be generated within the confines of the nation. If this form of collective identity was due to a highly abstractive leap from the local and dynastic to national and then to democratic consciousness, why shouldn't this learning process be able to continue?[59] (p. 102). And finally, suggests Habermas, turning to theories of cosmopolitan democracy, political legitimacy increasingly derives not from the expressed will of a precisely delimited political community but from processes of debate and discussion at a variety of levels (p. 111).[60]

Habermas's discussion of multiculturalism in *The Inclusion of the Other* re-emerges in some of his more recent writing on religion and in particular a situation in which 'the revival of religious energies, to which Europe alone seems to be immune, is associated with a fundamental critique of the post-metaphysical and nonreligious self-understanding of Western modernity'. He had previously taken a fairly conventional line that the major world religions had played a crucially important part in the development of critical social theory, broadly conceived, but that, as Max Horkheimer wrote in 1935, 'good will, solidarity with misery and the striving for a better world have cast off their religious mantle'.[61] Habermas's own position is of course post-metaphysical, in the sense that he denies any special role to philosophical insight into the nature of the world or humanity.[62] Neither religion nor philosophy can provide substantive foundations of moral reasoning: his 'discourse theory of morality', as he now prefers to call his discourse ethics, is intended as a reconstruction of the moral point of view as it has developed in human history. And like Hegel, he suggests at this time, we need to adopt a 'methodological atheism', though not any longer the 'militant *laicism*' of the young Hegelians.[63] As for his personal views, in a recent volume of interviews Habermas insists that he has grown 'old, but not pious',[64] and Axel Honneth suggests in the same volume that this direction in Habermas's thinking is motivated by a 'sociological realism' about the continued social importance of religion rather than any shift in his personal convictions.[65]

As Maeve Cooke noted however, Habermas had tended to oscillate between two different positions on religion. In the first, as he writes in *Texte und Kontexte* (p. 131), '. . . the ethics which have emerged out of the contexts of various world religions converge (*übereinkommen*) in the principles of a universalistic morality'. On the other, he sometimes defends a stronger thesis that religious traditions continue to provide important cognitive resources. This second theme has certainly come to the fore in Habermas's more recent work. His analysis has also been augmented by two further elements, one theoretical and the other practical-political. The theoretical issue is one raised by Rawls, with whose work Habermas increasingly engaged in the years before Rawls' death. Rawls was preoccupied with the question of the translation of religiously based arguments into political discussion.[66] The second issue is the rise of religious fundamentalism, on which Habermas had already written in relation to the United States and Germany in *The new Obscurity* but which was marked on a world scale by the terrorist attack of September 2001, on which he commented in a talk delivered the following month.

Habermas has tried to frame these issues in the, as he says, 'contentious'[67] concept of 'postsecular society' and the attempt to mediate 'between naturalism and religion' – the title of his collected essays on the subject.[68] The latter contrast crops up already in the 2001 speech, in which Habermas uses them to characterize the debate between science and organized religion over genetic engineering. This simple contrast, and the notion of a zero-sum game between science, or modernity as a whole, and religion, 'is inconsistent with a post-secular society which adapts to the fact that religious communities continue to exist in a context of ongoing secularization' (p. 104). The issue is complicated by the way in which the mutual accommodation of the secular and the religious is understood to take place in post-secular society. On the one hand, the religious have to accept that theirs is one belief system among others in 'a constitutional state grounded in a profane morality'. This means that they

> are required to split up their identities, as it were, into their public and private elements. They are the ones who have to translate their religious beliefs into a secular language before their arguments have any chance of gaining majority support . . . But only if the secular side, too, remains sensitive to the force of articulation inherent in religious languages will the search for reasons that aim at universal acceptability not lead to an unfair exclusion of religions from the public sphere, nor sever secular society from important resources of meaning'. (p. 109)

Habermas goes on to point out that the line between religious and secular reasons is imprecise, and that both sides should cooperate in determining it. It is difficult to disagree with this proposal. On the other hand, one can question whether in practice religious reasons are in fact excluded from political discussion in the ways Rawls and Habermas assumed. If I say that I oppose the provision of contraception because I am a Catholic, this may not be an *argument* for my choice, but it would be widely accepted as a prima facie valid reason for it. (You might try to talk me out of my beliefs, or to persuade me to interpret them more flexibly, but the rational connection between the belief and the political choice is at least an intelligible one.) Secondly, the extent to which modern polities and public spheres are expected to engage with specifically *religious* minorities is equally contentious, and determined in very different ways in modern states, even within Europe. France, for example, is a secular state; England has a state church headed by the monarch and a substantial presence of religious organizations and practices in the education system; in Germany the Protestant and Catholic churches and the Jewish religious communities are substantially funded via the public tax system.

Habermas approaches these issues in something like the terms of his earlier discussion of multiculturalism.[69] He also however wants to go beyond practical accommodation to religious and ethnic diversity in modern western societies to address 'the cognitive presuppositions that must be fulfilled if civic solidarity is to function effectively . . .'[70] (p. 6). Contemporary Europe's relatively secular configuration may be conducive to this sort of reflection; conversely, it might make it particularly offensive to religious fundamentalists.[71]

Europe is also the main theme in Habermas's most recent collection of political writings, *Ach, Europa* (2008) translated as *Europe: The Faltering Project* (2009). The title indicates a certain pessimism, as does that of one of the essays: 'The Politics of Europe in a Dead End'. In another, on 'The Role of Intellectuals and the Cause of Europe', he ask why the future of Europe, a theme which 'most concerns me today', is seen by others as 'abstract and boring'. We need to be concerned, he suggests, because if the question of the ultimate aim or *finalité* of the European Union is not decided soon, its future 'will be decided along the lines of neoliberal orthodoxy'.[72] Thus the process of European integration is not just important for Europe, but a contribution to the 're-regulation of the world society' pursued by some global social movements. National political parties 'have to reach out toward a European arena of action. And this arena, in turn, has to be programmatically opened up with the dual objective of creating a social Europe that can throw its weight onto the cosmopolitan scale'.[73]

Why should this matter? First of all, as we have seen, Habermas has long been committed to the cause of European integration. There is a specifically German background to this choice which he spells out in a speech made near Bonn, from where '. . . the Federal Republic achieved the goal of its sovereignty only in close connection with the political unification of Europe' (p. 90).[74] There is also a further dimension which is the main theme of this speech: the question of immigrants and foreign-born residents in Europe. He points out the interdependence of two issues: the transnational extension of civic solidarity *across* Europe and its extension to residents of foreign origin *within* individual member states.

> The more, for example in the Federal Republic, living with citizens of Turkish origin becomes a matter of course, the better we can also empathize with the situation of other European citizens – the different world of a wine-grower in Portugal or a plumber in Poland. The internal opening of closed-off cultures also opens them up to one another.[75]

If this is enough, as I believe it is, to demonstrate the importance of European integration for the internal integration and cohesion of individual states, there remain a set of more contingent and controversial questions about how to pursue the aim. This is not the place to discuss these issues in detail (I do this in the next chapter and also in 'Legality and Legitimacy'),[76] but it is worth bringing out the way in which they fit in with other dimensions of Habermas's thought. First, it is not surprising to find him continuing to insist on the need for the Union to formulate, and for the people of Europe to participate in, explicit constitutional choices. Having argued in vain that German reunification should take place in a more systematic constitutional framework, rather than a mere enlargement of the Federal Republic to include the territory of the GDR, Habermas was concerned that the EU should not adopt a similar fudge. There were of course strong tactical arguments against risking a constitutional convention,[77] and the result of the following five years looks like the worst of both worlds.

Following the second failure, in 2008, to smuggle through the constitutional project, it is tempting to agree with Habermas that what is needed is a Europe-wide referendum which might serve as a prelude to a more legitimate way of legislating within the EU on major issues. Andrew Arato however argues convincingly that this would be a mistake. As he says, it is odd that Habermas, as a theorist of deliberative democracy, should favour this form of decision-making, especially in relation to complex constitutional issues, in which 'whole documents can be rejected through a resistance to a few symbolic points coming from very different directions'.[78]

The second major issue is whether the Union should explicitly adopt a strategy of multi-level integration, in which some members, probably including the original six and as many others as wanted, would forge ahead in a federal direction while leaving one or more outer circles of less committed states. As Arato points out, any move towards a 'two-speed' Europe, such as the one comprising an inner circle of France, Germany, Italy and Spain which Habermas once envisaged, would reinforce the suspicion of Franco–German domination of the Union.[79] I would be anxious, like Arato (see above) about anything which reinforced and institutionalized divisions within Europe on these lines and thereby strengthened the position of the 'Eurosceptic' or, more accurately, xenophobic right and extreme right in the United Kingdom and elsewhere.

Cosmopolitan democratic theory, responding to the theories of globalization which emerged at the end of the 1980s, has been one of the most important recent foci of critical theory, at least in relation to Europe. David Held, who began his career with one of the key texts presenting critical theory to an English-language public, has been working since the beginning of the 1990s in this area, beginning with a book in 1995 and another co-edited with Daniele Archibugi.[80] In Germany, Hauke Brunkhorst also published a book in the same year on globalization and democracy and has since pursued the theme in relation to solidarity and with specific reference to the EU, as discussed in the next chapter.[81]

Beck, too, came to address the EU via earlier studies on globalization and cosmopolitanism. Like Bourdieu, Bauman, Giddens and Martin Albrow, who was one of the first sociologists to discuss globalization, Beck insisted that it should not be seen primarily as an economic process. Giddens, who had taken from Goffman and from ethnomethodology a stress on the 'knowledgeability' of human beings, incorporates this into his analysis of reflexive modernity and globalization. Beck, by contrast, uses the same term reflexivity to denote the production of unintended consequences, as in Ivan Illich's 'iatrogenic disease' (Illich, 1975). They converge, however, with one another (and with Bauman), on the juggernaut or, as Giddens put it, 'runaway world' aspect of globalization. Their political responses diverge, with Giddens hoping for the revitalization of dialogical democracy and what became the post-social-democratic politics of the 'Third Way', to Beck's less party-political 'reinvention of politics' through the revitalization of some of the more positive 'sub-political' spheres.

If, as Martin Hartmann suggests, there was a systematic reason why critical theorists like Habermas and Offe, gradually increasing their distance from neo-Marxism, took in the 1980s a closer interest in democratic theory and the political sphere, the cosmopolitan turn in the 1990s was clearly a response to globalization. As Beck put it, in characteristically flowery (or in this case leafy) language,

> The falling of leaves in autumn can't be prevented by looking the other way, and certainly not by insisting that you hate winter . . . even the most radical anti-cosmopolitan can re-erect the old boundaries only in theory, not in reality.[82]

It is worth noting that, whereas Held presents his cosmopolitan 'agenda' in normative terms, Beck, here as elsewhere in his work, avoids explicit normative commitments. As Jeff Alexander and Philip Smith have commented, there is something paradoxical about this approach, even to environmental risks.[83] And as Gerard Delanty writes, 'Cosmopolitanism as a theoretical approach suggests a critical attitude as opposed to an exclusively interpretative or descriptive approach to the social world.'[84] *The Cosmopolitan Vision* ends with a chapter on 'Cosmopolitan Europe: Reality and Utopia', pointing forward to Beck's book with Edgar Grande which appeared in the same year. Since this is substantially concerned with the EU I shall postpone discussion of it to the next chapter.

Cosmopolitan democratic critical theory has been particularly concerned with issues of migration. Preuss addressed the issue in 1985 in the context of European citizenship[85] and Offe in the context of group rights in an article of 1998.[86] Benhabib, too, came into this field via issues of multiculturalism and gender and has concentrated on it in her work over the past decade, beginning with her Horkheimer lectures of 1997 which were included in a revised form in *The Claims of Culture*.[87] Here she formulated the basic principles which have guided her work, that structures evolved in response to cultural pluralism and claims for minority rights are 'quite compatible with a universalist deliberative democracy model' under three conditions: 'egalitarian reciprocity, voluntary self-ascription and freedom of exit and association'. The first of these is self-explanatory; the other two specify that individuals should be free to choose whether and how to ascribe *themselves* to religious, ethnic or linguistic communities. 'Whether cultural groups can survive as distinct entities under these conditions is an open question, but I believe these conditions are necessary if legal pluralism in liberal-democratic states is to achieve the goals of cultural diversity as well as democratic equality, without compromising the rights of women and children of minority cultures.'[88]

Armed with these principles, Benhabib lucidly analyses some of the dilemmas of contemporary Europe and other regions of the world. In Chapter 6 of *The Claims of Culture*, she addresses issues of citizenship in Europe and, in particular, the different rights enjoyed by residents from other EU states and those from outside. She steers, as she says, 'a middle course between the radical universalism of open-borders politics on the one hand and sociologically antiquated conceptions of thick republican citizenship on the other'.[89] Democracies have to retain the right to define themselves and hence the bases under which they grant full political rights to others. In *The Rights of Others*, based on lecture series at Amsterdam and Cambridge, she pursues these themes. 'I want to argue that transnational migrations, and the constitutional as well as policy issues suggested by the movement of peoples across state borders, are central to interstate relations and therefore to a normative theory of global justice.'[90] Territorial rule remains the reference point for democratic theory, but the *demos* may need to be extended internally, notably to foreign residents,[91] and externally, to those affected by state policies.

> Popular sovereignty, which means that those who are subject to the law are also its authors, is not identical with territorial sovereignty. While the *demos*, as the popular sovereign, must assert control over a specific territorial domain, it can also engage in reflexive acts of self-constitution, whereby the boundaries of the *demos* can be readjusted. The politics of membership in the age of the disaggregation of citizenship rights is about negotiating the complexities of full membership rights, democratic voice, and territorial residence.[92]

In chapter 4 of the book, Benhabib explains in detail what disaggregation of citizenship amounts to in the EU, against the background of what she presents as a 'non-foundationalist human rights discourse'. By this she means an approach which Habermas, and probably Benhabib as well, would call a reconstruction:

> I will assume that rights claims are in general of the following sort: 'I can justify to you with good grounds that you and I should respect each

others' claims to act in certain ways and not in others, and to enjoy certain resources and services.'

Benhabib reformulates Kant's basic principle of right or justice, that which 'enables the freedom of each individual's will to coexist with the freedom of everyone else in accordance with a universal law'[93] in communicative terms as a right to justification.

> . . . to respect your capacity for communicative freedom – to accept or reject on the basis of reasons – means to respect your capacity for personal autonomy. Human rights, or basic rights, then, are the norms that would undergird and enable the exercise of your personal autonomy.[94]

This leads to a right in principle to membership of a political community, which cannot reasonably be refused to residents. Countries differ in the conditions they impose for naturalization; 'What would be objectionable from a moral point of view is the absence of *any* procedure or possibility for foreigners and resident aliens to become citizens at all . . .'[95] She concludes a very detailed survey of the situation with the observation that

> . . . there is a dynamic toward narrowing the divide separating human rights from citizens' rights, or basic rights from political rights . . . Precisely because first entry sets in motion a trajectory toward full integration, it is likely that future policy in the EU will be to restrict access to borders more severely rather than dismantling the rights of resident foreigners.[96]

Rather than bemoaning the disaggregation of citizenship, Benhabib argues that it can be handled in what she calls 'democratic iterations', defined as 'complex processes of public argument, deliberation, and exchange through which universalist rights claims are contested an contextualized, invoked and revoked, posited and positioned, throughout legal and political institutions, as well as in the associations of civil society'.[97] She illustrates this through a discussion of three controversies, two concerning headscarves in France and Germany and one, also in Germany, the right granted to long-term residents of Hamburg and Schleswig-Holstein to vote in local elections. In France, despite an initially missed opportunity to open up a debate on the issue, rather than simply allowing schools to ban pupils from wearing scarves, the decision of the Conseil d'Etat at the end of 1989 and the more severe legislation in 2004 and subsequently has opened up a continuing process of iterative democratic contestation. In such contestations, she suggests,

. . . women, who are learning to talk back to the state, will also engage and contest the very meaning of the Islamic traditions which they are now fighting to uphold. Eventually, these public battles will initiate private gender struggles about the status of women's rights within the Muslim tradition.[98]

In Germany, the case concerned a school-*teacher*, whose status as a state official seems to have formed the basis of the decision in 2003 by the Federal Constitutional Court to pass the buck back to the government of Baden-Württemberg. In the 1990 voting case too, the constitutional Court took a conservative line on the nationality issue but was trumped ten years later by the EU, whose citizens can now vote as residents of other member states in European and local elections (including, in the United Kingdom, elections to the Scottish Parliament and Welsh Assembly).

Laws like these can, and are changed, she concludes, in what one might see as a concretization of Habermas's claims for the mutual implication of law and democracy. 'But, while the scope of the authority of the laws can be reflexively altered, it is inconceivable that democratic legitimacy can be sustained without some clear demarcation of those in the name of whom the laws have been enacted from those upon whom the laws are not binding.' She concludes:

> The intuition that there may be a crucial link between territorial size and form of government is old in the history of western political thought, and it is one that I accept. Unlike communitarians and liberal nationalists, however, who view this link primarily as being based upon a cultural bond of identity, I am concerned with the logic of democratic representation, which requires closure for the sake of maintaining democratic legitimacy. Certainly, identification and solidarity are not unimportant, but they need to be leavened through democratic attachments and constitutional norms.[99]

A volume co-edited by Benhabib and based on a conference at Yale in 2003 brings together a number of critical theorists addressing issues of cosmopolitan democracy. Nancy Fraser asks how public sphere theory can be 'transnationalized' so as to 'serve as a critical theory in a post-Westphalian world'. The public sphere, she argues must satisfy the dual requirements of normative legitimacy and political efficacy, and this requires 'new transnational public powers, which can be made accountable to new democratic transnational circuits of public opinion'.[100] Craig Calhoun addresses the issue of 'Social solidarity as a problem for cosmopolitan democracy', restating his brilliant critique of 'the class consciousness of frequent travelers'. In an important counter to some incautious cosmopolitan claims, though not to Benhabib's more nuanced account, he stresses that in 'treating ethnicity as *essentially* (rather than partially) a choice of identifications . . . [one should not] . . . neglect the omnipresence of ascription and discrimination as determinations of individual identities'.[101] More fundamentally, he concludes,

> Strong Westphalian doctrines of sovereignty may always have been out of date. But just as it would be hasty to imagine that we are entering a postnational era – when all the empirical indicators are that nationalism is resurgent precisely because of asymmetrical globalisation – so it would be hasty to forget the strong claims to collective autonomy and self-determination of those who have been denied both, and the need for solidarity among those who are least empowered to realize their projects as individuals.[102]

Coming from the other direction, and focussing more on Europe, Veit Michael Bader launches a critique of 'liberal' and 'social democratic' nationalists, among whom he includes Offe, Streeck and Jöppke.[103] Several other contributors address issues of borders, citizenship and nationalism discussed above in relation to Benhabib's work.

In the same year in which *The Rights of Others* was published, Benhabib delivered the Tanner Lectures, published in 2006 as *Another Cosmopolitanism*, with comments by Jeremy Waldron, Bonnie Honig and Will Kymlicka. Benhabib ends her 'Reply' on a darker note.

> . . . whether we seek to tame the nation-state or to transcend it, there are certain developments through which the state is devolving its own powers and thus posing great dangers to its citizens. This devolution of the state's regulatory capacities is taking place, in large measure, as a consequence of the exigencies of global capitalism . . .

> . . . the transcendence of the nation-state is occurring hardly in the direction of cosmopolitanism but more in the direction of the privatization and corporatization of sovereignty.[104]

It would be hard to disagree with this diagnosis, which pushes us back to asking whether the EU should be seen as part of the solution or part of the problem, or perhaps both.[105] I pick up the threads of this discussion, as we have encountered it so far, in the next chapter.

Notes

1 Habermas, *Between Facts and Norms*.

2 Jürgen Habermas, *Law and Morality: The Tanner Lectures on Human Values*, VI, New York: Oxford University Press, 1988, p. 570.

3 Habermas, *Law and Morality*, p. 599.

4 Jürgen Habermas, *Justification and Application*, Cambridge: Polity, 1993, pp. 1–17.

5 Habermas, *Between Facts and Norms*, p. 165. These examples seem to raise more problems of demarcation than they resolve.

6 Ibid., p. 168.

7 Ibid., p. 179.

8 Ibid., 185.

9 Ibid., p. 360.

10 Ibid., pp. 370ff.

11 Ibid., pp. 384–7.

12 Ibid., p. 386.

13 Ibid., p. 442.

14 Ibid., pp. 386–7.

15 Review symposium on *Between Facts and Norms*, in *Deutsche Zeitschrift für Philosophie*, 41(2), 1993, pp. 321–64. Habermas responds to his critics in the 1994 'Postscript' on pages 447–62.

16 Habermas, *Between Facts and Norms*, p. 417.

17 Peter Dews, in *Deutsche Zeitschrift für Philosophie*, p. 363. Dews edited a volume of interviews with Habermas, *Autonomy and Solidarity*, London: Verso, 1996, 2nd edn, 1992, and *Habermas. A Critical Reader*, Oxford: Blackwell, 1999.

18 Habermas is of course well aware of this. As Dews notes, he has himself stressed the interdependence of justice and solidarity (*Erläuterungen zur Diskursethik*, p. 70; there is an English translation of this text ('Justice and Solidarity') in Thomas Wren (ed.), *The Moral Domain. Essays on the Ongoing Discussion between Philosophy and the Social Sciences*, Cambridge, MA: MIT Press, 1990, pp. 224–51. See, more recently, Nathalie Karagiannis (ed.), *European Solidarity*, Liverpool University Press, 2007.

19 The work of Gillian Rose is of course a brilliant exception. See also, more recently, Samantha Ashenden and Christopher Thornhill (eds), *Legality and Legitimacy*, Baden-Baden: Nomos, 2010; Daniel Chernilo, *The Natural Law Foundations of Modern Social Theory: A Quest for Universalism*. Cambridge University Press, forthcoming.

20 See, for example, the creation of Charter 77 in Czechoslovakia and Charter 88 in the United Kingdom; also Arato, *From Neo-Marxism to Democratic Theory*.

21 James Bohman, *Public Deliberation. Pluralism, Complexity, and Democracy*, Cambridge, MA and London: MIT Press, 1996, p. 2. As he says (p. 4), his book 'spans the Anglo American (primarily Rawlsian) and German (primarily Habermasian) literature on the subject of deliberative democracy.' See also John Dryzek, *Discursive Democracy. Politics, Policy, and Political Science*, Cambridge University Press; more recently Bohman, 'Toward a Critical Theory of Globalization. Democratic Practice and Multiperspectival Inquiry', *Concepts and Transformation*, 9(2), 2004, pp. 121–46; *Democracy across Borders. From Dêmos to Dêmoi*, Cambridge, MA: MIT Press, 2007.

22 Thomas McCarthy, *The Critical Theory of Jiirgen Habermas*, Cambridge: Polity, 1978.

23 A. Honneth, *Critique of Power*, Cambridge, MA: MIT Press. First published 1985; Seyla Benhabib, *Critique, Norm and Utopia*, New York: Columbia University Press, 1986.

24 Benhabib, *Critique, Norm and Utopia*, p. 346. See also, arguing along similar lines, Jay Bernstein's *Recovering Ethical Life. Jürgen Habemas and the Future of Critical Theory*, London: Routledge, 1996. Nancy Fraser has also moved from a feminist critique of critical theory to a variety of other topics, notably an important exchange with Honneth, discussed below.

25 Seyla Benhabib, 'Toward a Deliberative Model of Democratic Legitimacy', in Benhabib (ed.), *Democracy and Difference. Contesting the Boundaries of the Political*, Princeton University Press, 1996, pp. 67–94. See also, in particular, Iris Marion Young's contribution, 'Communication and the Other; Beyond Deliberative Democracy', pp. 120–35.

26 Benhabib, *Democracy and Difference*, p. 84. I discuss the practice of deliberative democracy in relation to the EU in the next chapter.

27 A. Honneth, (1982) 'Moral Consciousness and Class Domination: Some Problems in the Analysis of Hidden Morality', *Praxis International*, 2(1), pp. 12–24. Reprinted in Honneth, *Disrespect. The Normative Foundations of Critical Theory*, Cambridge: Polity, 2007, pp. 80–96. The Inter-University Centre was, as much as or more than Frankfurt, the crucible of third-generation critical theory, bringing together thinkers from West Germany and the English-speaking world. More importantly, of course, it was a meeting-point between East and West in a still divided Europe. The session I attended a couple of years later was probably fairly typical, including, for example, Wellmer from Germany, Ferenc Feher (then in Australia) and Mihaly Vajda from Hungary, and Andrew Arato, Jean Cohen, Joel Whitebook and Drusilla Cornell from the United States.

28 Honneth, *Disrespect*, p. 82. Here of course Honneth is implicitly referring to Habermas's classic analysis of the public sphere and its deterioration under conditions of modern democracy.

29 Honneth, *Disrespect*, p. 83.

30 Honneth, *The Struggle for Recognition*, Cambridge: Polity, 1995, p. 1.

31 'The Social Dynamics of Disrespect: On the Location of Critical Theory Today', pp. 63–79. Here p. 74.

32 See, for example, Fraser and Honneth, 2003, and the more hostile critiques by Lois McNay (2007, 2008).

33 Some of these are discussed later in this chapter.

34 Axel Honneth, *Reification. A New Look at an Old Idea.* With Commentaries by Judith Butler, Raymond Geuss and Jonathan Lear. Edited and Introduced by Martin Jay. The Berkeley Tanner Lectures 2005. New York: Oxford University Press, 2008.

35 As Joel Anderson (2009) notes, 'few outside Germany follow the Frankfurt School tradition of combining interpretations of classic texts . . . with both critical social theory and social scientific research'.

36 Honneth, 'Pathologies of the Social', in Honneth, *Disrespect*, pp. 3–48.

37 Ibid., p. 34.

38 Ibid., p. 42. Anthropology here means, of course, philosophical anthropology (see Honneth and Joas, *Social Action and Human Nature*, Cambridge: Cambridge University Press, 1980).

39 Honneth, 'Pathologies of the Social', p. 36.

40 Adorno, *Minima Moralia. Reflexionen aus dem beschädigten Leben*, Frankfurt: Suhrkamp, 1951. Translation London, New Left Books, 1974.

41 He had also addressed the specific issue of pathologies of communication; see the entry 'Sozialpathologie' by Martin Hartmann in the *Habermas-Handbuch*, pp. 368–71, which traces the theme into Honneth's work. See also the essay by Hartmann and Honneth, 'Paradoxien des Kapitalismus', *Berliner Debatte Initial*, 15(1), 2004, pp. 4–17 – the title is also that of a collective Frankfurt Institute volume, edited by Honneth: *Befreiung aus der Mündigkeit. Paradoxien des modernen Kapitalismus*, Frankfurt: Campus, 2002.

42 Honneth, *Pathologien der Vernunft*, p. 28. Translated as *Pathologies of Reason*, Columbia University Press, 2009.

43 Ibid., p. 30.

44 Habermas, *Between Facts and Norms*, p. 444.

45 Jürgen Habermas, *The Inclusion of the Other*, Cambridge: Polity, 1998.

46 Ibid., p. 208.

47 Ibid., p. 222.

48 Ibid.

49 Anticipated by some sceptical remarks about the future of the nation-state in his 1993 Postscript to *The Past as Future*. In the 1991 interview which makes up the main part of this book, he already remarked in passing, in an unusually speculative turn of phrase, that 'world history is giving a united Europe a second chance'.

50 Habermas, *The Inclusion of the Other*, p. 139.

51 Ibid., p. 144.

52 Habermas cites Jean-Marie Guéhenno, *La fin de la démocratie*, Paris: Flammarion, 1993. See also, more recently, Colin Crouch, *Postdemocracy*,

Cambridge: Polity, 2004 and Paul Ginsborg, *Democracy. Crisis and Renewal*, London: Profile Books, 2008.

53   Habermas, *The Inclusion of the Other*. See also 'Learning from Catastrophe' in *The Postnational Constellation*.

54   Habermas, *The Inclusion of the Other*, pp. 183–4.

55   Ibid., p. 184.

56   In the national case this tends to mean recovering control or influence: in the European or supranational case achieving it for the first time.

57   Habermas, *The Inclusion of the Other*, p. 99.

58   Ibid., p. 99.

59   Ibid., p. 102.

60   Ibid., p. 111.

61   Max Horkheimer, 'Gedanke zur Religion', in *Kritische Theorie*, Horkheimer, vol. 1, p. 375. See Maeve Cooke's excellent discussion of the theme of religion in Horkheimer and Habermas (which anticipates some more recent developments in Habermas' own thinking) in her essay 'Critical Theory and Religion' in D. Z. Phillips and T. Tessin (eds), *Philosophy of Religion in the 21st Century*, Basingstoke: Palgrave, 2000, pp. 211–43. Habermas was also interested, in a more historical way, in the role played by religious and in particular messianic motifs in the thought of Adorno, Benjamin, and Horkheimer.

62   As Cooke points out (p. 223, n. 73), Habermas suggests that Horkheimer's view of philosophy was also post-metaphysical. As he writes in an essay on Horkheimer republished in *Texte und Kontexte* (p. 92), 'For Horkheimer "materialism" always also had the connotation of being critical of philosophy: it stood for *postmetaphysical* thinking.' Cooke's underlying concern is that, as she argues in more recent work, '. . . the formal approach advocated by postmetaphysical thinking means that ethical, moral, and political choices cannot themselves supply participants in practical deliberations with the imaginative projections of the good life and the good society that are necessary to orient and to motivate practical deliberation about the proper goals of human action'. ('Salvaging and secularizing the semantic contents of religion: the limitations of Habermas's postmetaphysical proposal', *International Journal for the Philosophy of Religion*, 60 (2006), p. 202. See also Maeve Cooke, *Re-Presenting the Good Society*, Cambridge, MA: MIT Press, 2006 and R. J. Bernstein, 'Naturalism, Secularism, and Religion: Habermas's Via Media', *Constellations*, 17(1), 2010, pp. 155–66.

63   Cooke, *Texte und Kontexte*, p. 129.

64   'Jürgen Habermas; Ich bin alt, aber nicht fromm geworden', in Michael Funken (ed.), *Über Habermas. Gespräche mit Zeitgenossen*, Darmstadt: Wissenschaftliche Buchgesellschaft, 2008, pp. 181–90. The title quotation is on page 185.

65   Funken, op.cit., p. 42.

66 For an overview, see, for example, Melissa Yates, 'Rawls and Habermas on Religion in the Public Sphere', *Philosophy and Social Criticism*, 33(7) 2007, pp. 880–91.

67 'Die Dialektik der Säkularisierung', *Blätter für deutsche und internationale Politik*, 4, 2007, p. 33.

68 See also the exchange in *Philosophical Explorations*, 10(1) (March 2007). I am grateful to Daniel Steuer for drawing my attention to this.

69 See, for example, chapters 9 and 10 of the book: 'Religious Tolerance as Pacemaker for Cultural Rights' and 'Equal Treatment of Cultures and the Limits of Postmodern Liberalism.'

70 Jürgen Habermas, *Between Naturalism and Religion,* Cambridge: Polity, 2008, p. 6.

71 See also the observation by Fatemeh Hajihosseini (fn 68 below). On Europe's secularism, see Loek Halman and Veerle Draulans, 'How Secular is Europe?', *Bristish Journal of Sociology*, 57(6), 2006, pp. 263–88.

72 Habermas, *Ach, Europa,* p. 85.

73 Ibid., p. 112.

74 Ibid., p. 90.

75 Ibid., (p. 93) On migration, see the discussion of Preuss, Benhabib and others below.

76 William Outhwaite, 'Legality and Legitimacy in the European Union', in Chris Thornhill and Samatha Ashenden (eds), *Legality and Legitimacy: Normative and Sociological Approaches,* Baden-Baden: Nomos, 2010, pp. 279–90. See also Bowman, Jonathan, 2007. 'Challenging Habermas' Response to the EU Democratic Deficit', *Philosophy and Social Criticism*, 33(6), pp. 736–55.

77 See the chapters by Habermas and Philippe Schmitter in *The Shape of the New Europe,* Ralf Rogowski and Charles Turner (eds), Cambridge University Press, 2006.

78 'Europa und Verfassung', in Brunkhorst et al. (eds), *Habermas-Handbuch,* Stuttgart and Weimar: Metzler, 2009, p. 268. See also the entry by Christian Joerges, 'Europäische Staatsbürgerschaft', pp. 312–15.

79 'Europa und Verfassung', pp. 270–1. The Benelux countries might also wonder why they had been overlooked. And as Brunkhorst warns, this might lead to a lasting marginalisation of the Eastern periphery. (Brunkhorst, *Solidarität,* p. 230, n. 55; *Solidarity: From Civic Friendship to a Global Legal Community* (Cambridge, MA: MIT Press, 2005).

80 David Held, *Democracy and the Global Order. From the Modern State to Cosmopolitan Governance,* Cambridge: Polity, 1995; David Held and Daniele Archibugi (eds), *Cosmopolitan Democracy: Agenda for a New World Order,* Cambridge: Polity, 1995; see also Daniele Archibugi, David Held and Martin Köhler (eds), *Re-imagining Political Community. Studies in Cosmopolitan Democracy,* Cambridge: Polity, 1998.

81 Brunkhorst, *Solidarity. From Civic Friendship to a Global Legal Community,* Cambridge, MA: MIT Press, 2005. First published 2002. See also the

discussion of the book in *Philosophy and Social Criticism*, 32(7), pp. 795–838. On solidarity, see Jens Beckert et al., (eds), *Transnationale Solidarität. Chancen und Grenzen*, Frankfurt: Campus, 2004; Nathalie Karagiannis (ed.), *European Solidarity*, Liverpool: University Press, 2007.

82 Ulrich Beck, *The Cosmopolitan Vision*, Cambridge: Polity, 2006, p. 117. See Luke Martell, 'Beck's Cosmopolitan Politics', *Contemporary Politics*, 14(2), June 2008, pp. 129–43.

83 Jeff Alexander, 'Critical Reflections on "Reflexive Modernization"', *Theory, Culture and Society*, 13, 1996, pp. 133–8; Jeff Alexander and Philip Smith, 'Social Science and Salvation: Risk Society as Mythical Discourse', *Zeitschrift für Soziologie*, 25, 1996, pp. 251–62. This issue is discussed by Martin Hartmann in 'Widersprüche, Ambivalenzen, Paradoxien – Begriffliche Wandlungen in der neueren Gesellschaftstheorie', in Honneth (ed.), *Befreiung aus der Mündigkeit*, pp. 246–7. Beck takes a more explicit normative stance in his opening address to the German Sociological Association's 2008 conference, 'Remapping social inequalities I an age of climate change: for a cosmopolitan renewal of sociology', *Global Networks*, 10(2), 2010, pp. 165–81.

84 Gerard Delanty, *The Cosmopolitan Imagination. The Renewal of Critical Social Theory*, Cambridge University Press, 2009.

85 'Problems of a Concept of European Citizenship', *European Law Journal*, 1(3), November 1995, pp. 267–81; 'Migration: A Challenge to Modern Citizenship', *Constellations*, 4(3), 1998, pp. 307–19. See also Veit Michael Bader, 'Citizenship of the European Union. Human Rights, Rights of Citizens of the Union and of Member States', *Ratio Juris*, 12(2), June 1999, pp. 153–81.

86 '"Homogeneity" and Constitutional Democracy: Coping with Identity Conflicts through Group Rights', *Journal of Political Philosophy*, 6(2), June 1998, pp. 113–42.

87 *The Claims of Culture. Equality and Diversity in the Global Era*, Princeton University Press, 2002.

88 Ibid., pp. 19–20. In a footnote to the quoted passage she notes the very diverse views of immigrant groups in relation to schooling in minority languages and hence the inappropriateness of centrally imposed provision (as was the case in New York City schools at the time). In a later chapter (pp. 77–9) she criticizes the 'enclavist' policy towards minorities in the Netherlands.

89 Ibid., p. 153.

90 Seyla Benhabib *The Rights of Others. Aliens, Residents and Citizens*, Cambridge University Press, 2004, p. 1.

91 In *The Claims of Culture*, p. 79, she had commented favourably on a policy introduced in Amsterdam in 1999 to give 'city citizenship to all foreign residents and third-country nationals after a period of five years residency. Citizens of Amsterdam can vote as well as stand for and hold office, in citywide elections.' See Jean Tillie and Boris Slijper, 'Immigrant Political Integration and Ethnic Civic Communities in Amsterdam', in Seyla Benhabib, Ian Shapiro and Danilo Petranović (eds), *Identities, Affilaitions, and Alliances*, Cambridge University Press, 2007, pp. 206–25.

92 Benhabib, *The Rights of Others*, p. 47f. EU law is of course not directly 'authored' by the populations of member states but by the unelected Council of Ministers (ministers who are often, though not always, locally elected in the member States), with input from the Parliament, and also by the European Court of Justice itself.

93 Kant, *Metaphysics of Morals*, cited in *The Rights of Others*, p. 131.

94 Benhabib, *The Rights of Others*, p. 133. She notes that we also '. . . have moral obligations to those who cannot enter into discourses with us'.

95 Ibid., p. 141. Interestingly, she notes elsewhere (p. 156) that at the time of writing two EU countries, Greece and Luxemburg, did *not* permit naturalization. This has since changed.

96 Ibid., 167. This prediction has of course turned out to be right.

97 Ibid., 179. Cosmopolitanism, she insists (pp. 174–5), is not enough. 'Transnational networks without democratic attachments can enhance fundamentalism as well as terrorism.'

98 Ibid., p. 210.

99 Ibid.,p. 220.

100 Nancy Fraser, 'Transnationalizing the Public Sphere', in Seyla Benhabib, Ian Shapiro and Danilo Petranović (eds), *Identities, Affiliations, and Alliances*, Cambridge University Press, 2007, pp. 45–66. Somewhat surprisingly, she mentions the EU only in passing (p. 59) as an example of the difficulties posed by linguistic diversity.

101 'Social Solidarity and Cosmopolitan Democracy', in Seyla Benhabib, Ian Shapiro and Danilo Petranović (eds), *Identities, Affiliations, and Alliances*, Cambridge University Press, 2007, pp. 285–302.

102 Ibid.

103 'Building European Institutions: Beyond Strong Ties and Weak Commitments', in Seyla Benhabib, Ian Shapiro and Danilo Petranović (eds), *Identities, Affiliations, and Alliances*, Cambridge University Press, 2007, pp. 113–35. I shall return to this in discussing the politics of the EU.

104 Seyla Benhabib, *Another Cosmopolitanism*, edited and introduced by Robert Post, New York: Oxford University Press, 2006, pp. 176–7.

105 There is also the question raised by a perceptive reviewer of the book, whether a Europe which seems suspicious of its 'new generation of citizens and immigrants' is a promising place in which to expect the development of cosmopolitan universalism. (Fatemeh Hajihosseini, review in *German Law Journal*, 9(6), 2008, pp. 819–27).

6

Critical theory and the European Union

The editors of a recent volume on the sociology of the EU note the paradox that, whereas early accounts of European integration were centrally shaped by sociological perspectives such as those of Karl Deutsch and Ernst Haas[1], it is only in the past few years that it has become a major concern of social theory and empirical sociology. This is true also of critical theory. Habermas recalls that he came late to the study of the EU, having previously not been a 'Europe fan'.[2] He certainly made up for lost time, as we saw in the previous chapter. As Christian Geyer recently pointed out, he displays a greater passion for the future of Europe than for almost any other topic.[3]

Work on the EU by thinkers influenced by critical theory can be divided into three clusters:

- overviews such as those by Habermas himself and by Beck and Grande or Delanty and Rumford[4]

- accounts of deliberative democracy in the EU and in international politics more generally.[5]

- discussions of the European public sphere, European identity and so on.

Beck and Grande's book is closest to a manifesto. They begin with the ringing claim that 'Europe is today in Europe the last politically effective utopia.'[6] Theirs is explicitly intended as 'not least a *new critical theory of European integration*'.[7] They conceptualize the uneven advance of integration in the slogan of a Europe as a regime of 'secondary consequences', in which European society emerges 'behind the back of the actors'.[8] As for European civil society, they note the paradox of a civil society *from above* aiming to establish one from below.[9] European civil society offers the EU the opportunity of opening up a transnational space in such a way that it organises itself. Their argument, as in this case, typically takes the form of rejecting dilemmas and arguing for a logic of *both/and*, in which Europe brings together *both* citizens *and* states in a structure which is both imperial[10] and democratic. Europeanization is both vertical, with the development of supranational structures, and horizontal, in the opening up of states (and hence their citizens) to others.

In case this should begin to seem like an *un*critical account of European integration, they stress that Europe is suffering from a half-hearted or *deformed* cosmopolitanism, deformed economically by neoliberalism, politically by nationalism in the sense of the pursuit of their national interests by member states, and by bureaucracy in the sense of the strengthening of executives at the expense of parliament and citizens. Despite all this, however, there are positive pressures towards Europeanization and alliances such as that between the Commission and civil society organizations. Since a collapse into nationalist fragmentation or a scenario of stagnation have nothing to offer, the only attractive option is a 'cosmopolitan renewal of Europe based on four pillars: the strengthening of European civil society, the transition to a post-national model of democracy which gives European citizens a active role in European decision-making, a cosmopolitan approach to integration which recognizes national differences and the establishment of Europe 'as the driving force of a global cosmopolitanism and a member of a new transatlantic security community'.[11] This requires Europe-wide referendums;[12] it may also require a 'core Europe' to take the lead: '. . . only an avant-garde of integration is in a position to break up the nationalist self-misunderstanding of Europe and to open up a common transnational European space of action for all.'[13]

Beck's model of cosmopolitanism is the focus for several of the contributions to a recent volume edited by Anna Sophie Krossa and Roland Robertson. As the editors note in their Introduction, there is something paradoxical about Beck presenting his cosmopolitan vision of Europe with the slogan 'Move over America – Europe is back'.[14] Here again we see critical theory skirting the dangers of Eurocentrism, an evolutionary model whose model of modernity runs close to modernization theory, and a liberalism which abstracts from and is insensitive to people's attachments to place.[15]

Delanty and Rumford's book of 2005, like Beck and Grande's, is informed by the social theory of the last few decades – in particular, the revival of historical sociology and, more broadly, theories of modernity and, secondly, the growth of post-colonial theory and its application to European history in what is sometimes called the new direction in European Studies.[16] Like Beck and Grande, they are concerned to remedy the neglect of society in the literature on Europeanization. Their primary theoretical reference points are Habermasian and (other) forms of cosmopolitan theory. This points in particular to a focus on the public sphere rather than the more substantial notion of civil society.

> The dominant approach to viewing European civil society, which sees it either as the aggregation of national civil societies or the pet project of a European supra-state, is . . . deeply flawed . . . There are more compelling reasons to see European civil society as part of global civil society rather than an outcome of supra-national governance in the EU.[17]

What then of EU democracy? Erik Eriksen, who had co-authored an impressive book on Habermas and deliberative democracy,[18] has actively pursued the theme in relation to the EU, along with colleagues at the Norwegian research centre ARENA. A conference at Bergen in 1998 led to an influential edited book, as did another in Oslo in 2003. A deliberative approach, Erikson and Fossum argue, is particularly suitable for the politics of European integration precisely because of the EU's processual character and its imprecise contours and overlapping structures.

> Integration may occur through strategic bargaining or through functional adaptation. However, it may also occur through deliberation or what is commonly referred to as arguing. This latter type of integration is very important, as stability depends on learning and alteration of preferences. Deliberation, when properly conducted, ensures communicative processes where the force of the better argument will sway people to harmonize their action plans. To understand post-national integration, or integration beyond the nation-state, explanatory categories associated with deliberation are required, as supranational entities possess far weaker and less well-developed means of coercion – bargaining resources – than do states.[19]

Eriksen restates this principle in his conclusion to his more recent book:

> The many veto points, the lack of forceful compliance mechanisms, representation and problem-solving through committees and networks underscore the deliberative mode of decision-making. The infrequent use of majority vote – most decisions in the Council are unanimous – makes the EU into a kind of *consensus democracy.*[20]

This irenic image may seem at odds with the more familiar one of horse-trading in which, for example, I support your position of fishing quotas, in which I have no interest, in exchange for your support on a proposal for the decommissioning of nuclear reactors. Eriksen neatly summarizes this argument that, as Andersen and Burns put it, 'The EU is characterized by principles of *national representation, interest representation* and *representation of expertise.'*[21]

> It is maintained that the deliberations adhere to the logic of power rather than to the logic of arguments; self-interests rather than common interests dominate. It is the large Member States that have the most votes, and it is the economic-functional interests of the society whose voices are most easily heard, due to lobbying and considerable bargaining resources.

There is of course plenty of evidence for both perspectives, but a number of close observers of the EU have stressed the importance of emerging normative commitments and at least lip service to common objectives. A Thatcher-style inflexible insistence on national interest is likely to be counterproductive. Frank Schimmelfennnig, for example, has shown how existing member states found themselves drawn by previous commitments into reluctant support for eastern enlargement, even when they saw this as contrary to their national interest.[22] Eriksen, like several contributors to *Making the European Polity*, notes the importance of what he calls 'working agreements' – 'something in between bargained compromises and a rational consensus. A working agreement rests on reasonable reasons, but ones that do not convince all.'[23] This is undoubtedly a worthwhile enrichment to EU studies and deliberative democratic theory. The problem for the EU, however, is that often there is an inverse relation between the deliberative and the democratic dimensions. However exemplary the deliberations may be in the Council of Ministers or in the practices going under the name of the Open Method of Coordination, there is little about these that is democratic. Ministers, for example, may be simply appointed by, for example, the French president or, via the intermediation of the House of Lords, a British prime minister.[24]

These debates around the deliberative dimension of the EU overlap with a broader debate in international politics initiated by critical theorists in the late 1990s in response both to Haberma's theory of democracy and to his earlier formulation of his theory of communicative action. Known as the 'ZIB debate' from the initials of the journal in which it was largely conducted, it was part of a world-wide turn against 'realism' in international relations theory, including in Germany a research programme on 'communicative action in international relations' initiated by Harald Müller. An edited book of 2007, including a response by Habermas, examines the issues raised in this debate and takes them forward.

As Müller describes his research programme, it aimed

> . . . to identify processes of persuasion in international negotiations. Was it possible to find situations in which actors obeyed the 'force of the better argument', although their preferences at the opening of the negotiations lay in another direction?[25]

In an example taken from a conference he attended to monitor the nuclear non-proliferation treaty, in which a powerful delegation which had used procedural devices to obstruct the conference was 'shamed' into going along with the views of the majority, Müller describes something close to Eriksen's notion of 'working agreements'.

> The episode certainly does not constitute an ideal type of action oriented to understanding. It does however point to the power of argument against the background of a logic of diplomatic appropriateness.[26]

Eriksen's own contribution, which is also available in its original English version as an ARENA working paper, he develops the idea of 'working agreements' and illustrates it with the example of the constitutional convention and treaty.[27] Although the Convention failed to produce an acceptable constitution, in other respects it was quite an impressive deliberative assembly which may be remembered and even repeated when more immediately successful ventures are forgotten.[28] It was also one in which Old and New Europe met on relatively egalitarian and open terms; as Fraser Cameron (2004: 152) noted, 'it was difficult to distinguish speakers coming from existing or future member states'.[29]

The issue of constitutionalizing the EU takes us back to the fundamental questions of its future political shape and what Heidrun Friese and Peter Wagner termed 'The Nascent Political Philosophy of the European Polity'.[30] As in the more specific case of deliberative democracy, Europe becomes the terrain of debates in political philosophy shaped in relation to the national state. First, there is the issue debated between Habermas and the legal theorist Dieter Grimm of whether a Europe-wide democracy can meet anything like the expectations of the European national states. Here, as Friese and Wagner note, Claus Offe takes a position which one could call Eurosceptical if the term had not been attached to a much more fundamental rejection of the integration project. Whereas Habermas and others have justified further integration partly in terms of the need to preserve the European welfare state in a global context, Offe is more concerned with the impact on both democracy and the welfare state of what he called 'the stress of European integration'.[31]

Just as the solidarity which sustains redistribution in national welfare states may not extend to a transnational context, so the mutual trust which sustains democratic politics may stop at the state boundaries: '. . . political resources . . . will not be added, but will in contrast get lost on the way to "Europe"'.[32] Grimm, and to a lesser extent Offe, come close to the communitarian position which stresses the need for political communities to be embedded in a broader cultural context. Republicanism of the kind revived by Quentin Skinner stresses rather the self-definition and self-empowerment of a political community which may or may not be culturally homogeneous.[33] Both positions raise the stakes for European integration, suggesting scepticism in their stronger versions or caution and gradualism in weaker versions such as Richard Bellamy's 'cosmopolitan communitarianism'.[34] From positions such as these, Habermas is too bold in his organizational proposals and/or (the two are distinct) in his reliance on a notion of constitutional patriotism. For John Maynor, for example,

> By trying to extract any pre-political notions from their conception of citizenship, constitutional patriots are in danger of leaning too far towards a strict, status-based conception of citizenship that cannot be maintained because it contains an overly 'thin' conception of political identity based on rights.[35]

Writing in the aftermath of the failure of the constitutional treaty, Maynor notes that 'Curiously, a document that is meant, among other things, to enhance the democratic nature of the Union has failed to be endorsed democratically by its citizens.'[36] In fact, however, as Friese and Wagner show,[37] Habermas's position is a good deal richer than the mere term 'constitutional patriotism' suggests, and this was anyway always intended to capture much more than a mere identification with the wording and sentiments of the Grundgesetz. As concerns constitutions in the narrow sense, Habermas was of course twice bitten, first by the West German's government's refusal to properly constitutionalize reunification and second by the failure of the European constitution. But it is certainly arguable that in both cases the results might have been preferable, with a more considered approach to German unity and a constitution which most Europeans would have gone along with, if without great enthusiasm.

Offe and Preuss returned to the question of EU democratization in a wide-ranging article of 2006 which covers many of the broader issues discussed by Beck and Grande and Delanty and Rumford. The problem, they point out, in an argument made more fully by Vivien Schmidt in a book published in the same year,[38] is not just the lack of democracy in the EU but the fact that it undermines the democracy of the member-states.[39] Democracy requires not only that rulers be accountable to the ruled but also the 'active' characteristic that the rulers are able to formulate and implement policies. 'The latter condition applies to the EU level of rule as much as it does to the policy-making capacity of the governments of member states – a capacity that has been vastly decimated at the member state level by the process of EU integration, without being resurrected at the EU level itself.'[40] Rather than pursuing the illusory aim of turning the EU into a democratic state, it should recognize that it is more like a 'republican empire', linking together people who are not fused into a demos but cultivate 'solidarity grounded in the mutual recognition of otherness . . . the contribution of Europe to the problems of our world at the beginning of the twenty-first century.'[41] What this would look like in practice, given the sort of urgent practical issues which Offe in particular has addressed in the past years, remains of course open.

The EU is fated to steer an uneasy course between legalism and romanticism, and debates of the kind reviewed above are paralleled in the ongoing practice and rhetoric of European politics and debate. Closer to the romantic end of things is the ongoing discussion of European identity and here, too, critical theorists have played a major part. As Eder has commented, there was a tendency in the literature to assume that there must be a European identity and then to look for signs of it.[42] How far these centralized initiatives amount to the creation of a genuine European identity, assuming such a thing is anyway important,[43] is of course open to question.

The 1973 Copenhagen summit produced a paper on 'European identity', defined as being based on a 'common heritage' and 'acting together in relation to the rest of the world'. As Bo Stråth (2002) has suggested, the appeal to identity has in some ways replaced appeals to the notion of integration as a self-evident good. The EU's Eurobarometer tracked identity for a long time, tending only to show that a European identity came well after regional or national ones for most Europeans. The national differences were more interesting, with Britons and Turks least likely to affirm a European identity and Germans, along with Italians and other southern Europeans much more positive in their responses. Exposure to intra-European mobility through exchanges or migration had, unsurprisingly, a reinforcing effect.

Klaus Eder in particular has worked substantially on this topic, partly in conjunction with Bernhard Giesen and Willfried Spohn.[44] Much of the earlier work tended to focus on the topical issue of EU citizenship, which had been put on the policy agenda by the Maastricht Treaty and subsequent actions in the 1990s. This is in fact the focus of Eder and Giesen's edited book of 2001.[45] As they argue in their concluding chapter, citizenship can be seen as the 'foundation myth of a new European collective identity'[46]; 'The democratic discourse on citizenship has become the transnational master-narrative of democratic self-organization in Europe.'[47] The citizenship theme has sub-sequently become more muted, perhaps because the EU's citizenship policy was itself so half-hearted,[48] but the related theme of identity remains a major focus of work. Here Giesen tends to stress shared values in a Durkheimian way, while Eder places more emphasis on conflict and dissensus. In his own chapter in the edited book, he brings out the diversity of European culture.

> Although the code of cultural traditions in Europe represents a contradictory mixture of incompatible traditions, it obviously furthermore fulfils social-integrative functions . . . it follows that it is not the internal cohesion of a cultural code which makes social integration possible . . . What integrates is the fact that traditions are good for communication. Traditions are good in order to represent identity and difference.[49]

It is not possible, he emphasizes, simply to Europeanize a national form of consciousness; 'For Europe is no longer as obvious as the nation has been.'[50] At a European level the only realistic option is a minimalist conception of identity which is constantly reshaped. Echoing Renan's remark about *national* consciousness, Eder writes: '. . . the making of identity becomes daily political business.'[51]

In a later volume he edited with Willfried Spohn, Eder returns to this theme via a discussion of the critiques of the concept of identity which, as he recalls, Adorno called 'the prototype of ideology'.[52] Addressing the fraught issue of 'core' versus 'peripheral' Europeans, he concludes that '. . . the emerging transnational European society needs even more collective identity than national societies or any non-modern societies, because it is a system of social relations where social relations are mediated more than ever by cultural techniques.'[53] As he writes a little later in the chapter, '. . . there is no such "thing" as[54] a collective identity or a collective memory – these concepts rather grasp a moment in a permanent struggle of naming.'

In another essay of 2008, Eder returns to the theme of Europe as a 'trans-national space of cultural differences'. In implicit contrast to Habermas, he stresses that he does not understand

> a post-national situation in the sense that the national age is being replaced by a post-national age. Rather, I take the evolutionary view of emerging structures that are added to existing ones while changing their function.[55]

In the transnational situation of contemporary Europe, cultural differences are increased by migration, by the reaffirmation of ethnic identities and, most importantly, by the fact that the nation has itself become a case of cultural differences within an emerging transnational community; national sentiments have become normal cultural differences . . .

Thus the symbolic power that the nation-state had concentrated dissipates; what is left is the nation with a weakened state, left to play with its particularism in a transnational space which regulates the processes of inclusion and exclusion.[56]

The scene is the set for 'an increase in symbolic struggles'.[57] The most promising possible outcome is one involving a 'transnational unity of differences':

> In the transnational situation there is no longer a people on top of class, nation or ethnicity; there are rather a series of people (*demoi*) who identify at times with class, with nation or with ethnicity. The idea of a hierarchy of identifications is to be replaced by the idea of a network of cross-cutting identifications. These many *demoi* are held together by the reliability of an institutional framework they have accepted by voluntary agreement and which guarantees everybody the maximum fairness in real life.[58]

Eder's sociological realism and his focus on practices, including discursive practices, come out most strongly in his latest contribution.[59] He insists that one should not reduce identity to measurable identifications. An identity is something more sedimented:

> A collective identity is a semantic property of the social relations among a defined set of people. The set of people we are dealing with are the EU citizens. The thing that these EU citizens share is the national citizenship narrative.[60]

It therefore becomes an empirical question whether networks of European citizens will develop strong narratives around political and other issues at a European level.

'We can only wait for future events – for further opposition to the Lisbon Treaty, for weak performances on the stage of foreign or migration policy – to tell us about the robustness of the story that makes a political community and one day might also provide it with a collective identity.'[61]

Another Arena Working Paper, by Hans-Jörg Trenz, lends support to Eder's approach to European identity. Trenz brings together the constitutional debates in the EU from 2002 to 2007 with issues of identity and democracy. Rather than postulating a European identity 'as the basic infrastructure of a European democracy', he suggests that it should be seen rather 'as a contingent by-product of entering into democratic practice'.[62] In an approach which I discuss more fully later in this chapter in relation to the public sphere, Trenz examines the way in which the issues were framed in two quality newspapers in France and two in Germany. He found that in both countries in the debates up to 2005 instrumental justifications (in terms of power politics, interests or problem-solving) were much more prominent (close to 50%) than those invoking rights and democracy (around a third in Germany and a quarter in France) or identity and values (only 17% in Germany and 27% in France). Where it was used, identity language was diverse and fragmented; Trenz speaks of an 'identitarian Babel'.

As this chapter indicates, discussions of European identity tend to merge into questions about the existence of a European public sphere. Here, too, critical theory has substantially shaped the debates. As Michał Krzyżanowski, Anna Triandafyllidou and Ruth Wodak note, Habermas's *Structural Transformation of the Public Sphere* was a major influence, especially after it finally appeared in English in 1989, shortly followed by Nancy Fraser's paper of 2003 on 'Transnationalizing the Public Sphere'.[63] Work at Bremen by the late Bernhard Peters and others[64] and at Leeds, Bristol and Sussex by Paul Statham, who earlier worked with Eder on social movements and the media, has been particularly prominent. The most recent and perhaps most substantial study, that by Statham and Ruud Koopmans, covering seven West European states, illuminates not just the public sphere but many other areas of EU politics and civil society. In his own chapter in the volume, Paul Statham (2010: 292) concludes soberly that 'European civil society is . . . not only marginal compared with national civil society and the European executive, but also compared with globally operating NGOs . . . the substance of the EU's public sphere "deficit" consists in the overdomination by elite actors of Europeanized debates.'[65] rather than trying to arouse a largely dormant European civil society, or to increase the powers of a European Parliament which is inevitably remote from most voters, Statham suggests '. . . that the supranational European institutions holding power would be better off strengthening their communicative links to citizens and seeking legitimacy through national parliaments and media, rather than engaging in another round of top-down efforts to engage a remote and inattentive citizenry.'[66]

This would bring EU politics into line with a well-established finding of studies of European media. As Koopmans (2007: 185) comments, the weakness of a supranational media presence in Europe means that 'one therefore arrives naturally at a "Europeanization" approach . . . that focuses on the domestic aspect of European integration – in this case, the ways in which European integration affects debates in national news media.'[67] Michał Krzyżanowski, Anna Triandafyllidou and Ruth Wodak, in a volume concerned with a series of 'crisis moments' in late twentieth and early twenty-first century Europe, also stress the pervasive 'national filter' through which issues affecting Europe are presented.[68] The approach Statham suggests would probably work better in continental Europe than in the more detached countries of Scandinavia and, even more so, the United Kingdom.[69]

A related issue which is increasingly attracting attention is so-called 'Euroscepticism'. The term is slightly misleading, since it refers not so much to scepticism about particular policies or prospects as to a more whole-hearted rejection of integration and/or the main directions of policy in the EU.[70] Research has tended to focus on party politics, and in particular the question whether Euroscepticism functions more as a resource drawn on contingently and opportunistically by parties or as a more fundamental structuring feature of politics in Europe. There is certainly a tendency for fringe or peripheral parties of the left and right to adopt a Eurosceptical stance, but as Statham et al point out, the only core parties in their sample of seven countries gen- erating a 'hard' level of Eurocriticism are the British Conservatives and the conservative Swiss People's Party (SVP): 'committed Euroscepticism at the core of party systems is basically limited to two conservative parties in Britain and Switzerland'.[71] They conclude that 'What we are perhaps witnessing is the beginning of a process in which criticism of Europe becomes normalized within national party politics.'[72] This of course leaves open the question of a broader disenchantment with the EU. Trenz and de Wilde offer a useful overview in the light of the long-standing fact that European integration has always been more popular among elites than among populations as a whole and the shift from a 'permissive consensus' to a 'constraining dissensus'.[73]

If Europe, then, has not become 'an ethically charged notion in pan-Euro- pean public discourses', it is nevertheless striking that it has attracted such significant attention from thinkers in or influenced by the critical theory tradi- tion on both sides of the Atlantic. The 'Eurosociology' (in a broad sense of the term) of critical theory is an impressive example of its globalization – an issue I shall discuss briefly in the concluding chapter.

Notes

1 On Haas, see John Gerard Ruggie et al., 'Transformations in World Politics: The Intellectual Contributions of Ernst B. Haas', *Annual Review of Political Science*, 8, 2005, pp. 271–96.

2 Dews, *Habermas: Autonomy and Solidarity*.

3 'Habermas und Europa: sein Niveau entzündet', *Frankfurter Allgemeine Zeitung*, 25 June 2008. His intervention with Derrida against the second Iraq

war displayed a similar passion and even greater urgency and did of course itself include a specifically European reference. See Habermas, Jürgen and Jacques Derrida, 'February 15, or What Binds Europeans Together: A Plea for a Common Foreign Policy, Beginning in the Core of Europe', *Constellations*, 10(3), 2003, pp. 291–97.

4 Ulrich, Beck and Edgar Grande. *Cosmopolitan Europe*, Cambridge: Polity, 2007; Chris Rumford, *The European Union*, Oxford: Blackwell, 2002; Gerard Delanty and Chris Rumford, *Rethinking Europe: Social Theory and the Implications of Europeanization*, London: Routledge, 2005.

5 E. O. Eriksen and J. E. Fossum (eds), *Democracy in the European Union – Integration through Deliberation?*, London, 2000; Niesen, Peter and Herborth, Benjamin (eds), *Anarchie der kommunikativen Freiheit. Jürgen Habermas und die Theorie der internationalen Politik*, Frankfurt: Suhrkamp, 2007.

6 Ibid., p. 11. One version of their utopia is illustrated jokingly on p. 156.

7 Ibid., p. 47.

8 Ibid., p. 60

9 Ibid., p. 196.

10 Ibid., p. 364.

11 Ibid., p. 341

12 Ibid., p. 352.

13 Ibid., p. 374. On cosmopolitanism in relation to the 2004 Enlargement, see Outhwaite, 'The EU and its Enlargements: "Cosmopolitanism by Small Steps"' in Gerard Delanty (ed.), *Europe and Asia beyond East and West*, London: Routledge, 2006, pp. 193–202.

14 Anne Sophie Krossa and Roland Robertson (eds), *European Cosmopolitanism in Question*, Basingstoke: Palgrave, 2011, p. 3. See in particular the chapters by Andreas Langenohl and Jürgen Schraten.

15 The chapter by Craig Calhoun addresses this issue.

16 Chris Rumford (ed.), *Cosmopolitanism and Europe*, Liverpool University Press, 2007. See also Craig Calhoun, 'European Studies: Always Already There and Still in Formation,' *Comparative European Politics*, 1, 2003, pp. 5–20.

17 Delanty and Rumford, *Rethinking Europe*, p. 181. Both authors are more sensitive than Beck to the dangers of Eurocentrism; see in particular Delanty's edited volume *Europe and Asia beyond East and West*, (London: Routledge, 2006.

18 Erik O. Eriksen and Jarle Weigård, *Understanding Habermas. Communicative Action and Deliberative Democracy*, London: Continuum, 2003.

19 E. O. Eriksen and J. E. Fossum (eds), *Democracy in the European Union – Integration through Deliberation?*, London: Routledge, 2000, p. 3. They note later (p. 25, n. 4) that Ernst Haas, one of the fathers of integration theory, made deliberation a definitional property of supranational decision-making: '. . . a complex pattern of accommodation in which the participants refrain from unconditionally vetoing proposals and instead seek to attain agreement by means of compromises upgrading common interests.'

20 'Conclusion', in Eriksen, Erik Oddvar (ed.), *Making the European Polity. Reflexive Integration in the EU*, London: Routledge, 2005, p. 267.

21 S. S. Andersen and T. Burns, 'The European Union and the Erosion of Parliamentary Democracy: A Study of Post-parliamentary Governance', in S. S. Andersen and K. A. Eliassen (eds), *The European Union: How Democratic is it?*, London: Sage, 1996, p. 227, cited by Eriksen, 'Deliberative Supranatinalism in the EU', in Eriksen and Fossum, *Democracy in the European Union*, p. 56.

22 Frank Schimmelfennig, *The EU, NATO and the Integration of Europe*, Cambridge: Cambridge University Press, 2003; see also Milada Anna Vachudova, *Europe Undivided*, Oxford: Oxford University Press, 2005, pp. 244–5.

23 'Conclusion', in Erik Oddvar Eriksen (ed.), *Making the European Polity. Reflexive Integration in the EU*, London: Routledge, 2005, p. 267.

24 For a more optimistic view, see Bowman, Jonathan, 'Challenging Habermas' Response to the European Union Democratic Deficit', *Philosophy and Social Criticism*, 33(6), 2007, pp. 736–55.

25 Müller, 'Internationale Verhandlungen, Argumente und Verständigungshandeln. Verteidigung, Befunde, Warnung', in Niesen, Peter and Herborth, Benjamin (eds), *Anarchie der kommunikativen Freiheit. Jürgen Habermas und die Theorie der internationalen Politik*, Frankfurt: Suhrkamp, 2007, p. 200.

26 Müller, *Internationale Verhandlungen*, p. 208.

27 Eriksen, 'Deliberation and the Problem of Democratic Legitimacy in the EU', ARENA Working Paper 79, 2006. Reprinted in Niesen and Herborth, *Anarchie*, pp. 294–320.

28 Peter Norman, *The Accidental Constitution: The Story of the European Convention*, Brussels: EuroComment, 2005.

29 Fraser Cameron, (ed.), *The Future of Europe. Integration and Enlargement*, London: Routledge, 2004. Research by Ruth Wodak and her colleagues suggests however a rather more pessimistic assessment of the Convention. See M. Krzyżanowski (2005) '"European Identity Wanted": On Discursive and Communicative Dimensions of the European Convention', in R. Wodak and P. Chilton (eds), *A New Agenda for Critical Discourse Analysis: Theory, Methodology, and Interdisciplinarity*, Amsterdam, Philadelphia: J. Benjamins, pp. 137–63; F. Oberhuber, 'Deliberation or "Mainstreaming"? Empirically Researching the European Convention', op. cit., 2005, pp. 165–87; Krzyżanowski and Oberhuber, *(Un)Doing Europe? Discourses and Practices of Negotiating the EU Constitution*, Brussels: Peter Lang, 2007. Also Daniel Göler, *Deliberation, ein Zukunftsmodell europäischer Entscheidungsfindung? Analyse der Beratungen des Verfassungskonvents 2002–2003*, 2006.

30 Heidrun Friese and Peter Wagner, 'The Nascent Political Philosophy of the European Polity', *Journal of Political Philosophy*, 10(3), 2002, pp. 342–64.

31 'Demokratie und Wohlfahrtsstaat: Eine europäische Regimeform unter dem Stress der europäischen Integration', in Streeck (ed.), *Internationale Wirtschaft, nationale Demokratie*, Wolfgang Frankfurt: Campus, 1998, pp. 99–136; shorter version in English: 'The Democratic Welfare State in an Integrating Europe',

in Michael Greven and Louis Pauly (eds), *Democracy Beyond the State? The European Dilemma and the Emerging Global Order*, Lanham: Rowman and Littlefield, 2000, pp. 63–89. See also Offe, 'The European Model of "Social" Capitalism: Can it Survive European Integration?', in Max Miller (ed.), *Worlds of Capitalism. Institutions, Governance and Economic Change in the Era of Globalization*, London: Routledge, 2005, pp. 146–78.

32 Offe, 'Demokratie und Wohlfahrtsstaat', p. 99 (Friese and Wagner's translation, p. 346). There is certainly some evidence that people are more willing to contribute to the welfare of those they consider like themselves; see Philippe van Parijs (ed.), *Cultural Diversity versus Economic Solidarity*, Brussels: De Boeck Université (Bibliothèque scientifique Francqui), 2004. On the other hand, many Europeans trust the EU more than their national governments and sometimes people of other nationalities more than their own. Friese and Wagner (p. 347) conclude, reasonably enough, that '. . . Grimm and Offe fail to provide any convincing reason why relations of communication, trust and solidarity should not possibly grow further . . .'

33 On the problematic nature of this appropriation, see Joel Isaac, 'Republicanism; A European Inheritance?', *European Journal of Social Theory*, 8(1), February 2005, pp. 73–86.

34 Richard Bellamy, *Liberalism and Pluralism*, London: Routledge, 1999, p. 224. See also Richard Bellamy and Dario Castiglione, 'Democracy, Sovereignty and the Constitution of the European Union: The Republican Alternative to Liberalism', in Z. Bankowski and A. Scott (eds), *The European Union and its Order*, Oxford: Blackwell, 2000, pp. 170–90; also the discussion in Friese and Wagner, pp. 354–5.

35 Maynor, 'Constitutional Patriotism or Neo-republican Citizenship: A Way Forward for the EU?', in Per Mouritsen and Knud Erik Jørgensen (eds), *Constituting Communities. Political Solutions to Cultural Conflict*, Basingstoke: Palgrave, 2008, p. 194. See also Omid Payrow Shabani, 'Constitutional Patriotism as a Model of Postnational Political Association: The Case of the EU', *Philosophy and Social Criticism*, 32(6), pp. 699–718. For a critical discussion of the concept, see Jan-Werner Müller, *Constitutional Patriotism*, Princeton University Press, 2007 and Müller, 'Three Objections to Constitutional Patriotism', *Constellations*, 14(2), 2007, pp. 197–209.

36 Maynor, 'Constitutional Patriotism', p. 187.

37 Friese and Wagner, p. 356ff. See also Nanz, Patrizia, *Europolis. Constitutional Patriotism beyond the Nation State*, Manchester University Press, 2006.

38 Vivien Schmidt, *Democracy in Europe. The EU and National Polities*, Oxford University Press, 2006. See also Outhwaite, 'Legality and Legitimacy in the European Union', in Chris Thornhill and Samatha Ashenden (eds), *Legality and Legitimacy: Normative and Sociological Approaches*, Baden-Baden: Nomos, 2010, pp. 279–90.

39 Claus Offe and Ulrich Preuss (2006) 'The Problem of Legitimacy in the European Polity. Is Democratization the Answer?', in Colin Crouch and Wolfgang Streeck (eds), *The Diversity of Democracy. Corporatism, Social Order and Political Conflict*, Cheltenham: Edward Elgar, p. 177. See also

Preuss, The Constitution of a European Democracy and the Role of the Nation State', *Ratio Juris*, 12(4), December 1999, pp. 417–28; Europa als politische Gemeinschaft', in Gunnar Folke Schuppert and Ulrich Haltern (eds), *Europawissenschaft*, Baden-Baden: Nomos, 2005, pp. 495–539.

40 Offe and Preuss, 'Problem of Legitimacy', p. 179.

41 Ibid., p. 200.

42 Eder and Dubiel have stressed the importance of integration through regulated conflicts; see, for instance, Helmut Dubiel, 'Cultivated Conflicts', *Political Theory*, 26(2), April 1998, pp. 209–20.

43 Cathleen Kantner, *European Journal of Social Theory*, 9(4), November 2006, pp. 501–23.

44 See, for example, the Final Report, edited by Matthias L. Maier and Thomas Risse, of the Thematic Network 'Europeanization, Collective Identities and Public Discourses (IDNET)', Robert Schuman Centre for Advanced Studies, EUI, 2003. The project was coordinated by Risse and the partners included Jeffrey Checkel from ARENA, Giesen from Konstanz and Eder and Spohn from Berlin as well as Laura Benigni and Anna Triandafyllidou from Rome.

45 Klaus Eder and Bernhard Giesen (eds), *European Citizenship. Between National Legacies and Postnational Projects*, Oxford: Oxford University Press, 2001.

46 Ibid., pp. 262–6.

47 Ibid., p. 264.

48 For a comprehensive discussion, see Jo Shaw, *The Transformation of Citizenship in the European Union. Electoral Rights and the Restructuring of Political Space*, Cambridge University Press, 2007; also Jo Shaw, Richard Bellamy and Dario Castiglione (eds), *Making European Citizens*, Basingstoke: Palgrave, 2006. Barbara Einhorn, in her *Citizenship in Contemporary Europe*, Basingstoke: Palgrave, 2006, 2nd edn, 2010, uses the term in the broader sense of Eder and Giesen's volume.

49 Eder, 'Integration through Culture? The Paradox of the Search for a European Identity', in Eder and Giesen, pp. 222–44. Eder is also closer than most critical theorists to functionalist as well as evolutionary forms of analysis; see Trenz and Eder, 'The Democratising Dynamics of a Public Sphere: Towards a Theory of Democratic Functionalism', *European Journal of Social Theory*, 6, 2004, pp. 5–25; Klaus Eder, and Hans-Jörg Trenz, 'Prerequisites of Transnational Democracy and Mechanisms for Sustaining It: The Case of the European Union', in Beate Kohler-Koch and Berthold Bittberger (eds), *Debating the Democratic Legitimacy of the European Union* Lanham: Rowman and Littlefield, 2007, pp. 165–88.

50 Eder, 'Integration through Culture?', p. 230.

51 Ibid., pp. 238–9.

52 Klaus Eder, 'Remembering National Memories Together: The Formation of a Transnational Identity in Europe', in Eder and Willfried Spohn (eds), *Collective Memory and European Identity*, Klaus, Aldershot: Ashgate, 2005, pp. 187–220. The quotation is from Adorno's *Negative Dialektik*, p. 151. Eder also discusses the critique by Rogers Brubaker and F. Cooper, 'Beyond "Identity"', *Theory, Culture and Society,* 29, pp. 1–47.

53 Ibid., p. 205.

54 Ibid., p. 207.

55 Eder, 'Symbolic Power and Cultural Differences: A Power Model of Political Solutions to Cultural Differences', in Per Mouritsen and Knud Erik Jørgensen (eds), *Constituting Communities. Political Solutions to Cultural Conflict,* Basingstoke: Palgrave, 2008, p. 33.

56 Eder, 'Symbolic Power', p. 42.

57 Ibid., p. 44.

58 Ibid., p. 46.

59 Klaus Eder, 'Europe as a Narrative Network. Taking the Social Embeddedness of Identity Constructions Seriously', in Sonia Lucarelli, Furio Cerutti and Vivien A. Schmidt (eds), *Debating Political Identity and Legitimacy in the European Union,* London: Routledge, 2011, pp. 38–54. See also his earlier paper: 'Europe's borders. The narrative construction of the boundaries of Europe', *European Journal of Social Theory,* 9, 2006, pp. 255–71.

60 Eder, 'Europe as a Narrative Network', p. 42. As he notes (p. 41, n. 8), this is an approach pioneered by Karl Deutsch.

61 Eder, 'Europe as a Narrative Network', p. 51.

62 Hans-Jörg Trenz, 'In search for Popular Subjectness. Identity formation, constitution making and the democratic consolidation of the EU', *Arena Working Paper,* 7, April 2009, p. 1.

63 Anna Triandafyllidou, Ruth Wodak and Michał Krzyżanowski (eds), *The European Public Sphere and the Media: Europe in Crisis,* Basingstoke: Palgrave, 2009, p. 1.

64 Hartmut Wessler et al., *Transnationalization of Public Spheres.* Basingstoke: Palgrave Macmillan. See also Wessler (ed.), *Public Deliberation and Public Culture. The Writings of Bernhard Peters, 1993–2005,* Basingstoke: Palgrave Macmillan, 2008. The book has a preface by Habermas.

65 Paul Statham, 'What Kind of Europeanized Public Politics?', in Ruud Koopmans and Paul Statham (eds), *The Making of a European Public Sphere. Media Discourse and Political Contention,* Cambridge University Press, 2010, p. 292.

66 Ibid., p. 306.

67 Ruud Koopmans, 'Who inhabits the European public sphere? Winners and losers, supporters and opponents in Europeanised political debates', *European Journal of Political Research,* 46, 2007, p. 185.

68 Michał Krzyżanowski, Anna Triandafyllidou and Ruth Wodak, 'Conclusions: Europe, Media, Crisis and the European Public Sphere', in Anna Triandafyllidou, Ruth Wodak and Michał Krzyżanowski (eds), *The European Public Sphere and the Media. Europe in Crisis,* Basingstoke: Palgrave Macmillan, 2009, p. 262. As they also note (p. 268), '. . . the international character of the European Public Sphere does not support the conception of Europe as an ethically charged notion in pan-European public discourses.' See also Katharina Kleinen-von

Königslöw, 'Die Mehrfachsegmentierung der europäischen Öffentlichkeit', TranState Working Papers No. 138.

69 Statham's stress (p. 286) on the peculiarity of UK discourse on the EU is fully documented in the rest of the study, which covered five other member states (France, Germany, Italy, Netherlands and Spain) and one non-member, Switzerland.

70 As Statham et al note, '. . . growing criticism of Europe is not coterminous with emergent Euroscepticism. Significantly high Eurocriticisms among Dutch center parties in our sample were actually indicative of a normalized Europhile party politics.' Paul Statham, Ruud Koopmans, Anke Tresch and Julie Firmstone, 'Political Party Contestation. Emerging Euroscepticism or a Normalization of Eurocriticism?', in Koopmans and Statham (eds), *The Making of a European Public Sphere*, p. 273.

71 Statham et al., p. 271. See also Table 10.4, p. 264.

72 Ibid., p. 272.

73 Hans-Jörg Trenz and Peter de Wilde 'Denouncing European Integration. Euroscepticism as Reactive Identity Formation', Arena Working Paper 14, September 2009. See also Liesbet Hooghe and Gary Marks, 'A Post-functionalist Theory of European Integration: From Permissive Consensus to Constraining Dissensus', *British Journal of Political Science*, 39(1), 2008, pp. 1–23. Their Figure 4, p. 11, shows the gap between roughly constant elite support in 1996 across the member states and a 50 per cent difference in popular support ranging from Ireland to Sweden, while their Figure 3 shows the decline in support from around 46 per cent in the mid-1980s to the high 30s in 2003–05.

7

Conclusion: critical theory in Germany, Europe and North America: its continuing relevance

Charles Turner has brilliantly raised the interesting question of the relative importance of European and more specifically German motifs in Habermas's thought.[1] The same question can be raised in relation to critical theory as a whole. As we have seen, the first generation theorists focussed particularly on the German variant of fascism and its exceptionally virulent anti-Semitism, while of course locating it in the general fascistization of Europe. Their exile in the United States shaped their thought in all sorts of ways.[2] Two core associates of the Institute, Marcuse and Löwenthal, remained in the United States, as did a number of important thinkers less close to the core but, as noted in Chapter 1, often more engaged and insightful in their political analysis. As Hohendahl pointed out, the North American branch of critical theory substantially shaped its image there, and to some extent in Europe too, notably in the United Kingdom and France, until translations gradually began to come on stream in the 1970s.[3]

When they returned to Germany, Adorno and Horkheimer understandably directed most of their attention to specifically West German developments, just as Marcuse drew his examples for *One Dimensional Man* primarily from the United States. Habermas, too, was particularly preoccupied with the West German context, although his book on the public sphere covered the history of Europe as a whole and particularly of Britain. In his later work of the 1970s and 1980s, the focus tends to be on West Germany and, secondarily, on the United States, which he visited with increasing frequency.[4] Axel Honneth, in an interview with Habermas in 1981, suggested that his model of crises, concerning the relationship between system and life-world, might be 'too much centred on West Germany'.[5] Similarly, in their interview with Claus Offe, David Held and John Keane suggest that state theory has tended to overlook issues of territoriality, which had already been problematized in the rapprochement between sociology and international relations[6] and in the context of the growth of cosmopolitan democratic theory. Offe resists the criticism but refers ironically a little later in the interview to his alleged 'parochialism and domestic orientations'.[7]

Critical theory, as I have presented it here, is substantially rooted in Germany but also increasingly European in its focus and transatlantic in its protagonists. As the previous chapter documents, US-based scholars (though often with a European background) – such as Arato, Benhabib, Bohman, Cohen, Fraser, Rehg and others – have intervened to shape debates on post-communist constitutionalization, the future of the EU, and issues of social citizenship in Europe. The fact that Habermas engaged so fully with these issues has undoubtedly contributed to this development.

Susan Sontag provides an ironic memoir on transatlantic intellectual relations in her speech on receiving the Peace Prize of the German Booksellers' Association in 2003. She recalls growing up in the war years in Arizona, devouring what German literature she could obtain, while also fearing that German prisoners of war would escape from a camp in the north of the state and kill her. She then found that Fritz Arnold, her editor at the Hanser-Verlag, had been a prisoner in that same camp, keeping himself sane by reading English and American classics.[8] Critical theory too has gone global, as it has always been in one way or another, and its recent focus on the transformation of Europe is one important element of this process.

As we saw in particular in the last chapter, the stream of critical theory has merged with a number of other currents in various deltas of applied social research and theory. The work of Bernhard Peters is a good example. Personally close to Habermas, who supervised his PhD, Peters drew substantially from Habermas's theory of the public sphere as well as from other strands of Western Marxism, while remaining sceptical about some of the normative claims of discourse theory. He welcomed, and may have inspired, some of the ways in which Habermas modified his model to respond to such doubts.[9] An intellectual attachment to critical theory is not a question of creeds, conversion or apostasy; nor are such attachments always mediated by professional personal ties. Critical theory still exists, I think, as a broad theory family, with substantial continuities as well as divergences.

In this final chapter, I look more closely at the relationship between this 'Frankfurt' strand of critical theory and related theoretical families.[10] First, we should look at the relationship of contemporary critical theory to other neo-Marxist theories. Comparing the situation today with that in the 1970s, it is clear that the multiple versions of Marxism have become even more diversified and that a simple juxtaposition of critical theory and Marxism is no longer meaningful. Some Marxist writers continue to accuse Habermasian or other variants of critical theory of being non- or post-Marxist.[11] On the other hand, Göran Therborn, in *Marxism and Neo-Marxism*, argues that Habermas is closer to neo-Marxism, a category in which he includes, for example, Perry Anderson, than Adorno and Horkheimer. Among explicit post-Marxists, Chantal Mouffe has criticized Habermas for his excessive rationalism[12] and suspicion of rhetoric, though one may question how far they are apart in practice.[13]

The relation between critical theory and Foucault has already been mentioned in relation to Habermas's *Philosophical Discourse of Modernity* and Honneth's *Critique of Power*. Habermas came to revise many of his criticisms of Foucault, just as Foucault, shortly before his death, expressed considerable admiration for critical theory. Honneth argues convincingly for the complementarity of Habermas and Foucault, though essentially in an argument in which Habermas introduces a focus on social interaction, which is lacking both in earlier critical theory and in Foucault.[14] Habermas, however, Honneth goes on to argue, pays insufficient attention to questions of power and domination: these are of course central to Foucault's approach.[15] Thus Habermas 'does not admit acting groups in the categorial framework of his social theory; instead, he attaches the level of systems of action conceived as systems directly to the level of individual acting subjects . . .'[16] Honneth's own subsequently developed model is certainly an attempt to go beyond these limitations.

Although Honneth has not written substantially on Foucault since then, he published an article on Foucault and Adorno in *Critique*,[17] co-edited a conference volume on Foucault and himself contributed two chapters to it.[18] In the *Critique* article, he points out their common focus on domination and violence (*Gewalt*): 'For Adorno and for Foucault, the rationalisation of society means doing violence to the human body . . .'[19] If they nevertheless provide 'two forms of critique of modernity', it is because they differ in their analyses of what is done to the human subject:

. . . Adorno sees the totalitarian operations of control realised through the psychic manipulations of the mass media, that is, by the agencies of the culture industry, whereas Foucault believes that the integrating operations are secured rather through those corporal disciplinary procedures performed by such loosely related institutions as the school, the factory or the prison.[20]

Foucault's might therefore seem the more robust diagnosis, but whereas Adorno still wants to save the threatened subject, Foucault seems to write it off and is thus unable, within the terms of his theory, to thematize the suffering which concerns him *as* suffering.[21] In a subsequent article on the concept of critique in critical theory, Honneth stresses the impact of a 'genealogical' approach represented by Nietzsche for the early critical theorists and also by Foucault for the post-war generations:

The constructive grounding of a critical standpoint should secure a conception of rationality which establishes a systematic link between social rationality and moral validity. It should be shown reconstructively that this rationality potential determines social reality in the form of moral ideals. And these moral ideals should in turn be subject to the genealogical proviso that their original meaning may have been socially stretched to the point of unrecognizability. Only at this level, I fear, can one defend today what was once intended by the idea of social criticism in critical theory.[22]

The relationship between Foucauldian genealogy and critical theory has also been addressed, from a more Foucauldian perspective, by Samantha Ashenden and David Owen.[23] Ashenden and Owen have been concerned to correct misunderstandings of Foucauldian genealogy in the Critical Theory tradition and to stress the complementarity of genealogy, which he elucidates by means of a comparison with Wittgenstein's analysis of being captured by a particular conceptual 'picture', and the critique of ideology: '. . . just as *Ideologiekritik* is directed to freeing us from ideological captivity and false consciousness, so genealogy is directed to freeing us from aspectival captivity or restricted consciousness'.[24] Thus Nietzsche's genealogy of morality aimed to show that our received image of moral conduct has lost its meaning in the light of the death of God and has to be redrawn. Foucault, similarly, argues against our entrapment in a conception of power in terms of political sovereignty, in which we have not yet 'cut off the head of the king'.[25] He glosses this approach in a later text: genealogy '. . . will separate out, from the contingency that has made us what we are, the possibility of no longer being, doing, or thinking what we are, do, or think . . . seeking to give new impetus . . . to the undefined work of freedom.'[26]

The other major tradition of critical social theory is that initiated by Pierre Bourdieu. Habermas had great respect for Bourdieu, as indicated in an obituary he wrote, describing him as 'one of the last great sociologists of the twentieth century' and as someone who made nonsense of the idea of 'a barrier between political and intellectual engagement.'[27] He did not however engage directly with his work.[28] As in the case of Foucault, Derrida, Lyotard and others, it was left to subsequent generations to discern complementarities between Frankfurt critical theory and these other perspectives, themselves of course included under a broader rubric of 'critical theory' or just 'theory'. Honneth's *The Fragmented World of the Social* contains an essay on Bourdieu which stresses the importance of his work but criticizes his economistic or utilitarian model of action.[29] More recently, Simon Susen has provided a magisterial analysis of Habermas and Bourdieu and their complementary perspectives on the social. The possibilities of 'cross-fertilization' are essentially based in recognizing the coexistence of communicative and strategic action as pervasive features of social life.[30]

Bourdieu's analyses of the reproduction of class inequalities in the spheres of culture and ideology have of course much in common with Habermas's approach, and his focus on suffering in *The Weight of the World* also links him, in topic if not in methodology, with the work of the first generation critical theorists and also with Honneth's later work on disrespect. Bourdieu and Habermas diverged in their approach to globalization. Habermas, with his very German suspicion of nationalism, tended to stress the positive aspects of the 'postnational constellation', while Bourdieu polemicised against neoliberal '*pensée unique*'.[31] For him, globalization is essentially an ideological concept: '. . . not a new phase of capitalism but a "rhetoric" invoked by governments to justify their voluntary submission to the financial markets.'[32] Beck addressed the theme of globalization most substantially in *What is Globalization?* and in his subsequent analyses of 'world risk society'. Beck, as we saw, converges with Habermas in his enthusiasm for cosmopolitan democracy and for the project of European integration. For Bourdieu, Europe operates more as a platform on which to mount a political resistance to neoliberalism. As he wrote in 1998, among the 'collectives' resisting neoliberalism in the public interest a special place should belong to '. . . the state: the nation-state, or better yet the supranational state – a European state on the way toward a world state – capable of effectively controlling and taxing the profits earned in the financial markets and, above all, of counteracting the destructive impact that the latter have on the labour market.'[33] He restated this theme in 2001, in one of his last texts, the preface to *Firing Back*:

Paradoxically, it is *states* that have initiated the economic measures (of deregulation) that have led to their economic disempowerment . . . national states operate as *masks*, which . . . deflect mobilization, indignation, and protest from their true target.

Politics has been continually moving further and further away from the citizenry. But one has reason to believe that some of the aims of effective political action are located at the European level . . . And we may take as a goal to restore politics to Europe or Europe to politics by fighting for the democratic transformation of the profoundly undemocratic institutions with which it is presently endowed . . . If they are genuinely to be transformed, it can only be by a vast European social movement . . .[34]

A third critical perspective, emerging out of Bourdieu's, is that of Luc Boltanski and his various collaborators, notably Laurent Thévenot and Ève Chiapello. Boltanski, who had worked closely with Bourdieu in the early 1970s, set up a distinct research group, the 'Groupe de sociologie politique et morale', in 1984. Boltanski has tended to characterize his approach as a 'sociology of critique' (and, more recently, as a 'pragmatic sociology of critique'), as distinct from Bourdieu's 'critical sociology'. He is concerned, in other words, with the ways in which people engage in critique, rather as Goffman or ethnomethodologists examine the production of social order in everyday interaction. This is of course what Bourdieu was also doing – looking at the ways in which class inequalities are reproduced in culture: in forms of speech, consumption and so on. Where Boltanski differs from Bourdieu is in a greater emphasis on the contingency of social order, what in a recent interview is termed 'the fragility of reality'.[35] Working with Bourdieu, he says, he was more attracted to the practical and flexible application of his theoretical categories than to their more formal aspect which appeared in his published work and in that of his associates.[36] In his more recent work, he adds, he has become increasingly focussed on the way in which people experience domination and try to make coherent sense of their lives, whether by their personal interpretations of their situation and aspirations or by more political ones.[37]

Once again, a relationship which did not exist between Habermas and Bourdieu has been retrospectively created by later thinkers. Boltanski has had a substantial dialogue with Honneth; *De la Critique* was based on his Adorno Lectures in Frankfurt and, as we have seen, Honneth has also published a fair amount in France. Boltanski suggests, however, that their starting points are different: Honneth presupposes a philosophical anthropology based on the idea of a need for recognition, whereas Boltanski is concerned with a more contingent interplay of situations and interests.[38] Honneth, in turn, in a sensitive discussion of *On Justification* which welcomes Boltanski and Thévenot's focus on moral evaluation, argues that they 'have the tendency to always quickly bracket the structural-theoretical assumptions that are at the same time necessary for their argument . . . claims that refer to the ability of inter-subjectively shared norms and practices to create social structures in the form of institutions.'[39] In other words, Boltanski and Thévenot 'cannot leave it at a mere "sociology of critique". Driven by its own object, the analysis of society is propelled towards a critique of the forms of the social that it encounters.'[40]

De la critique seems to go further than Boltanski's earlier work towards recognizing the force of this line of criticism. Bourdieu's critical sociology, he writes, is 'the boldest enterprise ever attempted to combine in a single theoretical structure the most demanding requirements for sociological prac-tice and radically critical positions'.[41] For Bourdieu, 'sociology is both the instrument to describe domination and the instrument for emancipation from domination'.[42] Boltanski's argument is not with this aspiration but with the 'distance' which Bourdieu's sociology maintains from 'the critical capacities developed by actors in everyday situations. Boltanski's 'pragmatic sociology of critique', by contrast, fully recognizes the critical capacities of actors and the creativity with which they engage in interpretation and situated action.'[43] As he summarizes his argument in the following chapter,

> [t]he first programme, that of critical sociology, rests on compromise formations between distant (*surplombant*) sociological descriptions and normative stances, visions, aiming primarily to inform actors about the domination to which they are subjected without knowing it and to give them the resources to develop their critical capacities. The second – that of the pragmatic sociology of critique, starts instead from the actors' critical capacities and aims initially to use sociological methods to make them explicit. Then, secondly, it aims to establish normative positions . . . relying on modelling these ordinary critiques and the *moral sense* or the *sense of justice* which they display.[44]

Both programmes, he concludes, are concerned with the means by which actors attempt to overcome their subjection to domination and exploitation.

Of Boltanski's many works, the most relevant in the present context is per-haps a major study he published together with Thévenot: *On Justification*.[45] Building on their earlier work on the way in which people categorize posi-tions in the social structure and the way in which they argue for their assign-ments, they focus on the activity of critical justification and the frames of reference invoked in what they call 'tests' (*épreuves*). Analysing a set of man-uals for managers and, in one case, trade unionists, they identify six 'worlds': an 'inspired' world, in which greatness is measured in terms of creativity; a 'domestic' world, governed by hierarchies of personal dependence; a world of 'opinion' or fame; a 'civic' world, oriented to a conception of the public interest; a mercantile world, based on market principles; and an 'industrial' world, in which worth or greatness is measured by efficiency. Each of these frames of reference has a sphere or spheres in which it can legitimately be deployed. As Boltanski explained in a text which emerged from an interview,

> [i]f I say for example, 'I don't want anything to do with this student' and, if I am asked why, I reply 'because I don't like the way he looks', this is not a justification which will be considered acceptable in a faculty meeting.[46]

To give a rather fuller example, the series editor might argue for the publication of this book in any of the following terms:

1 It is very creative and original.

2 William is an old friend of mine, and it would be good to involve him in the project.

3 He has a major reputation.

4 It will be an important contribution to the scholarly field.

5 It will make a lot of money for the publisher.

6 It is an effective and readable presentation of useful material.

All six, in my experience, are invoked in discussions of this sort of, though 2 is only marginally acceptable, and the appropriateness of 3 might also be questioned. Anonymous 'double-blind' peer review, widely used in journals, is an attempt to exclude the operation of 2 and 3. The interest of this model is, I think, not so much in the precise number or specification of the various orders, but the ways in which speakers move between them.

Given the fact that the European Union is so substantially a discursive forum based on argument and justification,[47] it is surprising that Boltanski's approach has not been more widely invoked in the massive volume of literature devoted to it. To sketch out an analysis which David Spence and I will present in more detail in an article on which we are currently working, member state representatives must, for example, steer an intermediate path between the naked pursuit of what they perceive as their national interest and a wholly selfless devotion to the common European good. It is equally unacceptable for a minister to say in the Council that he or she is only concerned with the national interest (though Thatcher came close to this) as it is to go home and say that, although the result of the meeting has been disastrous for their own member state, the decisions taken were in the general interest of the Union and that's what really matters. The tension between national (member state) and Union interest is fundamental to the EU. It is in part structural, in the formal division between servants of the Community such as the European Commissioners and Commission officials and the judges of the European Court, on the one hand, and the ministers and permanent representatives of the member states, on the other, with members of the Parliament located somewhere in between.[48] Much, however, depends on informal accommodations between incumbents of these various positions, as stressed, for example, by Keith Middlemas in his masterly study of 'the informal politics of the European Union.[49] In Middlemas's analysis:

> Informal politics are defined not so much by the players' status – any who wish and can establish credentials to the satisfaction of others can enter – as by the mode chosen to establish relationships. All players can choose between formal and informal modes and shades of grey between them. There is no dividing line – only a spectrum. Rules and conventions are policed on both sides, with many nuanced penalties for infringement.
>
> . . . To a minimum extent, all players, like member states themselves, must demonstrate an element of altruism (European-mindedness) as well as basic self-interest . . .[50]

Thomas Risse has paved the way for an approach of this kind from the direction of Habermasian critical theory as applied to international relations. In a substantial article of 2000,[51] he argued that the contrast, often drawn in the existing literature between what March and Olsen called 'logic of consequentalism', following rational choice approaches, and a 'logic of appropriateness', oriented to situational norms and other constraints,[52] might usefully be complemented by a third logic of argumentation or, in Habermasian terms, communicative action. In some situations, negotiators change their minds, or at least their positions, in response to arguments and discussion in ways which go beyond what look like their interests or the formal requirements of the situation. He gives the example of Gorbachev's concession in relation to German membership of NATO, which astonished his own delegation.[53] In other cases, such as debates over human rights violations, there may be an international public audience to which negotiators have to orient their positions.

Arguing processes are more likely to occur both in negotiating settings and in the public sphere,

> the more actors are uncertain about their interests and even identities

the less actors know about the situation in which they find themselves and about the underlying 'rules of the game' ('common knowledge'), and

the more apparently irreconcilable differences prevent them from reaching an optimal rather than a merely satisfactory solution for a widely perceived problem ('problem solving').[54]

These issues have been discussed in relation to EU politics in the previous chapter. What an approach drawing on Boltanski might contribute is a sharper focus on modes of justification, which would also be a way of extending a Habermasian perspective to engage with questions of the legitimate use of rhetoric, of which Habermas himself is notoriously suspicious. Studies by linguists, for example those by Ruth Wodak and colleagues, are increasingly feeding into the Europeanist mainstream.[55] This is one of several promising avenues of what Simon Susen calls 'cross-fertilisation' between Frankfurt critical theory and related programmes.[56]

Axel Honneth, in his introduction to the first volume of the Institute's new book series, wrote that it should not give the impression that the authors were 'well on the way to revive the programme of interdisciplinary social research originally initiated by Horkheimer'. They were not likely to presuppose 'a unitary theory of society which would make it possible to link the various disciplines in such a way that they would enable analysis of society as a whole.'[57] Yet something surely remains of this original aspiration in the more diversified research in critical theory being continued in Frankfurt and elsewhere in the world.

Notes

1 Charles Turner, 'Jürgen Habermas: European or German?', *European Journal of Political Theory*, 3(3), 2004, pp. 293–314.

2 See, for example, T. W. Adorno, 'Scientific Experiences of a European Scholar in America', in Donald Fleming and Bernard Bailyn (eds), *The Intellectual Migration: Europe and America 1930–1960*, Cambridge: Harvard University Press, 1969, pp. 338–70; Löwenthal, Leo, *Mitmachen wollte ich nie: Ein autobiographisches Gespräch mit Helmut Dubiel*, Frankfurt: Suhrkamp, 1980, translated as *An Unmastered Past: The Autobiographical Reflections of Leo Lowenthal*, Berkeley: University of California Press, 1987; Martin Jay, *Permanent Exiles. Essays on the Intellectual Migration from Germany to America*, New York: Columbia University Press, 1985. Jay notes (p. 41) that Adorno wrote to Löwenthal: 'I believe 90 percent of all that I've published in Germany was written in America.'

3   Peter Uwe Hohendahl, 'Reappraisals of Critical Theory: The Legacy of the Frankfurt School in America', in Hohendahl (ed.), *Reappraisals: Shifting Alignments in Postwar Critical Theory,* Ithaca: Cornell University Press, 1991, pp. 198–228.

4   He said in a preface to his first lecture on returning to Frankfurt University in 1983 that one of the reasons why he was always glad to teach at US universities 'is that no-one there knows in advance and imputes to me what I have to say.' ('Bemerkungen zu Beginn einer Vorlesung', *Die Neue Unübersichtlichkeit,* p. 210.

5   'The Dialectics of Rationalization', in Peter Dews (ed.), *Habermas. Autonomy and Solidarity,* London: Verso, 2nd edn, 1992, p. 117.

6   See, in particular, Anthony Giddens' *The Nation-State and Violence,* Cambridge: Polity, 1985, followed by Michael Mann's trilogy on *The Sources of Social Power,* Cambridge: Cambridge University Press, 1986 and the work of Martin Shaw.

7   Offe, *Contradictions,* pp. 270–4.

8   'Literature is Freedom', reprinted in Daniel Levy, Max Pensky and John Torpey (eds), *Old Europe, New Europe, Core Europe. Transatlantic Relations after the Iraq War,* London: Verso, 2005, pp. 220–2.

9   Hartmut Wessler and Lutz Wingert, 'Introduction', in Wessler (ed.), *Public Deliberation and Public Culture The Writings of Bernhard Peters, 1993–2005,* Basingstoke: Palgrave Macmillan, 2008, pp. 1–17.

10   See also my article on 'Canon Formation in Late Twentieth Century British Sociology ', *Sociology,* 46(3), 2009, pp. 1–17 and my forthcoming edited book on modern social thought.

11   See, for example, Gérard Raulet, 'La théorie critique de l'<école de Francfort>. Du néo-marxisme au <post-marxisme> (pp. 141–58) and Jacques Bidet, 'Habermas en-deçà de Marx' (pp. 447–60) in Jacques Bidet and Eustache Kouvélakis (eds), *Dictionnaire Marx contemporain,* Paris: Presses Universitaires de France, 2001. Bidet's critique includes the conciliatory suggestion (p. 159) that 'The theoretical reorganisation which he proposes, oriented to the idea of communication as an experience characterised by the triple demand of truth, justice and identity, can be understood or taken up as the very idea of communism.' (my translation) Jean-Marie Vincent similarly suggests that Adorno went beyond Marx in his critique of economism, while also falling short in other respects ('Adorno et Marx', in Jacques Bidet and Eustache Kouvélakis (eds), *Dictionnaire Marx contemporain,* Paris: Presses Universitaires de France, 2001, p. 368).

12   See the discussion of agonistic and deliberative democracy in the previous chapter.

13   See, for example, Kari Karppinen, Hallvard Moe and Jakob Svensson, 'Habermas, Mouffe and Political Communication. A Case for Theoretical Eclecticism', *Javnost – the Public,* 15(3), (2008), pp. 5–12.

14   Axel Honneth, *Kritik der Macht,* Frankfurt: Suhrkamp, 1988, p. 224; tr. p. 269.

15 Ibid., pp. 295–6; tr. p. 270.

16 Ibid., p. 314; tr. p. 285.

17 Axel Honneth, 'Foucault und Adorno. Zwei Formen einer Kritik der Moderne', in Honneth, *Die zerrissene Welt des Sozialen*, Frankfurt: Suhrkamp, 1990, pp. 73–92; tr. *The Fragmented World of the Social* <New York: SUNY Press, 1995, pp. 121–31.

18 Axel Honneth and Martin Saar (eds), *Michel Foucault. Zwischenbilanz einer Rezeption*, Frankfurt: Suhrkamp, 2003.

19 Honneth, *The Fragmented World of the Social*, p. 122.

20 Ibid., p. 128.

21 Ibid., p. 131.

22 Honneth, *Pathologien der Vernunft*, p. 69.

23 See, in particular, their contributions to Ashenden, Samantha and David Owen (eds), *Foucault contra Habermas*, London: Sage, 1999. See also Owen's contribution to the debate in the *European Journal of Philosophy*, 10(2), 2002.

24 Owen, 'Criticism and Captivity: On Genealogy and Critical Theory', *European Journal of Philosophy*, 10(2), 2002, p. 220. For an example of Wittgenstein's approach, see his *Philosophische Grammatik*, §154: 'Denk doch einmal gar nicht an das Verstehen als *"seelischen* Vorgang"! – Denn das ist die Redeweise, die dich verwirrt . . .' (*Philosophical Grammar*, p.)

25 Foucault, *Discipline and Punish*, Harmondsworth: Penguin, 1978, pp. 88–9.

26 Foucault, in P. Rabinow (ed.), *Ethics: The Essential Works: Vol. 1*, Harmondsworth: Penguin, 1997, pp. 315–16, quoted by Owen, 'Criticism and Captivity', p. 224.

27 'Pierre Bourdieu', *Frankfurter Rundschau*, 25 January 2002; translated as 'Humaniste engagé', *Le Monde*, 26 January 2002.

28 For a list of passing mentions, see Simon Susen, *The Foundations of the Social*, Oxford: Bardwell Press, 2007, p. 234 and notes. As Susen notes, Bourdieu referred a good deal more often to Habermas, though mostly in negative terms.

29 'The Fragmented World of Symbolic Forms: Reflections on Pierre Bourdieu's Sociology of Culture', in *The Fragmented World of the Social*, pp. 184–201.

30 Susen, *Foundations*, esp. pp. 254–68. For a rather different perspective on Bourdieu, see Nedim Karakayali, 'Reading Bourdieu with Adorno: The Limits of Critical Theory and Reflexive Sociology', *Sociology*, 38(2), pp. 351–68. Karakayali's account draws on that by Gillian Rose, *The Melancholy Science: An Introduction to the Thought of Theodor W. Adorno*, Basingstoke, Macmillan, 1978. For Rose (p. 143), reflexive sociology is shaped by 'an epistemological concern with the ground of its own activity arising from a critical awareness of the way in which conventional sociology "constitutes" its object in its theorizing.' It therefore 'repeats more or less explicitly what positivism does implicitly, namely bases truth or reality on the analysis of consciousness, and thereby reduces social reality to a demonstrably constricted consciousness of it'. This theme is developed in a different way in Habermas's later critiques of the early Frankfurt School's entrapment in 'the philosophy of consciousness' in his *Theory of Communicative Action* and *Philosophical Discourse of Modernity*; Rose's own alternative is presented in her *Hegel Contra Sociology*, London: Athlone, 1981.

31   This is the dominant theme of one of the relatively rare issues of the *Actes* (vol. 119, September 1997) devoted to the economy; see in particular Neil Fligstein, 'Rhétorique et réalités de la "mondialisation"'. See also the issues of the *Actes* (vols 114, September 1996 and 115, December 1996) on 'new forms of domination in work.' Much of Bourdieu's more polemical work was published, for obvious reasons, in the daily and weekly press. See the articles cited below, also his critique of Hans Tietmeyer: 'L'architecte de l'euro passe aux aveux', *Le Monde diplomatique*, March 1997, p. 19; reprinted as 'The Thoughts of Chairman Tietmeyer', in Bourdieu, *Acts of Resistance. Against the New Myths of Our Time*, Cambridge, Polity, 1998, pp. 45–51. A recent issue of the *Actes* (166–7, March 2007) contains some interesting material on the EU, including an article by Didier Georgakakis and Marine Lassalle. Georgakakis also edited a special issue of *Regards Sociologiques* ('Sur l'Europe', No. 27/28, 2004), in which he regrets (p. 3) the lack of a Bourdieusian approach to the EU. He had earlier edited a special section of the journal *Politix* (vol. 11, no. 43, Troisième trimestre, 1998), pp. 5–91.

32   Pierre Bourdieu et Loïc Wacquant, 'La nouvelle vulgate planétaire', *Le Monde diplomatique*, May 2000, pp. 6–7; tr. as 'New Liberal Speak: Notes on the new planetary vulgate', *Radical Philosophy*, January–February 2001. See also Lucia Re, 'Approches européennes de la "mondialisation"', *Jura Gentium. Revue de philosophie du droit international et de la politique globale*, 1 (1) 2005.

33   'L'essence du néoliberalisme', *Le Monde diplomatique*, March 1998; tr. by Jeremy Shapiro as 'The Essence of Neoliberalism', Caracas, Biblioteca electrónica, www.analytica.com/biblioteca/bourdieu/neoliberalism.asp See also, for example, his speeches to Greek trade unionists and researchers in 1996 and again in 2001: 'Le mythe de la "mondialisation" et l'État social européen', GSEE, Athens, October 1996, reprinted in *Contre-Feux*, Paris, Raisons d'Agir, 1998, *Acts of Resistance: Against the New Myths of Our Time*, Cambridge: Polity, 1998, pp. 29–44; 'Pour un savoir engagé', *Le Monde diplomatique* Feb. 2002, p. 3; tr. as 'For a Scholarship with Commitment', in *Firing Back. Against the Tyranny of the Market 2*, London: Verso, 2003, pp. 17–25. Also his appeals for a European social movement (Pour un mouvement social européen', *Le Monde diplomatique*, June 1999; tr. in *Firing Back. Against the Tyranny of the Market 2*, London: Verso, 2003, pp. 53–63; 'Pour des États Généraux du Mouvement Social Européen', *Le Monde* 28 April 2000).

34   *Firing Back*, pp. 14–15. Something like this diagnosis has been brilliantly presented by Vivien Schmidt, in *Democracy in Europe. The EU and National Polities*, Oxford University Press, 2006; see also my chapter on , 'Legality and Legitimacy in the European Union', in Chris Thornhill and Samatha Ashenden (eds), *Legality and Legitimacy: Normative and Sociological Approaches*, Baden-Baden: Nomos, 2010, pp. 279–90.

35 Juliette Rennes and Simon Susen, 'La fragilité de la réalité. Entretien avec Luc Boltanski', *Mouvements* No. 64, October–December 2010, pp. 150–64. See also Luc Boltanski and Axel Honneth, 'Soziologie der Kritik oder Kritische Theorie? Ein Gespräch mit Robin Celikates', in Rahel Jaeggi and Tilo Wesche (eds), *Was ist Kritik?*, Frankfurt am Main: Suhrkamp, 2009, pp. 81–114.

36 Rennes and Susen, 'La fragilité de la réalité', pp. 151–2.

37 Ibid., p. 155.

38 Ibid., p. 158.

39 Honneth, 'Dissolutions of the Social: On the Social Theory of Luc Boltanski and Laurent Thévenot', *Constellations*, 17(3), 2010, p. 385.

40 Ibid. See also Simon Susen, 'Quelques réflexions sur *De la critique* de Luc Boltanski', forthcoming [ref].

41 Boltanski, *De la critique*, pp. 39–40.

42 Ibid., p. 40.

43 Boltanski, *De la critique*, p. 74; tr. p. On Boltanski's very informal use of the term 'pragmatic', see his response to Rennes and Susen, 'La fragilité de la réalité', pp. 150–1.

44 Boltanski, *De la critique*, pp. 83–4.

45 Luc Boltanski and Laurent Thévenot. *On Justification. Economies of Worth*, translated by Catherine Porter, Princeton University Press, 2006. First published in 1991. See also: Berten, André (1993) 'D'une sociologie de la justice à une sociologie du droit. À propos des travaux de L. Boltanski et L. Thévenot', *Recherches sociologiques*, 24(1–2), pp. 69–89; Luc Boltanski and Laurent Thévenot 'Finding One's Way in Social Space: A Study Based on Games', *Social Science Information*, 22(4/5), 1983, pp. 631–80; Luc Boltanski and Laurent Thévenot, *Les économies de la grandeur*, Paris: Cahiers du CEE, Presses Universitaires de France, 1987; Luc Boltanski and Laurent Thévenot, 'The Sociology of Critical Capacity', *European Journal of Social Theory*, 2(3), 1999, pp. 359–77; Luc Boltanski and Laurent Thévenot, 'The Reality of Moral Expectations: A Sociology of Situated Judgement', *Philosophical Explorations*, 3(3), 2000, pp. 208–31; Axel Honneth, 'Dissolutions of the Social: On the Social Theory of Luc Boltanski and Laurent Thévenot', *Constellations*, 17(3), 2010, 376–89; Thévenot, Laurent, 'L'action qui convient', in Patrick Pharo and Louis Quéré (eds), *Les formes de l'action*, Paris: Éditions de l'École des Hautes Études en Sciences Sociales, 1990, pp. 39–69; Thévenot, Laurent, 'Un pluralisme sans relativisme? Théories et pratiques du sens de la justice', in Joëlle Affichard and Jean-Baptiste de Foucauld (eds), *Justice sociale et inégalités*, Paris: Esprit, 1992, pp. 221–53; Thévenot, Laurent (1998) 'À l'épreuve des grands principes', *Sciences Humaines*, 79, pp. 20–3.

46 Cécile Blondeau and Jean-Christophe Sevin, 'Entretien avec Luc Boltanski, une sociologie toujours mise à l'épreuve', *ethnographiques.org*, Numéro 5, April 2004.

47 This is also reflected in the literature on the EU, both in specifically discourse analytic approaches such as those of Ruth Wodak and others and, more broadly, in works such as that by Sonia Lucarelli, Furio Cerutti and Vivien

A. Schmidt (eds), *Debating Political Identity and Legitimacy in the European Union*, London: Routledge, 2011.

48 On the Parliament, see, for example, Nils Ringe, *Who Decides and How? Uncertainty and Policy Choice in the European Parliament*, Oxford: Oxford University Press, 2009.

49 Keith Middlemas, *Orchestrating Europe. 'The Informal Politics of the European Union*, London: Fontana, 1995.

50 Middlemas, *Orchestrating Europe*, p. xx.

51 Thomas Risse, '"Let's Argue!"': Communicative Action in World Politics', *International Organization*, 54(1), Winter 2000, pp. 1–39.

52 James G. March and Johan P. Olsen, *Rediscovering Institutions*, New York: Free Press, 1989; 'Institutional Perspectives on Political Institutions', *Governance*, 93, pp. 247–64; 'The Institutional Dynamics of International Political Orders', *International Organization*, 52, 1998, pp. 943–69. See also, for critiques of their position, Ole Jacob Sending, 'Constitution, Choice and Change: Problems with the "Logic of Appropriateness" and its Use in Constructivist Theory', *European Journal of International Relations*, 8, 2002, pp. 443–70; Kjell Goldmann, 'Appropriateness and Consequences; The Logic of Neo-Institutionalism', *Governance*, 18(1), January 2005, pp. 35–52. See also Julian Clark and Alun Jones, '"Telling Stories about Politics": Europeanization and the EU's Council Working Groups', *Journal of Common Market Studies*, 49(2), 2011, pp. 341–66.

53 Risse, 'Let's Argue!' pp. 23–8.

54 Ibid., p. 33.

55 See, for example, another recent article by Clark and Jones, 'The Spatialising Politics of European Political Practice: Transacting "Eastness" in the European Union', *Environment and Planning D: Society and Space*, 29, 2011, pp. 291–308, which refers substantially to Wodak's work.

56 Susen, *Foundations of the Social*, pp. 17, 20, 25, 223–73, 303, 312–13.

57 Honneth, 'Einleitung', *Befreiung aus der Mündigkeit*, p. 11.

Bibliography

Abendroth, Wolfgang, et al. (1968) *Die Linke antwortet Jürgen Habermas,* Frankfurt, Europäische Verlagsanstalt.

Adorno, Theodor W, et al. (1950) *The Authoritarian Personality,* New York, Harper and Row.

— (1951) *Minima Moralia. Reflexionen aus dem beschädigten Leben,* Frankfurt, Suhrkamp. Translated as *Minima Moralia* London, New Left Books, 1974.

— (1972) 'Spätkapitalismus oder Industriegesellschaft?', *Gesammelte Schriften,* vol. 8, Frankfurt, Suhrkamp.

— (1969) 'Scientific Experiences of a European Scholar in America', in Donald Fleming and Bernard Bailyn (eds), *The Intellectual Migration: Europe and America 1930–1960,* Cambridge, Harvard University Press, p. 338ff.

— (1972) 'Spätkapitalismus oder Industriegesellschaft?', *Gesammelte Schriften,* vol. 8, Frankfurt, Suhrkamp.

Adorno, T. W., Albert, H., Dahrendorf, R., Habermas, J., Pilot, H. and Popper, K. R. (1976) *The Positivist Dispute in German Sociology,* London, Heinemann.

Albrecht, Clemens, et al. (1999) *Die intellektuelle Gründung der Bundesrepublik. Eine Wirkungsgeschichte der Frankfurter Schule,* Frankfurt, Campus Verlag.

Aly, Götz (2008) *Unser Kampf 1968: Ein Irritierter Blick Zurück,* Berlin, Fischer.

Anderson, Perry (1976) *Considerations on Western Marxism,* London, New Left Books.

Arato, A. (1982) 'Critical Sociology and Authoritarian State Socialism', in J. B. Thompson and D. Held (eds), *Habermas: Critical Debates,* London, Macmillan, pp. 196–218.

— (1984) 'Autoritärer Sozialismus und die Frankfurter Schule', in Axel Honneth and Albrecht Wellmer (eds), *Die Frankfurter Schule und die Folgen,* Alexander von Humboldt-Stiftung, Symposium Berlin, De Gruyter, 1986, pp. 193–206.

— (2000) *Civil Society, Constitution and Legitimacy,* Lanham, MD, Rowman and Littlefield.

Arato, Andrew and Eike Gebhardt (eds) (1978) *The Essential Frankfurt School Reader,* Oxford, Blackwell.

Arato, A. and Jean Cohen (1992) *Civil Society and Democratic Theory,* Cambridge, MIT Press.

Arato, Andrew (2009) 'Europa und Verfassung', in Hauke Brunkhorst, Regina Kreide and Cristina Lafont (eds), *Habermas-Handbuch,* Stuttgart and Weimar, Metzler, pp. 263–72.

Arnason, Johann (1971) *Von Marcuse zu Marx,* Frankfurt, Suhrkamp.

— (1979) 'A Review of Jürgen Habermas, Zur Rekonstruktion des historischen Materialismus', *Telos* 39, 201–18.

— (1993) *The Future that Failed. Origins and Destinies of the Soviet Model*, London and New York, Routledge.

Ash, Timothy Garton (1993) *In Europe's Name. Germany and the Divided Continent*, London, Jonathan Cape.

Ashenden, Samantha and David Owen (eds) (1999) *Foucault contra Habermas*, London, Sage.

Bader, Veit Michael (1999) 'Citizenship of the European Union. Human Rights, Rights of Citizens of the Union and of Member States', *Ratio Juris* 12(2), June 153–81.

Bahro, Rudolf (1978) *The Alternative in Eastern Europe*, London, NLB. Original edition 1977.

Bartosch, Ulrich and Klaudius Gansczyk (eds) (2008) *Weltinnenpolitik für das 21. Jahrhundert: Carl-Friedrich von Weizsäcker verpflichtet*, Hamburg and London, Lit.

Bavaj, Riccardo (2010) '"Western Civilization" and the Acceleration of Time. Richard Löwenthal's Reflections of a Crisis of "the West" in the Aftermath of the Student Revolt of "1968"', in *Themenportal Europäische Geschichte* www.europa.clio-online.de/2010/Article=435.

Beck, Ulrich (1992) *Risk Society,* London, Sage.

— (2003) 'Toward a New Critical Theory with a Cosmopolitan Intent', *Constellations* 10(4), 453–68.

— (2006) *The Cosmopolitan Vision*, Cambridge, Polity.

— (2008) 'Jenseits von Klasse und Nation: Individualisierung und Transnationalisierung sozialer Ungleichheiten, '*Soziale Welt* 59, 301–25.

— (2010) 'Remapping Social Inequalities in an Age of Climate Change: For a Cosmopolitan Renewal of Sociology', *Global Networks* 10(2), 165–81.

Beck, Ulrich and Edgar Grande (2007) *Cosmopolitan Europe*, Cambridge, Polity.

Beckert Jens et al. (eds) (2004) *Transnationale Solidarität. Chancen und Grenzen*, Frankfurt, Campus.

Benhabib, Seyla (1980) *Critique, Norm and Utopia,* New York, Columbia University Press.

— (1986) 'The Generalized and the Concrete Other: The Kohlberg-Gilligan Controversy and Feminist Theory', *Praxis International*, 5(4).

— (1992) *Situating the Self. Gender, Community and Postmodernism in Contemporary Ethics,* Cambridge, Polity.

— (2002) 'Citizens, Residents, and Aliens in a Changing World: Political Membership in the Global Era', in Ulf Hedetoft and Mette Hjort (eds), *The Postnational Self. Belonging and Identity*, Minneapolis, University of Minnesota Press, pp.85–119.

— (2004) *The Rights of Others*, Cambridge, Cambridge University Press.

— (2005) 'Beyond Interventionism and Indifference. Culture, Deliberation and Pluralism', *Philosophy and Social Criticism* 31(7), 753–71.

Benhabib, Seyla and Drucilla Cornell (eds) (1987) *Feminism and Critique: Essays on the Politics of Gender in Late-Capitalist Societies,* Cambridge, Polity.

— (2006) *Another Cosmopolitanism*, New York, Oxford University Press.

— 'Verteidigung der Moderne', in *Habermas-Handbuch,* Hauke Brunkhorst et al. (eds), pp.240–54.

Benhabib, S. and F. Dallmayr (eds) (1990), *The Communicative Ethics Controversy*, Cambridge, MA, MIT Press.
Benjamin, Walter (1979) 'Theories of German Fascism', 1930, translated in *New German Critique* 17, 120–8.
Berger, Johannes (1981) 'Changing Crises-types in Western Societies', *Praxis International* 1(3), 230–9.
— (2005) 'Social Institutions, Technological Progress and Economic Performance', in Max Miller (ed.), *Worlds of Capitalism. Institutions, Governance and Economic Change in the Era of Globalization*, London, Routledge, pp. 33–56.
Bernstein, R. J. (ed.) (1985) *Habermas and Modernity*, Oxford, Blackwell.
— (1986) *Philosophical Profiles,* Cambridge, Polity.
— (1991) *The New Constellation: The Ethical Horizons of Modernity/ Postmodernity,* Cambridge, Polity.
— (2010). 'Naturalism, Secularism, and Religion: Habermas's Via Media', *Constellations* 17(1), 155–66.
Berten, André (1993) 'D'une sociologie de la justice à une sociologie du droit. À propos des travaux de L. Boltanski et L. Thévenot', *Recherches sociologiques* 24(1–2), 69–89.
Bidet, Jacques (2001) 'Habermas en-deçà de Marx', in Jacques Bidet and Eustache Kouvélakis (eds), *Dictionnaire Marx contemporain*, Paris, Presses Universitaires de France, pp. 447–60.
Björk, Micael (2005) 'A Plea for Detached Involvement: Norbert Elias on Intellectuals and Political Imagination in Inter-war Germany', *History of the Human Sciences* 18(2), 43–61.
Bogusz, Tanja (2010) *Zur Aktualität von Luc Boltanski*, Wiesbade, VS Verlag.
Bohman, James (2004) 'Toward a Critical Theory of Globalization. Democratic Practice and Multiperspectival Inquiry', *Concepts and Transformatcon* 9(2), 121–46.
— (1996) *Public Deliberation: Pluralism, Complexity, and Democracy*, Cambridge, MIT Press.
— (2004) 'Constitution Making and Democratic Innovation. The European Union and Transnational Governance', *European Journal of Political Theory* 3(3), July, 315–37.
— (2005) 'Rights, Cosmopolitanism and Public Reason. Interactive Universalism in *The Claims of Culture*', *Philosophy and Social Criticism* 31(7), 715–26.
— (2007) 'Toward a Critical Theory of Globalization. Democratic Practice and Multiperspectival Inquiry', *Concepts and Transformation* 9(2), 2004, 121–46. *Democracy across Borders. From Dêmos to Dêmoi*, Cambridge, MA, MIT Press.
Boltanski, Luc and Laurent Thévenot (1983) 'Finding One's Way in Social Space: A Study Based on Games', *Social Science Information* 22(4/5), 631–80.
— (1987) *Les économies de la grandeur*, Paris, Cahiers du CEE, Presses Universitaires de France.
— (1999) 'The Sociology of Critical Capacity', *European Journal of Social Theory* 2(3), 359–77.

— (2000) 'The Reality of Moral Expectations: A Sociology of Situated Judgement', *Philosophical Explorations* 3(3), 208–31. Boltanski, Luc and Laurent Thévenot, *On Justification. Economies of Worth*, translated by Catherine Porter, Princeton University Press, 2006. First published in 1991.

Bonss, Wolfgang and Axel Honneth (eds) (1982), *Sozialforschung als Kritik*, Frankfurt, Suhrkamp.

Borkenau, Franz (1940) *The Totalitarian Enemy*, London, Faber.

Borradori, Giovanna (ed.) (2003) *Philosophy in a Time of Terror. Dialogues with Jürgen Habermas and Jacques Derrida*, Chicago, Chicago University Press.

Bottomore, Tom (1984) *The Frankfurt School*. Chichester, Ellis Horwood and London, Tavistock.

Bourdieu, Pierre et Loïc Wacquant (2000) 'La nouvelle vulgate planétaire', *Le Monde diplomatique*, May 2000, 6–7.

Bourdieu, Pierre (1998) 'L'essence du néoliberalisme', *Le Monde diplomatique*, March; translated by Jeremy Shapiro as 'The Essence of Neoliberalism', Caracas, Biblioteca electrónica, www.analytica.com/biblioteca/bourdieu/neoliberalism.asp

— 'Le mythe de la "mondialisation" et l'État social européen', GSEE, Athens, October 1996, reprinted in *Contre-Feux*, Paris, Raisons d'Agir, 1998, translated as *Acts of Resistance: Against the New Myths of our Time*, Cambridge, Polity, 1998.

— (1997) 'Larchitecte de l'euro passe aux aveux', *Le Monde diplomatique*, March, p. 19.

— (1998) *Acts of Resistance: Against the New Myths of our Time*, Cambridge, Poljty, 1998.

— (1999) 'Pour un mouvement social européen', *Le Monde diplomatique*, June.

— (2000) 'Pour des États Généraux du Mouvement Social Européen', *Le Monde* 28 April 2000.

Bourdieu, Pierre et Loïc Wacquant (2000) 'La nouvelle vulgate planétaire', *Le Monde diplomatique*, May 2000, pp. 6–7; tanslated as 'NewLiberalSpeak: Notes on the New Planetary Vulgate', *RadicalPhilosophy*, Jan–Feb 2001.

— (2001) 'Pour un savoir engagé', *Le Monde diplomatique*, February, p. 3.

— (2003) *Firing Back. Against the Tyranny of the Market 2*, London, Verso.

Bowman, Jonathan (2007) 'Challenging Habermas' Response to the European Union Democratic Deficit', *Philosophy and Social Criticism* 33(6), 736–55.

Bronner, Stephen Eric (1994) *Of Critical Theory and its Theorists*, Oxford, Blackwell.

Brunkhorst, Hauke (2002) 'Verfassung ohne Staat? Das Schicksal der Demokratie in der europäischen Rechtsgenossenschaft', *Leviathan* 30(4), 530–43.

— (2005) *Solidarity. From Civic Friendship to a Global Legal Community*, Cambridge, MA, MIT Press. First published 2002.

— (2006) 'The Legitimation Crisis of the European Union', *Constellations* 13(2), 165–80.

— (2007) 'Zwischen transnationale Klassenherrschaft und egalitäre Konstitutionalisierung. Europas zweite Chance', in Nessen and Herborth (eds), pp. 321–49.

— Regina Kreide and Cristina Lafont (eds) (2009), *Habermas-Handbuch*, Stuttgart and Weimar, Metzler.

Calhoun, Craig (ed.) (1992) *Habermas and the Public Sphere,* Cambridge, MA, MIT Press.

— (2003) 'European Studies: Always Already There and Still in Formation', *Comparative European Politics* 1, 5–20.

Carnoy, Martin (1984) 'The German Debate', in Carnoy, *The State and Political Theory,* Princeton University Press, chapter 5.

Cerrutti, Furio (1984) 'Philosophie und Sozialforschung. Zum ursprünglichen Programm der kritischen Theorie', in Axel Honneth and Albrecht Wellmer (eds), *Die Frankfurter Schule und die Folgen,* Alexander von Humboldt-Stiftung, Symposium Berlin, De Gruyter, 1986, pp. 246–58.

Chernilo, Daniel. forthcoming.

Christ, Peter and Ralf Neubauer (1991) *Kolonie im eigenen Lande. Die Treuhand, Bonn und die Wirtschaftskatastrophe der fünf neuen Länder,* Neuwied, Rowohlt.

Clark, Julian and Alun Jones (2011) '"Telling Stories about Politics": Europeanization and the EU's Council Working Groups', *Journal of Common Market Studies* 49(2), 341–66.

— (2011) 'The Spatialising Politics of European Political Practice: Transacting "Eastness" in the European Union', *Environment and Planning D: Society and Space* 29, 291–308.

Cohen, Jean and Andrew Arato (1992) *Civil Society and Political Theory,* Cambridge, MA, MIT Press.

Connerton, Paul (ed.) (1984) *Critical Sociology,* Harmondsworth, Penguin, 1976.

Connolly, W. (ed.) *Legitimacy and the State,* Oxford, Blackwell.

Cooke, Maeve (2000) 'Critical Theory and Religion', in D. Z. Phillips and T. Tessin (eds), *Philosophy of Religion in the Twenty-First Century,* London, Palgrave, pp. 211–43.

— (2006) *Re-Presenting the Good Society,* Cambridge, MA, MIT Press.

— (2006) 'Salvaging and Secularizing Secularizing the Semantic Contents of Religion: The Limitations of Habermas's Postmetaphysical Proposal', *International Journal for the Philosophy of Religion* 60, 187–207.

— (2006) 'Säkulare Übersetzung oder Postsäkulare Argumentation? Habermas über Religion in der demokratischen Öffentlichkeit', in R. Langthatler and H. Nagl-Docekal (eds), *Jürgen Habermas über Religion,* Vienna/Berlin, Oldenbourg, pp. 342–66.

Crouch, Colin (2004) *Postdemocracy,* Cambridge, Polity.

Delanty, Gerard (2009) *The Cosmopolitan Imagination. The Renewal of Critical Social Theory,* Cambridge, Cambridge University Press.

— (2011) 'Varieties of Critique in Sociological Theory and their Methodological Implications for Social Research', *Irish Journal of Sociology* 19(1), 68–92.

Delanty, Gerard and Piet Strydom (eds) (2003) *Philosophies of Social Science: The Classic and Contemporary Readings,* Buckingham, Open University Press.

Dews, Peter (1987) *Logics of Disintegration: Post-Structuralist Thought and the Claims of Critical Theory,* London, Verso.

— (ed.) (1999) *Habermas: A Critical Reader,* Oxford, Blackwell.

Demirović, A. (1999) *Der nonkonformistische Intellektuelle. Die Entwicklung der kritischen Theorie zur Frankfurter Schule.* Frankfurt, Suhrkamp.

Drieschner, Michael (1996) 'Die Verantwortung der Wissenschaft. Ein Rückblick auf das Max-Planck-Institut zur Erforschung der Lebensbedingungen der wissenschaftlich-technischen Welt (1970–1980)', in T. Fischer and R. Seising (eds), *Wissenschaft und Öffentlichkeit'*, Frankfurt, Peter Lang, pp. 173–98.

Dubiel, Helmut (1988) *Kritische Theorie der Gesellschaft*, Weinheim and Munich, Juventus, 3rd edn, 2001.

— (1985) *Was ist Neokonservatismus?*, Frankfurt, Suhrkamp.

— (1994) 'Ihre Zeit in Gedanken erfasst. Entwicklungsstufen kritischer Theorie', in Institut für Sozialforschung, *Mitteilungen*, Heft 4, 5–13.

— (1998) 'Cultivated Conflicts', *Political Theory* 26(2), April, 209–20.

— (1998) 'The Duture of Citizenship in Europe', *Constellations* 4(3), 368–73.

— (1999) *Niemand ist frei von der Geschichte. Die nationalsozialistische Herrschaft in den Debatten des deutschen Bundestages*, Munich, Carl Hanser, 1999.

Dubiel, Helmut and Günther Frankenberg (1983) 'Entsorgung der Vergangenheit. Widerspruch gegen eine neokonservative Legende', *Die Zeit* 18 March 1983.

Eder, Klaus (1976) *Die Entstehung staatlich organisierter Gesellschaften*, Frankfurt, Suhrkamp, 2nd edn, 1980.

— (1985) *Geschichte als Lernprozess? Zur Pathogenese politischer Modernität in Deutschland*, Frankfurt, Suhrkamp.

— (1993) *The New Politics of Class: Social Movements and Cultural Dynamics in Advanced Societies*, London, Sage.

— (2000) 'Zur Transformation nationalstaatlicher Öffentlichkeit in Europa,' *Berliner Journal für Soziologie* 10(2), 167–84.

Eder, K. and B. Giesen (eds) (2001) *Collective Memory and European Identity. The Effects of Integration and Enlargement*, Aldershot, Ashgate.

— (2002) 'Europäische Säkularisierung – ein Sonderweg in die postsäkulare Gesellschaft', *Berliner Journal für Soziologie* 3, 343.

— (2006) 'Europe's Borders. The Narrative Construction of the Boundaries of Europe', *European Journal of Social Theory* 9, 255–71.

Eder, K. and B. Giesen (eds) (2001) *European Citizenship between National Legacies and Postnational Projects*, Oxford, Oxford University Press.

— (2008) 'Symbolic Power and Cultural Differences: A Power Model of Political Solutions to Cultural Differences', in Per Mouritsen and Knud Erik Jørgensen (eds), *Constituting Communities. Political Solutions to Cultural Conflict*, Basingstoke, Palgrave, pp. 31–53.

— (2011) 'Europe as a Narrative Network. Taking the Social Embeddedness of Identity Constructions Seriously', in Sonia Lucarelli, Furio Cerutti and Vivien A. Schmidt (eds), *Debating Political Identity and Legitimacy in the European Union*, London, Routledge, 2011, pp. 38–54.

Eder, Klaus and Hans-Jörg Trenz (2007) 'Prerequisites of Transnational Democracy and Mechanisms for Sustaining It: The Case of the European Union', in Beate Kohler Koch and Berthold Bittberger (eds), *Debating the Democratic Legitimacy of the European Union* Lanham, Rowman and Littlefield, pp. 165–88.

Elias, Norbert (1989) *Studien über die Deutschen*, Frankfurt: Suhrkamp. Tr. as *The Germans* Cambridge, Polity, 1996.

Elster, J., C. Offe and U. Preuss with Frank Boenker, Ulrike Goetting and Friedbert W. Rueb. *Institutional Design in Post-Communist Societies: Rebuilding The Ship at Sea*, Cambridge, Cambridge University Press, 1998.

Eriksen, E. O. and J. E. Fossum (eds) (2000) *Democracy in the European Union – Integration Though Deliberation?*, London, Routledge.

Eriksen, Erik Oddvar (ed.) (2005) *Making the European Polity. Reflexive Integration in the EU*, London, Routledge.

— (2009) *The Unfinished Democratization of Europe*, Oxford, Oxford University Press.

— (2010) 'European Transformation. A Pragmatic Approach', Arena Working Paper 7, August.

— (2011) 'Reflexive Integration: A Perspective on the Transformation of Europe', in Gerard Delanty and Stephen P. Turner (eds), *A Handbook of Contemporary Social and Political Theory*, London, Routledge, pp. 417–27.

Fehér, F. (1982) 'Paternalism as a Mode of Legitimation in Soviet-type Societies', in Rigby, T. H. and Fehér, F. (eds), *Political Legitimation in Communist Regimes*, London, Macmillan, pp. 64–81.

Fehér, F., A. Heller and G. Márkus (1983) *Dictatorship Over Needs*, Oxford, Blackwell.

Fligstein, Neil (1997) 'Rhétorique et réalités de la "mondialisation"', *Actes de la recherche en sciences sociales*, 119, September 1997.

Forrester, John (ed.) (1985) *Critical Theory and Public Life*, Cambridge, MA, MIT Press.

Fossum, John Erik and Hans-Georg Trenz (2006) 'When the People Come in: Constitution-making and the Belated Politicisation of the European Union', European Governance Papers (EUROGOV) No. C-06-03, http://www.connex-network.org/eurogov/pdf/egp-connex-C-06-03.pdf

— (1978) *Discipline and Punish*, Harmondsworth, Penguin.

— (1997) *Ethics: The Essential Works: Vol. 1*, ed., P. Rabinow, Harmondsworth, Penguin, pp. 315–16.

Frank, Arthur (1992) 'Only by Daylight: Habermas's Postmodern Modernism', *Theory, Culture and Society* 9(3), 149–65.

Frank, Manfred (1988) *Die Grenzen der Verständigung: Ein Geistergespräch zwischen Lyotard und Habermas*, Frankfurt, Suhrkamp.

Frankenberg, G. and U. Rödel (1981) *Von der Volkssouveränität zum Minderheitenschutz*, Frankfurt, Europäische Verlagsanstalt.

Fraser, Nancy (1985) 'Toward a Discourse Ethic of Solidarity', *Praxis International* 5(4), 425–9.

Friese, Heidrun and Peter Wagner (2002) 'The Nascent Political Philosophy of the European Polity', *Journal of Political Philosophy* 10(3), 342–64.

Fromm, Erich (ed.) and Bonss, W. (1984) *The Working Class in Weimar Germany*, Leamington Spa, Berg.

Geis, Anna, and David Strecker (eds) (2005) *Blockaden staatlicher Politik. Sozialwissenschaftliche Analysen im Anschluss an Claus Offe*, Frankfurt and New York, Campus.

Georgakakis, Didier (ed.), Special issue, *Politix* 11(43), Troisième trimestre, 1998, pp. 5–91.

— (ed.) (2004) 'Sur l'Europe', *Regards Sociologiques*, no. 27/28.

Georgakakis, Didier and Marine Lassalle (2007) 'Genèse et structure d'un capital institutionnel européen. Les très hauts fonctionnaires de la Commission européenne, *Actes de la recherche en sciences sociales*, pp. 166–7, March.

Giddens, Anthony (1985) *The Nation-State and Violence*, Cambridge, Polity.

Goldmann, Kjell (2005) 'Appropriateness and Consequences; The Logic of Neo-Institutionalism', *Governance* 18(1), January, 35–52.

Guldimann, Tim (1984) *Moral und Herrschaft in der Sowjetunion*, Frankfurt: Suhrkamp Frankfurt am Main, Suhrkamp.

Gutmann, Amy (1992) *Multiculturalism and the Politics of Recognition*, Princeton University Press.

Habermas, Jürgen, L. von Friedeburg, C. Oehler and F. Weltz (1961) *Student und Politik*, Neuwied, Luchterhand.

Habermas, Jürgen (1962) *Strukturwandel der Offentlichkeit*, Neuwied/Berlin, Luchterhand, 2nd edn, Frankfurt, Suhrkamp, 1989. Translated as *The Structural Transformation of the Public Sphere*, Cambridge, Polity, 1989.

Habermas, Jürgen (1986) *Theorie und Praxis*, Neuwied/Berlin, Luchterhand, 1963. Translated as *Theory and Practice*, Cambridge, Polity.

— (1986) *Technik und Wissenschaft als Ideologic*, Frankfurt, Suhrkamp, 1968. Part translated in Jurgen Habermas, *Toward a Rational Society*, Cambridge, Polity.

— (1986) *Erkenntnis und Interesse*, Frankfurt, Suhrkamp, 1968. Translated as *Knowledge and Human Interests*, Cambridge, Polity.

— (1971) *Zur Logik der Sozialwissenschaften*, 2nd edn, Frankfurt, Suhrkamp. Translated as *On the Logic of the Social Sciences*, Cambridge, Polity, 1990.

— (1973) 'A Postscript to *Knowledge and Human Interests*', *Philosophy of the Social Sciences* 3(2), 157–89.

— (1976) *Legitimationsprobleme im Spatkapitalismus*, Frankfurt, Suhrkamp, 1973) Translated as *Legitimation Crisis*, London, Heinemann.

— (1976) 'What does a Crisis Mean Today?', *Social Research* (Winter 1973), repr. in P. Connerton (ed.), *Critical Sociology*, Harmondsworth, Penguin.

— (1973) *Kultur und Kritik*, Frankfurt, Suhrkamp.

— (1974) 'The Public Sphere', *New German Critique*, 3.

— (1974) 'Konnen komplexe Gesellschaften eine vernünftige Identität ausbilden?', in J. Habermas and D. Henrich, *Zwei Reden*, Frankfurt, Suhrkamp.

— (1987) *Theorie des kommunikativen Handelns*, 2 vols, Frankfurt, Suhrkamp, (1981) Translated by Thomas McCarthy as *The Theory of Communicative Action*, vol. 1, London, Heinemann, 1984, repr. Cambridge, Polity, vol. 2, Cambridge, Polity.

— (1991) *Zur Rekonstruktion des historischen Materialismus*, Frankfurt, Suhrkamp, 1976. Part translated in *Communication and the Evolution of Society*, Cambridge, Polity.

— (1982) 'A Reply to My Critics', in J. B. Thompson and D. Held (eds), *Habermas: Critical Debates*, London, Macmillan, pp. 219–83.

— (1983) *Philosophical-Political Profiles*, London, Heinemann.

— (1982) The Entwinement of Myth and Enlightenment', *New German Critique* 26, 13–20.

— (1990) *Moralbewusstsein und kommunikatives Handeln*, Frankfurt, Suhrkamp, 1983. Translated as *Moral Consciousness and Communicative Action*, Cambridge, Polity.

— (1984) *Vorstudien and Ergänzungen zur Theorie des kommunikativen Handelns*, Frankfurt, Suhrkamp.

— (1986) 'Drei Thesen zur Wirkungsgeschichte der Frankfurter Schule', in Axel
   Honneth and Albrecht Wellmer (eds), *Die Frankfurter Schule und die Folgen*,
   Alexander von Humboldt-Stiftung, Symposium 1984, Berlin, De Gruyter,
   pp. 8–12.
— (1985) 'Moral und Sittlichkeit: Hegels Kantkritik im Lichte der Diskursethik',
   Merkur 39(12), December.
— (1985) 'Modernity – an Incomplete Project', repr. in Hal Foster (ed.),
   Postmodern Culture, London, Pluto.
— (1985) *Die neue Unubersichtlichkeit*, Frankfurt, Suhrkamp. Translated as *The
   New Conservatism*, Cambridge, Polity, 1989.
— (1985) *Der Philosophische Diskurs der Moderne*, Frankfurt, Suhrkamp Translated
   as *The Philosophical Discourse of Modernity*, Cambridge, Polity, 1990.
— (1986) 'A Kind of Settlement of Damages (Apologetic Tendencies)', *New
   German Critique* 44 (Spring–Summer, 1988), pp. 25–39. First published in
   Die Zeit, 11 July 1986.
— (1986) *Autonomy and Solidarity*, ed. Peter Dews, London, Verso, 2nd edn,
   London, Verso, 1992.
— (1988) *Nachmetaphysisches Denken*, Frankfurt, Suhrkamp. Translated as
   Postmetaphysical Thinking, Cambridge, Polity, 1992.
— (1989) Towards a Communication Concept of Rational Will Formation', *Ratio
   Juris* 2 (July 1989), 144–54.
— (1989) 'Volkssouveränität als Verfahren', *Merkur* 43(6), 465–77.
— (1990) *Die nachholende Revolution*, Frankfurt, Suhrkamp.
— (1990) 'Remarks on the Discussion', *Theory, Culture and Society* 7(4), 127–32.
— (1988) *Law and Morality: The Tanner Lectures on Human Values* VI,
   217–79.
— (1991) *Erläuterungen zur Diskursethik*, Frankfurt, Suhrkamp. Translated as
   Justification and Application, Cambridge, Polity, 1993.
— (1991) *Vergangenheit als Zukunft*, ed. Michael Heller, Zurich, Pendo, 2nd,
   expanded edn Munich, Piper, 1993. Translated as *The Past as Future*, Lincoln,
   University of Nebraska Press, 1994.
— (1992) *Faktizität und Geltung*, Frankfurt, Suhrkamp, Translated as *Between
   Facts and Norms*, Cambridge, Polity, 1996.
— (1995) *Die Normalität einer Berliner Republik*, Frankfurt, Suhrkamp.
Habermas, 'A Kind of Settlement of Damages (Apologetic Tendencies)', *New
   German Critique* 44 (Spring–Summer) 1988, 25–39.
— (2001) *Die postnationale Konstellation*, Frankfurt, Suhrkamp, 1998. Translated
   as *The Postnational Constellation*, Cambrdge, Polity.
— (1998) *Die Einbeziehung des Anderen*, Frankfurt, Suhrkamp, 1996. Translated
   as *The Inclusion of the Other*, Cambridge, Polity.
— (1998) *On the Pragmatics of Communication*, edited by Maeve Cooke,
   Cambridge, MA, MIT Press and Cambridge, Polity.
— (2003) *Wahrheit und Rechtfertigung*, Frankfurt, Suhrkamp, 1999. Translated
   as *Truth and Justification*, Cambridge, Polity.
— (2008) *Ach, Europa*, Frankfurt, Suhrkamp.
— (2001) 'A Constitution for Europe?', *New left Review* 11, September/October
   2001, pp. 5–26.
— (2004) *Der gespaltene Westen*, Frankfurt, Suhrkamp.

— (2007) 'Die Dialektik der Säkularisierung', *Blätter für deutsche und internationale Politik* 4, 33–46.

— (2003) *Die Zukunft der menschlichen Natur*, Frankfurt, Suhrkamp, 2001. Translated as *The Future of Human Nature*, Cambridge, Polity.

— (2001) *Glauben und Wissen. Friedenspreis des Deutschen Buchhandels 2001*, Frankfurt, Suhrkamp. Reprinted in Habermas, *The Future of Human Nature*, pp. 101–15.

— (2001) *Kommunikatives Handeln und detranszendentalisierte Vernunft*, Stuttgart, Reklam.

— (2002) 'Pierre Bourdieu', *Frankfurter Rundschau*, 25 January 2002. Translated as 'Humaniste engagé', *Le Monde*, 26 January 2002.

— (2003) 'Toward a Cosmopolitan Europe', *Journal of Democracy* 14(4), 86–100.

— (2001) *Zeit der Übergänge,* Frankfurt, Suhrkamp.

— (2003) *Zeitdiagnosen. Zwölf Essays 1980–2001*, Frankfurt, Suhrkamp, 2003.

— (2005) *Zwischen Naturalismus und Religion*, Frankfurt, Suhrkamp. Translated as *Between Naturalism and Religion*, Cambridge, Polity, 2008.

Habermas, Jürgen and Luhmann, Niklas *Theorie der Gesellschaft oder Sozialtechnologie: Was leistet die Systemforschung?*, Frankfurt, Suhrkamp.

— (1998) *The Inclusion of the Other*, Cambridge, Polity.

— (1961) Ludwig von Friedburg, Christoph Oehler and Friderich Weltz, *Student und Politik*, Neuwied, Luchterhand.

— (1989) *Strukturwandel der Offentlichkeit*, Neuwied/Berlin, Luchterhand, 1962, 2nd edn, Frankfurt, Suhrkamp, 1989. Translated as *The Structural Transformation of the Public Sphere*, Cambridge, Polity.

— (1968) (ed.), *Antworten auf Herbert Marcuse*, Frankfurt, Suhrkamp. 'Stichworte zum Legtimationsbegriff – eine Replik', in Habermas, *Zur Rekonstruktion des historischen Materialismus*, pp. 329–37.

Habermas, Jürgen and Jacques Derrida (2003) 'February 15, or What Binds Europeans Together: A Plea for a Common Foreign Policy, Beginning in the Core of Europe', *Constellations* 10(3), 291–97.

Hall, John (ed.) *Civil Society–Theory, History, Comparison*, Oxford, Polity.

Halman, Loek and Veerle Draulans (2006) 'How Secular is Europe?', *British Journal of Sociology* 57(6), 263–88.

Harrington, Austin (2007) 'Habermas and the Post-Secular Society', *European Journal of Social Theory* 10(4) November, 547.

Hartmann, Martin 'Widersprüche, Ambivalenzen, Paradoxien – Begriffliche Wandlungen in der neueren Gesellschaftstheorie', in Honneth (ed.) *Befreiung aus der Mündigkeit*, pp. 221–51.

Heller, A. (1988) 'On Formal Democracy', in Keane, J. *Civil Society and the State*, London, Verso, pp. 129–46.

Hinrichs, Karl, Herbert Kitschelt and Helmut Wiesenthal (eds) (2000) *Kontingenz und Krise. Institutionenpolitik in kapitalistischen und postsozialistischen Gesellschaften. Claus Offe zu seinem 60 Geburtstag*, Frankfurt/New York, Campus Verlag.

Hohendahl, Peter (1985) 'Habermas' Critique of the Frankfurt School', *New German Critique* 35, 3–26.

Hohendahl, Peter Uwe (1991) 'Reappraisals of Critical Theory: The Legacy of the Frankfurt School in America', in Hohendahl (ed.), *Reappraisals: Shifting*

Alignments in Postwar Critical Theory, Ithaca, Cornell University Press, pp. 198–228.

Honneth, A. (1982) 'Moral Consciousness and Class Domination: Some Problems in the Analysis of Hidden Morality', *Praxis International* 2(1), 12–24.

— (1985) 'Diskursethik und implizites Gerechtigkeitskonzept', in Emil Angehrn and Georg Lohmann (eds), *Ethik und Marx*, Königstein, Hain Verlag.

— (1985/1992) *Critique of Power*, Cambridge, MA, MIT Press. First published 1985.

— (1992/1995) *The Struggle for Recognition*, Cambridge, Polity.

Honneth, A. and H. Joas (1980/1988) *Social Action and Human Nature*, Cambridge, Cambridge University Press.

— (2000) *Disrespect. The Normative Foundations of Critical Theory.* Cambridge: Polity, 2007. First published as *Das Andere der Gerechtigkeit*, Frankfurt, Suhrkamp.

— (ed.) (2002) *Befreiung aus der Mündigkeit. Paradoxien des modernen Kapitalismus*, Frankfurt, Campus.

— (2008) *Reification. A New Look at an Old Idea.* With Commentaries by Judith Butler, Raymond Geuss and Jonathan Lear. Edited and Introduced by Martin Jay. The Berkeley Tanner Lectures 2005. New York, Oxford University Press.

— *Pathologien der Vernunft. Geschichte und Gegenwart der kritischen Theorie.* Frankfurt, Suhrkamp, 2007. Translated as *Pathologies of Reason*, Columbia University Press, 2009.

— (2010) 'Dissolutions of the Social: On the Social Theory of Luc Boltanski and Laurent Thévenot', *Constellations* 17(3), 376–89.

— (ed.) (2002) *Befreiung aus der Mündigkeit. Paradoxien des gegenwätigen Kapitalismus*, Frankfurt, Campus.

Hooghe, Liesbet and Gary Marks (2008) 'A Postfunctionalist Theory of European Integration: From Permissive Consensus to Constraining Dissensus', *British Journal of Political Science* 39(1), 1–23.

Horkheimer, Max (1932) 'Vorwort', *Zeitschrift für Sozialforschung* I(1–2), I–IV.

— (1933) 'Vorwort', *Zeitschrift für Sozialforschung* II(2), 161.

— (1934) *Dämmerung*. Translated by Michael Shaw as *Dawn and Decline. Notes 1926–1931 and 1950–1969*, New York, Seabury, 1978.

— (1937) 'Tradionelle und kritische Theorie', *Zeitschrift für Sozialforschung* VI(2), 245–94.

Horkheimer, 'Die Juden und Europa' (1939) *Zeitschrift für Sozialforschung* 8 (1/2), 115–37.

Horkheimer, Max and Theodor W. Adorno (1972/1979) *Dialectic of Enlightenment,* London, Verso, First published 1947.

Inglehart, R. F. (1977) *The Silent Revolution: Changing Values and Political Styles among the Western Mass Publics,* Princeton, NJ, Princeton University Press.

Jäger, Wolfgang (1973) *Offentlichkeit und Parlamentarismus: Eine Kritik an Jürgen Habermas,* Stuttgart, Kohlhammer.

Jay, Martin (1973) *The Dialectical Imagination. A History of the Frankfurt School and the Institute for Social Research 1923–50*, London, Heinemann.

— (1985) 'The Jews and the Frankfurt School: Critical Theory's Analysis of Anti-Semitism', *New German Critique* 19, Winter 1980, pp. 17–149. Reprinted in

Jay, *Permanent Exiles. Essays on the Intellectual Migration from Germany to America*, New York, Columbia University Press, pp. 90–100.

Joas, Hans and Helmut Steiner (eds) (1989) *Machtpolitischer Realismus und pazifistische Utopie. Krieg und Frieden in der Geschichte der Sozialwissenschaften*, Frankfurt, Suhrkamp.

Joas, Hans and Martin Kohli (eds) (1993) *Der Zusammenbruch der DDR. Soziologische Analysen*, Frankfurt, Suhrkamp.

Joas, Hans (2003) *War and Modernity*, Cambridge, Polity Press.

— (2005) 'A Pragmatist from Germany', in Alan Sica and Stephen Turner (eds), *The Disobedient Generation. Social Theorists in the Sixties*, Chicago University Press, pp. 156–75.

— 'Die Religion der Moderne', *Die Zeit*, 42/2005, p. 94.

Karagiannis, Nathalie (ed.) (2007) *European Solidarity*, Liverpool, Liverpool University Press.

Karakayali, Nedim (2004) 'Reading Bourdieu with Adorno: The Limits of Critical Theory and Reflexive Sociology', *Sociology* 38(2), 351–68.

Kellner, Douglas (1984) *Herbert Marcuse and the Crisis of Marxism*, Basingstoke, Macmillan.

— (1989) *Critical Theory, Marxism and Modernity*, Cambridge, Polity.

Kirchheimer, Otto (1978) 'Changes in the Structure of Political Compromise', *Studies in Philosophy and Social Science* 9(2), 1941, 264–89. Reprinted in Andrew Arato and Eike Gebhardt (eds), *The Essential Frankfurt School Reader*, Oxford, Blackwell, pp. 49–70.

Kommunistischer Bund (1973) *Kampf dem Faschismus. Nachdruck von Texten zur Faschismus-Frage aus den 20er und 30er Jahren*, Hamburg, J. Reents Verlag.

Konrád G. (1984) *Antipolitics*, London, Harcourt, Brace Jovanovich.

Konrád G. and I. Szelényi (1979) *The Intellectuals on the Road to Class Power*, Brighton, Harvester.

Koopmans, Ruud (2007) 'Who Inhabits the European Public Sphere? Winners and Losers, Supporters and Opponents in Europeanised Political Debates', *European Journal of Political Research* 46, 183–210.

Korte, Hermann 'Norbert Elias', in Dirk Kaesler (ed.) (2000), *Klassiker der Soziologie 1. Von Auguste Comte bis Norbert Elias*, Munich, Beck, pp. 321–2.

Kracauer, Siegfried (1998) *Die Angestellten. Aus dem neuesten Deutschland*, Frankfurt, Societäts-Verlag, 1930. Translated by Quintin Hoare as *The Salaried Masses. Duty and Distraction in Weimar Germany*, London, Verso.

Krossa, Anne Sophie and Roland Robertson (eds) (2012) *European Cosmopolitanism in Question*, Basingstoke, Palgrave.

Kunneman, Harry (1991) *Der Wahrheitstrichter: Habermas und die Postmoderne*, Frankfurt, Campus.

Lassman, Peter (1984) 'Social Structure, History and Evolution', *Economy and Society* 13(1).

Levy, Daniel, Max Pensky and John Torpey (eds) (2005) *Old Europe, New Europe, Core Europe. Transatlantic Relations after the Iraq War*, London, Verso.

Lowenthal, Leo (1980) *Mitmachen wollte ich nie: Ein autobiographisches Gespräch mit Helmut Dubiel*, Frankfurt.

Lubasz, H. (1977) 'Marx's Initial Problematic: The Problem of Poverty', *Political Studies* XXIV, 1, 24–42.

Lyotard, Jean-François (1984) *The Postmodern Condition: A Report on Knowledge*, Manchester, Manchester University Press.

Mann, M. (1975) 'The Ideology of Intellectuals and Other People in the Development of Capitalism', in L. N. Lindberg, R. Alford, C. Crouch and C. Offe (eds), *Stress and Contradiction in Modern Capitalism*, Lexington, MA, D. C. Heath.

Mannheim, Karl (1943) *Diagnosis of Our Times: Wartime Essays of a Sociologist*, London, Kegan Paul, Trench, Trubner & Co.

March, James G. and Johan P. Olsen (1989) *Rediscovering Institutions*, New York, Free Press.

— (1996) 'Institutional Perspectives on Political Institutions', *Governance* 93, 247–64.

— (1998) 'The Institutional Dynamics of International Political Orders', *International Organization* 52, 943–69.

Marinopoulou, Anastasia, *The Concept of the Political in Max Horkheimer and Jürgen Habermas*, Athens, Nissos, 2008.

Marcuse, Herbert (1958) *Soviet Marxism. A Critical Analysis*, New York, Columbia University Press.

— (1964) *One Dimensional Man*, Boston, MA, Beacon Press.

— (1975) *Zeit-Messungen*, Frankfurt, Suhrkamp.

Martell, Luke (2008) 'Beck's Cosmopolitan Politics', *Contemporary Politics* 14(2), June, 129–43.

Mattick, Paul (1972) *One Dimensional Man in Class Society*, New York, Herder and Herder.

McCarthy, Thomas (1978) *The Critical Theory of Jiirgen Habermas*, Cambridge, Polity.

McNay, L. (2007) *Against Recognition*, Cambridge, Polity.

— (2008) 'The Trouble with Recognition: Subjectivity, Sufffering, and Agency', *Sociological Theory* 26(3), September, 271–95.

Maynor, John (2008) 'Constitutional Patriotism or Neo-republican Citizenship: A Way Forward for the EU?', in Per Mouritsen and Knud Erik Jørgensen (eds), *Constituting Communities. Political Solutions to Cultural Conflict*, Basingstoke, Palgrave, pp. 187–207.

Meuschel, Sigrid 'Integration durch Legitimation? Zum Problem der Sozialintegration in der DDR', in Ilse Spittmann-Rühle and Gisela Helwig (eds), *Ideologie und gesellschaftliche Entwicklung in der DDR. Achtzehnte Tagung zum Stand der DDR-Forschung in der Bundesrepublik Deutschland, 28 bis 31 Mai 1985*, Köln, Edition Deutschland-Archiv, 1985, pp. 15–29.

— (1992) *Legitimation und Parteiherrschaft: Zum Paradox von Stabilität und Revolution in der DDR, 1945–1989*, Frankfurt, Suhrkamp.

— (1993) Überlegungen zu einer Herrschafts- und Gesellschaftsgeschichte der DDR', *Geschichte und Gesellschaft* 19, 5–15.

— (2000) The Other German Dictatorship: Totalitarianism and Modernization in the German Democratic Republic', *Thesis Eleven* 63, 53–62.

Meyer, Gerhard (1932) 'Neuere Literatur über Planwirtschaft', *Zeitschrift für Sozialforschung* I 3(1), 379–400.

Michnik, Adam (2009) 'Verteidigung der Freiheit. Reflexionen über 1989', *Osteuropa* 2–3.

Middlemas, Keith (1995) *Orchestrating Europe. 'The Informal Politics of the European Union*, London, Fontana.

Mouritsen, Per and Knud Erik Jørgensen (eds) (2008) *Constituting Communities. Political Solutions to Cultural Conflict*, Basingstoke, Palgrave.

Mudde, Cas (2006) 'Anti-System Politics', in Paul Heywood, Erik Jones, Martin Rhodes and Ulrich Sedelmeier (eds), *Developments in European Politics*, Basingstoke, Palgrave, pp. 178–95.

Müller, Harald (2007) 'Internationale Verhandlungen, Argumente und Verständigungshandeln. Verteidigung, Befunde, Warnung', in Niesen, Peter and Herborth, Benjamin (eds), *Anarchie der kommunikativen Freiheit. Jürgen Habermas und die Theorie der internationalen Politik*, Frankfurt, Suhrkamp, pp. 199–223.

Müller, Jan-Werner (2007) *Constitutional Patriotism*, Princeton, Princeton University Press.

— 2007, 'Three Objections to Constitutional Patriotism', *Constellations* 14(2), 197–209.

Müller, Tim (2007) *Krieger und Gelehrte. Herbert Marcuse und die Denksysteme im Kalten Krieg*, Hamburg, Hamburger Edition.

Müller-Doohm, Stefan (2005) 'Theodor W. Adorno and Jürgen Habermas–Two Ways of Being a Public Intellectual: Sociological Observations Concerning the Transformation of a Social Figure of Modernity', *European Journal of Social Theory* 8(3), 269–80.

Müller-Doohm, Stefan (ed.) (2000) *Das Interesse der Vernunft. Rückblicke auf das Werk von Jürgen Habermas seit 'Erkenntnis und Interesse'*, Frankfurt, Suhrkamp.

Müller-Doohm, Stefan and Stefan Bird-Pollan (2010) 'Nation State, Capitalism, Democracy: Philosophical and Political Motives in the Thought of Jürgen Habermas', *European Journal of Social Theory* 13(4) November, 443–57.

Narr, W. D. and Claus Offe (1975) *Wohlfahrtsstaat und Massenloyalität*. Cologne, Kiepenheuer & Witsch.

Nanz, Patrizia (2006) *Europolis. Constitutional Patriotism Beyond the Nation-State*, Manchester University Press.

Negt, Oskar (1968) 'Einleitung', in *Die Linke antwortet Jürgen Habermas*, Frankfurt, Europäische Verlagsanstalt, pp. 17–32.

Negt, Oskar and Alexander Kluge (1993) *The Public Sphere and Experience*, Minneapolis, Minnesota University Press. First published 1972.

Niesen, Peter and Benjamin Herborth (eds) (2007). *Anarchie der kommunikativen Freiheit. Jürgen Habermas und die Theorie der internationalen Politik*, Frankfurt, Suhrkamp.

Nullmeier, Frank (2009) 'Spätkapitalismus und Legitimation', in Hauke Brunkhorst et al. (eds), *Habermas-Handbuch*, Stuttgart Weimar, Metzler, pp. 188–99.

Ó Tuama, Séamus (ed.) (2009) *Critical Turns in Critical Theory*, London, I. B. Tauris.

Offe, Claus (1968) 'Kapitalismus: Analyse als Selbsteinschüchterung', in *Die Linke antwortet Jürgen Habermas,* Frankfurt, Europäische Verlagsanstalt, pp. 106–12.

— (1968) 'Technik und Eindimensionalitat. Eine Version der Technokratiethese?', in Jürgen Habermas (ed.), *Antworten auf Herbert Marcuse,* Frankfurt, Suhrkamp, pp. 73–88.

— (1984) 'Ungovernability: On the Renaissance of Conservative Theories of Crisis', in Jürgen Habermas (ed.), *Observations on the Spiritual Situation of the Age,* Cambridge, MA, MIT Press. First published 1979. Also reprinted in Offe, *Contradictions of the Welfare State,* pp. 65–87.

— (1981) 'Some Contradictions in the Modern Welfare State', *Praxis International* 1, 3 pp. 219–29. Reprinted in Offe, *Contradictions of the Welfare State,* pp. 147–61.

— (1984) *Arbeitsgesellschaft – Strukturprobleme und Zukunftsperspektiven,* Frankfurt, Campus.

— (1984) *Contradictions of the Welfare State,* London, Hutchinson.

— (1985) *Disorganized Capitalism,* Cambridge, Polity.

— (1987) 'Toward a Theory of Late Capitalism', in V. Meja, D. Misgeld and N. Stehr (eds), *Modern German Sociology,* New York, Columbia University Press, pp. 324–39.

— (1989) 'Kommunistischer Kapitalismus', *Die Zeit,* 8 December.

— (1996) 'Wohlstand, Nation, Republik. Aspekte des deutschen Sonderweges vom Sozialismus zum Kapitalismus', in Hans Joas and Martin Kohli (eds), *Der Zusammenbruch der DDR,* pp. 282–301. Expanded English version in Offe, *Varieties of Transition. The East European and East German Experience,* Cambridge, Polity Press, pp. 10ff.

— (1996) *Varieties of Transition. The East European and East German Experience,* Cambridge, Polity.

— (1996). *Modernity and the State. East, West,* Cambridge, Polity.

— (1996) 'Designing Institutions in East European Transitions', in Robert Goodin (ed.), *The Theory of Institutional Design,* New York, Cambridge University Press, pp. 199–226.

— 'The European Model of "Social" Capitalism: Can it Survive European Integration?', in Max Miller (ed.), *Worlds of Capitalism. Institutions, Governance and Economic Change in the Era of Globalization,* London, Routledge, pp. 146–78.

Offe, Claus and Ulrich Preuss (2006) 'The Problem of Legitimacy in the European Polity. Is Democratization the Answer?', in Colin Crouch and Wolfgang Streeck (eds), *The Diversity of Democracy. Corporatism, Social Order and Political Conflict,* Cheltenham, Edward Elgar, pp. 175–204.

Outhwaite, William (1987) *New Philosophies of Social Science: Realism, Hermeneutics and Critical Theory,* London, Macmillan.

— (ed.) (1996), *The Habermas Reader,* Cambridge, Polity.

— (1998) 'Habermas: Modernity as Reflection', in Brian Cheyette and Laura Marcus (eds), *Modernity, Culture and 'the Jew',* Cambridge, Polity.

Outhwaite, W. and T. Bottomore (eds) (1993), *The Blackwell Dictionary of Twentieth-Century Social Thought,* Oxford, Blackwell.

Outhwaite, William and Larry Ray (2005) *Social Theory and Postcommunism,* Oxford, Blackwell.

— (2006) 'The EU and its Enlargements: "Cosmopolitanism by Small Steps"'
in Gerard Delanty (ed.), *Europe and Asia beyond East and West*, London,
Routledge, pp. 193–202.

— (2010) 'Legality and Legitimacy in the European Union', in Chris Thornhill
and Samatha Ashenden (eds), *Legality and Legitimacy: Normative and
Sociological Approaches*, Baden-Baden, Nomos, pp. 279–90.

Owen, David (2002) 'Criticism and Captivity: On Genealogy and Critical Theory',
European Journal of Philosophy 10(2), 216–30.

Pensky, Max (2000) 'Cosmopolitanism and the Solidarity Problem: Habermas on
National and Cultural Identities', *Constellations* 7(1), 64–79.

— (ed.) (2005) *Globalizing Critical Theory*, Lanham and Oxford, Rowman and
Littlefield.

Pierson, Chris (1991) *Beyond the Welfare State?*, Cambridge, Polity.

Pollock, F. (1929) *Die planwirtschaftlichen Versuche in der Sowjetunion 1917–1927*
Leipzig, Hirschfeld. Reprinted in Archiv sozialistischer Literatur, 21, Frankfurt,
Verlag Neue Kritik, 1971.

Pollock, F. (ed.) (1955) *Gruppenexperiment; Ein Studienbericht.* Frankfurt:
Europäische Verlags-Anstalt.

Preuss, Ulrich (1969) *Das politische Mandat der Studentenschaft*, Frankfurt,
Suhrkamp.

— (1984) *Politische Verantwortung und Bürgerloyalität. Von den Grenzen der
Verfassung und des Gehorsams in der Demokratie*, Frankfurt, Fischer.

— (1992–93) 'Constitutional Powermaking for the New Polity: Some
Deliberations on the Relations between Constituent Power and the
Constitution', *Cardozo Law Review* 14, 639–60.

— (1990) *Constitutional Revolution. The Link between Constitutionalism
and Progress*, Atlantic Highlands, NJ, Humanities Press, 1995. Earlier
version published as *Revolution, Fortschritt und Verfassung*, Klaus
Wagenbach.

— (1995) 'Patterns of Constitutional Evolution and Change in Eastern Europe',
in Joachim Jens Hesse and Nevil Johnson (eds), *Constitutional Policy and
Change in Europe*, Oxford, Oxford University Press, pp. 95–126.

— (1998) 'Migration: A Challenge to Modern Citizenship', *Constellations* 4(3),
307–19.

— (1999) 'The Constitution of a European Democracy and the Role of the Nation
State', *Ratio Juris* 12(4) December 1999, 417–28.

— (2005) Europa als politische Gemeinschaft', in Gunnar Folke Schuppert
and Ulrich Haltern (eds), *Europawissenschaft*, Baden-Baden, Nomos,
pp. 495–539.

— (2006/07) 'Perspectives on Post-Conflict Constitutionalism; Reflections on
Regime Change Through External Constitutionalization', *New York School
Law Review* 51, 467–94.

— (2007) The Exercise of Constituent Power and Central and Eastern Europe',
in Martin Loughlin and Neil Walker (eds), *The Paradox of Constitutionalism*,
Oxford, Oxford University Press, pp. 211–28.

— (2008) Constitutionalism in Fragmented Societies: The Integrative Function
of Liberal Constitutionalism and its Challenges', in Joakim Nergelius

(ed.), *Constitutionalism – New Challenges. European Law from a Nordic Perspective*, Leiden and Boston, Martinus Nijhoff, pp. 93–102.

— 'German Unification: Expectations and Outcomes', Hertie School of Governance – Working Papers No. 48, November 2009.

Radkau, Joachim (2009) *Max Weber*, Cambridge, Polity. First published 2005.

Rasmussen, David M. (1990) *Reading Habermas*, Cambridge, MA, Blackwell. (Includes bibliography of recent works on Habermas.)

Raulet, Gérard (2001) 'La théorie critique de l'<école de Francfort>. Du néo-marxisme au <post-marxisme>, in Jacques Bidet and Eustache Kouvélakis (eds), *Dictionnaire Marx contemporain*, Paris, Presses Universitaires de France, pp. 141–58.

Ray, Larry (1993) *Rethinking Critical Theory: Emancipation in the Age of Global Social Movements*, London, Sage.

— (2009) 'At the End of the Postcommunist Transformation? Normalization or Imagining Utopia?, *European Journal of Social Theory* 12(3), August, 321–36.

Re, Lucia (2005) 'Approches européennes de la "mondialisation", *Jura Gentium. Revue de philosophie du droit international et de la politique globale* 1, 1.

Reder, Michael and Josef Schmidt (2008) *Ein Bewusstsein von dem, was fehlt*, Frankfurt, Suhrkamp.

Rennes, Juliette and Simon Susen (2010) 'La fragilité de la réalité. Entretien avec Luc Boltanski', *Mouvements* no. 64, October–December, pp. 150–164.

Ringe, Nils (2009) *Who Decides and How? Uncertainty and Policy Choice in the European Parliament*, Oxford, Oxford University Press.

Risse, Thomas (2000) '"Let's Argue!": Communicative Action in World Politics', *International Organization* 54(1) Winter, 1–39.

Rockmore, Tom (1989) *Habermas on Historical Materialism*, Bloomington and Indianapolis, Indiana University Press.

Rödel, U., G. Frankenberg and H. Dubiel (1989) *Die demokratische Frage*, Frankfurt, Suhrkamp.

Roderick, Richard (1986) *Habermas and the Foundations of Critical Theory*, London, Macmillan.

Rorty, Richard (1979) *Philosophy and the Mirror of Nature*, Princeton, NJ, Princeton University Press.

Rose, Gillian (1978) *The Melancholy Science: An Introduction to the Thought of Theodor W. Adorno*, Basingstoke, Macmillan.

— (1981) *Hegel Contra Sociology*, London, Athlone.

Rüb, Friedbert (1995) 'Die drei Paradoxien der Konsolidierung der neuen Demokratien in Mittel- und Osteuropa', in Hellmut Wollmann, Helmut Wiesenthal and Frank Bönker (eds), *Transformation sozialistischer Gesellschaften: Am Ende des Anfangs*, *LEVIATHAN* Sonderheft 15, 1995, Opladen, Westdeutscher Verlag, pp. 509–37.

Rumford, Chris (2002) *The European Union*, Oxford, Blackwell.

Sarotte, Mary (2009) *1989. The Struggle to Create Post-Cold-War Europe*, Princeton, Princeton University Press.

Schimmelfennig, Frank and Hanno Scholtz (2010) 'Legacies and Leverage: EU Political Conditionality and Democracy Promotion in Historical Perspective', *Europe-Asia Studies* 62(3), 443–60.

Schmidt, Alfred (1993) 'Max Horkheimer's Intellectual Physiognomy', in Seyla Benhabib, Wolfgang Bonß and John McCabe (eds), *On Max Horkheimer. New Perspectives,* Cambridge, MIT Press, pp. 25–47.

Schmidt, Vivien (2006) *Democracy in Europe. The EU and National Polities,* Oxford University Press.

Sending, Ole Jacob (2002) 'Constitution, Choice and Change: Problems with the "Logic of Appropriateness" and its Use in Constructivist Theory', *European Journal of International Relations* 8, 443–70.

Sensat, Julius (1979) *Habermas and Marxism,* Beverly Hills, CA, Sage.

Sitton, John (2003) *Haberrmas and Contemporary Society,* New York, Palgrave Macmillan.

Skillington, Tracey (2009) 'Linking Knowledge, Communication and Social Learning: Critical Theory's Immanent Critique of Capitalism's Administrative State', in Séamus Ó Tuama (ed.), *Critical Turns in Critical Theory,* London, I. B. Tauris, pp. 119–39.

Smith, David (1998) 'The Ambivalent Worker', *Social Thought and Research* 21(1–2), 35–83.

Sontag, Susan (2005) 'Literature is Freedom', reprinted in Daniel Levy, Max Pensky and John Torpey (eds), *Old Europe, New Europe, Core Europe. Transatlantic Relations after the Iraq War,* London, Verso, pp. 220–2.

Specter, Matthew G. (2010) *Habermas. An Intellectual Biography,* New York, Cambridge University Press.

Stamm, Karl-Heinz (1988) *Alternative Öffentlichkeit: Die Erfahrungsproduktion neuer sozialen Bewegungen,* Frankfurt and New York, Campus.

Statham, Paul (2010) 'What Kind of Europeanized Public Politics?', in Ruud Koopmans and Paul Statham (eds), *The Making of a European Public Sphere. Media Discourse and Political Contention,* New York, Cambridge University Press, pp. 277–306.

Statham, Paul, Ruud Koopmans, Anke Tresch and Julie Firmstone (2010) 'Political Party Contestation. Emerging Euroscepticism or a Normalization of Eurocriticism?', in Koopmans and Statham (ed.), *The Making of a European Public Sphere,* pp. 245–73.

Stockman, Norman (1978) 'Habermas, Marcuse and the *Aufhebung* of Science and Technology', *Philosophy of the Social Sciences* 8(1), 15–35.

Strydom, Piet (1992) 'The Ontogenetic Fallacy: The Immanent Critique of Habermas' Developmental Logical Theory of Evolution', *Theory, Culture and Society* 9(3), 65–93.

Susen, Simon (2007) *The Foundations of the Social. Between Critical Theory and Reflexive Sociology,* Oxford, Bardwell.

Szelényi, Ivan (1980) 'Whose Alternative?', *New German Critique* 20 (Spring/ Summer), 117–34.

— *Theory, Culture and Society,* 7 (1990) special issue on critical theory.

Teltschik, Horst (1991) *329 Tage,* Berlin, Siedler.

Therborn, G. (1971) 'Jürgen Habermas: A New Eclectic', *New Left Review* 67(May–June), 69–83.

Thévenot, Laurent (1990) 'L'action qui convient', in Patrick Pharo and Louis Quéré (eds), *Les formes de l'action,* Paris, Éditions de l'École des Hautes Études en Sciences Sociales, pp. 39–69.

— (1992) 'Un pluralisme sans relativisme? Théories et pratiques du sens de la justice', in Joëlle Affichard and Jean-Baptiste de Foucauld (eds), *Justice sociale et inégalités*, Paris, Esprit, pp. 221–53.

— (1998) 'À l'épreuve des grands principes', *Sciences Humaines* 79, 20–3.

Thompson, J. B. and D. Held (eds) (1982) *Habermas: Critical Debates,* London, Macmillan.

Tomka, Béla (2005) 'The Politics of Institutionalized Volatility: Lessons from East Central European Welfare Reforms', Woodrow Wilson International Center.

Toniolatti, Edoardo, 'Complex Identities. Seyla Benhabib Between Feminism and Discourse Ethics', *Philosophy Today* (forthcoming).

Trenz, Hans-Jörg and Klaus Eder (2004) 'The Democratising Dynamics of a Public Sphere: Towards a Theory of Democratic Functionalism', *European Journal of Social Theory* 6, 5–25.

Trenz, Hans-Jörg (2009) 'In Search for Popular Subjectness. Identity Formation, Constitution Making and the Democratic Consolidation of the EU', Arena Working Paper 7, April.

Trenz, Hans-Jörg and Peter de Wilde (2009) 'Denouncing European Integration. Euroscepticism as Reactive Identity Formation', Arena Working Paper 14, September.

Triandafyllidou, Anna, Ruth Wodak and Michał Krzyżanowski (eds) (2009) *The European Public Sphere and the Media: Europe in Crisis*, Basingstoke, Palgrave.

Tribe, Keith (1986) 'Franz Neumann in der Emigration: 1933–1942', in Axel Honneth and Albrecht Wellmer (eds), *Die Frankfurter Schule und die Folgen*, Alexander von Humboldt-Stiftung, Symposium 1984, Berlin, De Gruyter, pp. 259–74.

Tully, James (1995) *Strange Multiplicity: Constitutionalism in an Age of Diversity*, Cambridge, Cambridge University Press.

Turner, Charles (2004) 'Jürgen Habermas: European or German?', *European Journal of Political Theory* 3(3), 293–314.

Turner, Stephen and Dirk Käsler (eds) (1992) *Sociology Responds to Fascism*, London, Routledge.

Ulmen, G. L. (1978) *The Science of Society. Toward an Understanding of the Life and Work of Karl August Wittfogel*, The Hague, Mouton.

Vincent, Jean-Marie (2001) 'Adorno et Marx', in Jacques Bidet and Eustache Kouvélakis (eds), *Dictionnaire Marx contemporain*, Paris, Presses Universitaires de France, pp. 357–68.

Vozlensky, M. (1985) *Nomenklatura. The Ruling Class of the USSR,* London, Overseas Publishing House.

Weber, Max (1978) *Economy and Society,* Berkeley, University of California Press.

Wellmer, Albrecht (1974) *Critical Theory of Society,* New York, Seabury. First published 1969.

— (1986) 'Die Bedeutung der Frankfurter Schule heute', in Axel Honneth and Albrecht Wellmer (eds), *Die Frankfurter Schule und die Folgen*, Alexander von Humboldt-Stiftung, Symposium 1984, Berlin, De Gruyter, pp. 25–34.

— (1985) 'On the Dialectic of Modernism and Postmodernism', *Praxis International* 4(4), 337–62.

— (1991) *The Persistence of Modernity,* Cambridge, Polity.

Wessler, Hartmut (ed.) (2008) *Public Deliberation and Public Culture. The Writings of Bernhard Peters, 1993–2005*, Basingstoke, Palgrave Macmillan.
— (2008) *WestEnd. Neue Zeitschrift für Sozialforschung* 5(2).
White, Stephen (1988) *The Recent Work of Jürgen Habermas: Reason, Justice and Modernity,* Cambridge, Cambridge University Press.
White, Stephen (ed.) (1995) *The Cambridge Companion to Habermas,* Cambridge, Cambridge University Press.
Wiggershaus, Rolf (1994) *The Frankfurt School,* Cambridge, Polity. First published 1986.
Wingert, Lutz and Klaus Günther (2001) *Die Öffentlichkeit der Vernunft und die Vernunft der Öffentlichkeit. Festschrift für Jürgen Habermas*, Frankfurt, Suhrkamp.
Wittfogel, K. A. (1932a) 'Warum Hitler seine Konkurrenz zerschlug', *Der Rote Aufbau*, Nr. 13, reprinted in Kommunistischer Bund, *Kampf dem Faschismus,* Hamburg: J. Reents Verlag, 1973, pp. 217–21.
— ('Hans Petersen') (1932b) 'Wer finanziert Hitler?', *Der Rote Aufbau*, Nr. 13, reprinted in Kommunistischer Bund, *Kampf dem Faschismus,* Hamburg, J. Reents Verlag, 1973, pp. 222–5.
— (1932c) 'Die Demagogie der Frühprogramme des Faschismus', *Der Rote Aufbau*, Nr. 16, reprinted in Kommunistischer Bund, *Kampf dem Faschismus,* Hamburg, J. Reents Verlag, 1973, pp. 245–56.
Wolf, Christa (1990) *Im Dialog. Aktuelle Texte*, Frankfurt, Luchterhand.
Wren, Thomas (ed.) (1990) *The Moral Domain. Essays on the Ongoing Discussion between Philosophy and the Social Sciences,* Cambridge, MA, MIT Press.
Young, Iris Marion (1987) 'Impartiality and the Civic Public: Some Implications of Feminist Critiques of Moral and Political Theory', *Praxis International* 5(4) (1986), p. 398. Reprinted in Seyla Benhabib and Drucilla Cornell (eds), *Feminism and Critique: Essays on the Politics of Gender in Late-Capitalist Societies,* Cambridge, Polity.
Yurchak, A. (2006) *Everything Was Forever, Until It Was No More. The Last Soviet Generation,* Princeton and Oxford, Princeton University Press.
Žižek, S. (2001) *Did Somebody Say Totalitarianism?*, London, Verso.
Zurn, C. (2005) 'Recognition, Redistribution, and Democracy: Dilemmas of Honneth's Critical Social Theory', *European Journal of Philosophy* 13(1), 89–126.
— (2009) 'Social Pathologies as Second-Order Disorders', in Danielle Petherbridge (ed.), *The Critical Theory of Axel Honneth,* Leiden, Brill.

Index